The incredible true story of a breathtaking rescue in the frenzied final hours of the U.S. evacuation of Afghanistan—and how a brave Afghan mother and a compassionate American officer engineered a daring escape—from the #1 *New York Times* bestselling author of 13 Hours

When the U.S. began its withdrawal from Afghanistan and the Afghan Army instantly collapsed, Homeira Qaderi was marked for death at the hands of the Taliban. A celebrated author, academic, and champion for women's liberation, Homeira had achieved celebrity in her home country by winning custody of her son in a contentious divorce, a rarity in Afghanistan's patriarchal society. As evacuation planes departed above, Homeira was caught in the turmoil at the Kabul Airport, trying and failing to secure escape for her and her eight-year-old son, Siawash, along with her parents and the rest of their family.

Meanwhile, a young American diplomat named Sam Aronson was enjoying a brief vacation between assignments when chaos descended upon Afghanistan. Sam immediately volunteered to join the skeleton team of remaining officials at Kabul Airport, frantically racing to help rescue the more than 100,000 stranded Americans and their Afghan helpers. When Sam learned that the CIA had established a secret entrance into the airport two miles away from the desperate crowds crushing toward the gates, he started bringing families directly through, personally rescuing as many as fifty-two people in a single day.

On the last day of the evacuation, Sam was contacted by Homeira's literary agent, who persuaded him to help her escape. He needed to risk his life to get them through the gate in the final hours before it closed forever. He borrowed night-vision goggles and enlisted a Dari-speaking colleague and two heavily armed security contract "shooters." He contacted Homeira with a burner phone, and they used a flashlight code signal borrowed from boyhood summer camp. For her part, Homeira broke Sam's rules and withstood his profanities. Together they braved gunfire by Afghan Army soldiers anxious about the restive crowds outside the airport. Ultimately, to enter the airport, Homeira and Siawash would have to leave behind their family and everything they had ever known.

The Secret Gate tells the thrilling, emotional tale of a young man's courage and a mother and son's skin-of-the-teeth escape from a homeland that is no longer their own.

Mitchell Zuckoff is the author of eight previous works of nonfiction, including the #1 *New York Times* bestseller *13 Hours*, as well as *Frozen in Time* and *Lost in Shangri-La*. As a member of the *Boston Globe* Spotlight Team, he was a finalist for the Pulitzer Prize in investigative reporting. Zuckoff's honors include the Livingston Award for International Reporting, the Winship/PEN New England Award for Nonfiction, and the Heywood Broun Memorial Award. His work has appeared in *The New Yorker*, *The New York Times*, and numerous other publications.

The Secret Gate · Mitchell Zuckoff
Random House · Hardcover · 04/25/23 · $28.99/$38.99C · 9780593594841

D1003138

THE
SECRET
GATE

THE
SECRET
GATE

A True Story of Courage and Sacrifice
During the Collapse of Afghanistan

MITCHELL ZUCKOFF

RANDOM HOUSE
NEW YORK

Published in the United States by Random House,
an imprint and division of Penguin Random House LLC, New York.

RANDOM HOUSE and the HOUSE colophon are registered
trademarks of Penguin Random House LLC.

Hardback ISBN 9780593594841
Ebook ISBN 9780593594865

Printed in the United States of America on acid-free paper

randomhousebooks.com

9 8 7 6 5 4 3 2 1

ScoutAutomatedPrintCode

FIRST EDITION

Book design by Ralph Fowler

For Suzanne

CONTENTS

CONTENTS

AUTHOR'S NOTE

At a dangerous time, in a dangerous place,
two strangers took the most dangerous leap of all.
They trusted each other.

This is a true story.

2-page map TK

THE
SECRET
GATE

1

HOMEIRA

ONE BRIGHT SUMMER morning in 2021, Homeira Qaderi hurried her eight-year-old son Siawash out the door of their Kabul apartment. To speed their exit, she made him a promise that set his heart racing: tonight, after school, we'll fight the Taliban.

The electricity was out again in the middle-class Fourth District near Kabul University, so Homeira ignored the elevator and followed Siawash down ten flights of stairs.

The temperature hovered around eighty degrees Fahrenheit when they stepped outside at 7 A.M. that Tuesday, August 3. Mother and son turned a corner into a cobblestone alley where a van waited to take him to a private international school that taught classes in English. As Siawash scrambled inside, Homeira heard him boast to his friends about her daring battle plan.

Homeira watched the van drive off, praying as always that a suicide attack wouldn't kill him.

She returned to the apartment building where she'd remade her life. Where she regained her balance after Siawash's father divorced her for challenging his decision to take a second wife. Where, after a forced separation, she was raising Siawash to be an enlightened Afghan man. Where she earned fame, fans, and deadly enemies as an author and activist. And where she intended to spend the rest of her days writing more books and campaigning for women's equality in a city she loved for its beauty and its possibilities, despite its dangers and its flaws.

Kabul-jan, she called it, using the Farsi term of endearment for "my dear Kabul."

Homeira breathed heavily as she scaled the last of more than a hundred steps in her headscarf and long-sleeved blouse. Inside her apartment, she moved with a dancer's grace, unwrapping her shawl to reveal a cascade of thick brown hair that fell to her waist. Homeira was thirty-eight but looked younger, with high cheekbones, full lips, and large brown eyes that expressed her every volcanic emotion. A shade taller than five feet, she typically wore three-inch heels, which she removed to climb the stairs. She remained barefoot inside her four-bedroom sanctuary.

The sunny apartment reflected a life that would have been unimaginable for a single mother in Afghanistan even a few years earlier. She purchased it with earnings from her first book published in English, an acclaimed memoir of her girlhood during the Soviet-Afghan War of the 1980s and under the Taliban's vicious rule in the 1990s. The book doubled as a love letter to Siawash during their three painful years apart. The title alone made her a heroine to progressives and an infidel to extremists: *Dancing in the Mosque*.

Every detail of Homeira's home delighted her: shiny wood floors with hand-knotted rugs; a tufted white couch where Siawash did his homework while she read; a high-ceilinged office with a desk fit for a prime minister; an old-fashioned gramophone to play dance music when no men were nearby; an exercise room that served as home to Siawash's pet turtle; shelves brimming with books, honors, and diplomas; a plant-filled balcony; and windows that faced north to the blue domes of a Shiite shrine and, four miles beyond, to Kabul International Airport.

Homeira went to the kitchen for a handful of grapes and a large cup of *sheer chai,* tea with boiled milk, to kick-start her day. As she poured the pink tea, the room filled with scents of rosemary and eucalyptus. She carried it to her office, where a silver MacBook laptop on her desk connected her to a world spinning out of control.

The previous night, Homeira spoke by phone with her father, Wakil Ahmad. They were ethnically Pashtun, the same tribe that spawned the Taliban, but the family scorned the fundamentalist insurgents and their repressive, misogynistic interpretation of Islam. Wakil Ahmad was his celebrity daughter's biggest supporter. He lived with his wife, Homeira's mother Ansari, and four of Homeira's five younger siblings in Herat, an oasis city near the border with Iran, five hundred miles west of Kabul. During the war with the Russians that consumed much of Homeira's childhood, her father and several uncles fought among the militants known as mujahideen. Since then, Wakil Ahmad made a threadbare living teaching literature, with a special fondness for Russian novels.

Internet phone service was spotty in Herat, so Wakil Ahmad had climbed to his roof to speak with Homeira. The call broke up repeatedly, but each time they connected Homeira heard gunshots from nearby clashes between the Afghan Army and the Taliban. Unconfirmed reports circulated that the Taliban had laid siege to Herat, Afghanistan's third-largest city, as its fighters sought to expand recent gains in rural areas, with an eye toward provincial capitals and Kabul.

The call with her father confirmed Homeira's fears: the suicide bombers, as she called them, were approaching her family's door.

HOMEIRA'S WORRIES ABOUT her family and her country were rooted in a tortured history that long predated the chaotic summer of

2021.

An abbreviated account begins in late 2001, when American troops invaded Afghanistan to destroy the al-Qaeda terrorists who planned the 9/11 attacks and to topple the Taliban government that sheltered them. Within weeks the Taliban fled Kabul. Al-Qaeda leaders were killed or forced into hiding. But that was just the start. For nearly two decades, the United States and its close allies remained in Afghanistan to prevent the return of the Taliban and al-Qaeda, while working to create democracy, build the economy, combat endemic corruption, and champion women's rights. The Taliban, meanwhile, returned to its guerrilla origins to battle Afghan, U.S., and NATO troops.

As years passed, Americans' support for the war faded. So did hope for a stable, prosperous, modern Afghanistan. One U.S. president after another struggled to find a path to victory or a dignified exit. In February 2020, President Donald J. Trump approved a deal with the Taliban to withdraw the last U.S. forces. In exchange, the Taliban promised "to prevent the use of Afghan soil" by terrorists. In April 2021, President Joe Biden agreed to follow through on that bargain, but delayed the departure date by four months, to the twentieth anniversary of 9/11. The Taliban treated the impending American withdrawal as an invitation to try to overthrow the democratically elected Afghan government and seize power.

Initially, Homeira felt confident that the Afghan Army, some three hundred thousand soldiers strong, trained and equipped by the United States and NATO, would crush the ragtag Taliban militia, which had perhaps a quarter as many men. She dreaded the deaths of Afghan troops and the collateral killings of civilians, and she even regretted the loss of individual Talib lives. But she hoped the post-American war between the Taliban and the Afghan military would be like a monsoon, passing quickly and leaving her country's new democratic foundations intact.

Lately, though, as the withdrawal deadline approached and the Taliban steadily gained ground, doubts crept in. After the phone call with her father, Homeira posted on social media, where she had more than a half-million followers across several platforms: "What is going on in Herat?"

Within minutes, two high-ranking government officials sent her similar messages. Both claimed reports of Taliban forces sweeping into Herat and other provincial capitals—including Lashkar Gah and Kandahar in the south—were false rumors spread by troublemakers. The officials' messages alarmed Homeira more. They were either lying or oblivious.

At her desk in the morning light, with the electricity restored and her internet connection strong, Homeira scrolled through news and social media sites. She recoiled at photos of women and children fleeing Herat ahead of oncoming Taliban fighters. Homeira understood the impulse: the long, hard memories of Afghan women had again set them in motion.

While ruling Afghanistan from 1996 to 2001, the Taliban had cruelly imposed its interpretation of seventh-century Islamic sharia law. Among other harsh decrees, women and girls were excluded from workplaces and schools, stripped of civil and legal rights, and banished from public life unless shrouded by burqas and escorted by male relatives. Punishments were swift, without limit or appeal. Stonings, public executions, and amputations were Taliban specialties.

Homeira's tea grew cold as she stared at the images from Herat. She realized her family's neighbors, some of whom she likely knew, had already been transformed into refugees of war. A shiver passed through her, though she resolved not to show or express fear publicly.

Homeira spent the lonely hours of Siawash's school day fretting about her family and her country. She struggled to concentrate, unable to add a single sentence to the short story she was writing. She fretted about her finances, which had dwindled as she went without a full-time job while working on her next book. Her savings had eroded further from countless days in court trying to force her ex-husband to provide financial support, a colossal long shot. Even in the new, more moderate Afghan republic, divorced women were shunned, stigmatized as "unclean," and ignored by judges. A disturbing number considered suicide by self-immolation to be a viable alternative to the dishonor of divorce.

Homeira checked the clock as she awaited Siawash's return. He disliked the food at school, so she returned to the kitchen to cook a family favorite: *kitchiri,* a mixture of basmati rice, mung beans, spices, and onions she stirred on the stove until it turned golden brown. Soon her urban apartment smelled like the adobe Herat kitchen of Nanahjan, her beloved grandmother.

Shortly before 4 P.M., Siawash burst through the door too excited to eat, having spent all day anticipating their promised clash with the Taliban. The sight of her precocious son lifted Homeira's spirits. He had apple cheeks and his mother's soulful eyes. A lock of dark hair draped onto his forehead. His round glasses made him look at once studious and impish, a comic scholar.

Homeira insisted that Siawash try a few bites of *kitchiri.* As he ate, they resumed a conversation they'd begun that morning. Homeira tried to explain Afghan politics, religious zealotry, and sectarian war in a comprehensible way for an eight-year-old boy. It helped that Siawash had already absorbed Homeira's revulsion for the Taliban. A video on her phone from two years earlier showed Siawash strumming a guitar and singing, "You damned Talibs. One day you will burn this country to the ground."

Still, she worried about how much space the barbarians occupied in his mind. He knew details of beheadings. He kept track of death tolls. He knew why supposed infidels were flogged, stoned, or burned. His knowledge came from Homeira and also from television, his friends, and social media. Homeira sometimes regretted allowing him to use Facebook, where he saw all manner of horrors. But more powerful than her worry about Siawash being traumatized was her desire that he understand and reject the twisted medieval forces around them.

As daylight ebbed, Homeira explained that Siawash's most advanced lesson in battling the enemies of modernity would come that night. To a westerner, Homeira's activism might seem benign, but in Kabul her plan constituted a radical act of courage.

"At nine P.M.," Homeira told him, "you have to come on the balcony and we'll shout *Allahu Akbar!*" She said the strategy of demonstrators yelling "God is great!" from balconies, rooftops, and streets had originated in Herat and spread nationwide.

Siawash was confused.

He knew that Taliban fighters screamed *Allahu Akbar!* when they sawed off someone's head, or detonated a suicide bomb, or horsewhipped a woman for meeting a boyfriend. It was their signature cry when they committed hideous acts in the name of purifying the country. Screaming their slogan seemed to Siawash like a vote of support.

"Why are we shouting *Allahu Akbar*?" he asked. "What's going to happen?"

To fight the fanatics, Homeira told him, we must reclaim that phrase as a celebration of life instead of a shriek of death.

"We, the people of Kabul, all the people of Afghanistan, are going to speak out against the Taliban and say, 'We are Muslims. We are more Muslim than they are. We have principles, we are valuable, we are against killing people.'" Their protest would rally all good people in Afghanistan, she said, raising morale to finally defeat the Taliban.

The thought of participating in such important business thrilled Siawash.

Homeira didn't tell him that she expected the demonstration to be symbolic at best, futile at worst. She also didn't scare her son by admitting that her participation would enrage her critics and multiply the death threats against her. In recent months, the Taliban had targeted numerous female judges, journalists, intellectuals, and activists for assassination, many of whom Homeira knew personally or by reputation.

As nighttime approached, Homeira and Siawash were joined by the three young sons of Homeira's uncle Abo Ismael, one of her mother's brothers. A dozen years older than Homeira, Abo Ismael was a doctor who lived with his wife Samrina and their children on the building's fourth floor. The boys ran into the apartment to play with Siawash and eat Homeira's *kitchiri*. Close in age with Siawash, they called Homeira "auntie" despite being her cousins.

"We're going to go on the balcony and shout *Allahu Akbar!*" Siawash announced.

Shocked, the oldest turned to Homeira. "Auntie, can women shout *Allahu Akbar?* Can they scream on the balcony?"

"Why not, jan?" she said. "If the Talibs get here, women are the first ones who'll be treated awfully. I have to stand up to them. If they get here, they'll flog us. They won't let me talk about my books. If they see me on the street they'll make me wear a burqa."

The boys burst out laughing at the thought of fashionable, colorful Homeira in a shapeless black shroud, her face hidden behind a mesh veil.

"You won't be able to see anything!" one of the boys said. "You'll trip and fall ten times with every step!"

After a noisy game of darts her uncle's sons returned home. Siawash went to work. He charged a wireless microphone. He combed his hair and traded his Western clothes for a long white shirt and loose white pants, a traditional outfit called a *shalwar kameez,* to be sure he'd stand out in the darkness. Homeira chose a dark dress with beaded cuffs. She covered her hair with a blue silk scarf, pinning it securely so it wouldn't slip off and fuel the insults of those who already condemned her as immodest.

As his excitement intensified, Siawash asked, "Why do Talibs kill people?"

The question caught Homeira off guard. She blurted out her first thought: "Because Talibs didn't go to school and have no education. They don't know killing people is bad."

"So why didn't their parents send them to school?" he persisted.

"Because their parents didn't go to school."

Siawash considered this.

"So," he said, "the parents of the parents of their parents didn't go to school either?"

"Yes," Homeira said, "because there weren't many schools back then."

Siawash brightened. With a child's innocence, he proposed a solution. "There are schools now. They can come to my school and learn English. We also have music and dance."

"Siawash-jan," Homeira said, "Talibs behead anyone who dances or plays music."

She instantly regretted saying it. Siawash looked like he'd been slapped.

"So they'll behead us because of music and dance if they come to our school?"

"Don't say that," she said. "First, Talibs are not coming. Second, if they do come, your school will no longer have dance and music classes."

"What about our music teacher?"

"He'll be teaching other lessons."

Drained, Homeira persuaded Siawash to watch a movie while they waited for 9 P.M. He tried, but couldn't relax. He went to the guest room to practice shouting at the top of his lungs, telling Homeira he wanted to be heard beyond the mountains that ringed Kabul.

"They need to hear that this is Siawash's voice," he said, "so when Talibs hear it they know it's Siawash and they'll get scared." She took pleasure in his excitement, even as she wished his biggest concerns were school, friends, toys, and his turtle.

When the appointed hour approached, Homeira led Siawash next door to a smaller, sparsely furnished apartment owned by one of her younger brothers, Jaber, who worked at the presidential palace as an aide to President Ashraf Ghani. Homeira knew that Jaber, who was twenty-nine, would be working late or joining the *Allahu Akbar* protesters in the streets.

One appeal of Jaber's balcony was an unobstructed view of the blue-domed Sakhi Shrine and the sprawling cemetery surrounding it, which would allow their voices to carry. But Homeira had another motive she didn't tell Siawash: her bravery had limits. Her immediate concern wasn't the Taliban. Despite the events in Herat, she still doubted the turbaned killers with Kalashnikov rifles would ever reach Kabul. Instead, she felt anxious about her neighbors. Homeira's own balcony faced a building directly across the alley, and she didn't want to endure scorn from traditional men who thought a woman had no right to raise her voice.

Homeira behaved much bolder when it came to social media, which she used as an outlet for her feelings and a megaphone for her causes. With help from a female neighbor, Homeira and Siawash prepared to share a video of their protest live on Facebook.

At the stroke of 9 P.M., they stepped to the railing of Jaber's balcony. Dots of white light twinkled in the distance from homes and cellphones, illuminating a mile-high mountain known as TV Hill for its forest of broadcast towers. The Facebook video captured them yelling *Allahu Akbar!* dozens of times into the night sky. Siawash's voice boomed through the wireless microphone as Homeira draped an arm around his shoulders. When they heard the voices of other protesters, Homeira and Siawash punched their fists into the air with each shout.

Comments flooded Homeira's Facebook page. Her father's note affected her the most.

"My child," he wrote, "I, too, said *Allahu Akbar* and I cried."

An Afghan man acknowledging tears was rare, but Homeira understood. "He had been in war," she'd say, "and now he was seeing his daughter and grandson were still doing the same thing, and nothing had changed." Later, Wakil Ahmad called Homeira to express his pride. She wept with joy.

A journalist from Reuters contacted Homeira for permission to share the video globally. She agreed despite the risks, but asked that Siawash's face be blurred.

When the shouting was over, Homeira and Siawash returned to their apartment triumphant. After more dinner, she tried to settle him to sleep. As Homeira tucked him in, Siawash begged to see the recording. He watched it repeatedly, until she took away the phone.

"Do you think Talibs feared our *Allahu Akbar* tonight?" he asked. "Do you think they heard me?"

She kissed and hugged him. "I promise they heard you and they saw you shouting *Allahu Akbar*," she said.

Siawash closed his eyes and said good night. Before Homeira could leave, his eyes flew open. He asked a question that gutted her.

"Mom, what if Talibs come to my school tomorrow and kill me?"

IN SIAWASH'S QUESTION, Homeira heard an echo of her own early life.

On the morning of her birth, her mother told her, men filled the streets of Kabul shouting *Allahu Akbar!* to rally resistance to the Soviet invasion. During the nearly four decades that followed, Homeira's entire lifetime, the country experienced little respite from war.

Homeira's family left Kabul for Herat when she was an infant. One of her earliest memories was of her grandmother, her nanah-jan, tightening her hijab during a Soviet air raid, so she wouldn't risk going to hell by dying with her head uncovered. Afterward, Homeira made a game of searching for bullet holes on the outer walls of the house where she lived with her parents, four aunts, her father's parents, and each newly arrived sibling. One Soviet bullet never reached the house. It killed her teenage Aunt Zahra as she led Homeira through their yard toward the safety of their basement. Homeira's younger sister Zahra was named in tribute.

As a small child, Homeira laughed when she saw a Russian soldier's bare bottom as he pressed his hand against a neighbor girl's mouth. She told the story to her family, expecting to amuse them, too. One of her mujahideen uncles punched a wall. Her grandfather wiped away tears.

"In this land," her nanah-jan explained, "it is better to be a stone than to be a girl."

Nanah-jan also told her: "A girl should have fear in her eyes." Homeira stood before a mirror and turned her eyelids inside out, but couldn't find any. That troubled her mother, who called Homeira *osiyangar,* a rebel.

To escape the war, the family fled to Iran when Homeira was four. One of her most haunting memories was her father's shouted command—"Run, Homeira!"—as smugglers led them toward the Iranian border at night. He ran alongside her, carrying her baby brother Mushtaq and a bundle of their clothes. She fell and bruised her face, but got back on her feet with her father's help. When they reached a refugee camp, her mother tried to explain the cost of leaving one's homeland: "It means becoming a stranger in a foreign country. It means dying alone."

Two hungry years later, they returned to Herat, after the defeated Soviets learned why Afghanistan is called the "graveyard of empires." Although the Soviets lost, Afghans filled most of the actual graves. More than a million civilians died and many more were wounded. Millions became refugees. Cities were leveled and the economy barely functioned.

Homeira's house somehow survived amid a moonscape of bomb craters. Two captured uncles returned home, one missing a kidney, the other missing fingernails. During the next two years of relative quiet, Homeira played with friends, earned a reputation for mischief, and tested the patience of her mother and grandmother. Her father quietly tolerated Homeira's antics, encouraging her to explore her intellect beyond sewing and bearing children. When schools reopened, Homeira discovered a love of reading and storytelling. Her mother nicknamed her Scheherazade, after the Sultan's wife who narrates *One Thousand and One Nights.*

At twelve, she caught the predatory eye of a religious leader at their mosque, who exposed himself as Homeira collected water from a river. Later she caught him molesting a child and told her father, who rallied neighbors to expel him from their community.

Meanwhile, fighting returned to Afghanistan, this time a civil war among a half dozen mujahideen armies divided among ethnic and tribal lines. As she listened to the BBC with her father, Homeira first heard the word Taliban. She tracked the extremists' rise to power via news reports and local whispers. Homeira expected its fighters to resemble the beefy Russian soldiers with their crisp uniforms and high boots. When Talibs arrived in Herat in 1995 she saw they were skinny men with long beards, their clothing rags, their eyes ringed with black kohl.

The Taliban's victory forced women and teenage girls into the shadows, forced to wear burqas when they ventured outside their homes. At thirteen, banned from attending school, Homeira followed her mother's suggestion and turned their kitchen into a clandestine classroom to teach younger girls to read and write. Her father provided a blackboard he borrowed from the boys' school where he taught. Less helpful was her brother Mushtaq, who interrupted Homeira's lessons by shouting, "The Taliban are here!" Frightened girls hid notebooks inside Qurans until they heard Mushtaq laughing at his prank.

Over the next year of war, drought, and famine, thousands of displaced rural Afghans streamed into Herat. Many settled in tents on a bombed-out, scorpion-infested wasteland across the Injil River from Homeira's house. Refugee girls befriended the girls from Homeira's kitchen school, and soon they begged to learn, too. The kitchen was too small, but Homeira had an idea: she could teach them in a large tent the refugees used as a mosque. After the refugee girls' parents promised to keep it a secret, Homeira's father carried the blackboard back and forth daily between their home and the mosque tent. If anyone asked, Homeira's lessons consisted only of Quran readings.

Homeira blossomed inside the secret school. In the sweltering heat, shielded by thick canvas walls, she shed her burqa. Refugee boys joined the lessons, addressing Homeira as *Moalem Sahiba,* Madam Teacher.

One summer day, Homeira's students told her of a wedding the night before where celebrants had secretly defied the Taliban's prohibition on dancing. With promises of silence from all the students, two girls offered to teach Homeira to dance. She stood guard at the tent flap as her students spun and swayed, their slender arms swirling like smoke, their fingers fluttering like windblown leaves. "It was magical," Homeira wrote of the defiant day that gave her memoir its title. "The mosque was transformed. We were all laughing and clapping."

The noise attracted two Talib guards from a checkpoint near the refugee camp. Homeira had barely enough time to pull on her burqa and quiet the children. When the Talibs demanded an explanation, Homeira said several boys were chanting Quran verses while the rest clapped in encouragement. The dubious Talibs left her with a warning: don't do it again. "I believe that on that day in that sacred place," she wrote, "God smiled on us and loved us more than ever before."

But joyful days were few. The Taliban's cruelty took a particularly heavy toll on women and girls. Homeira often visited the burn ward of Herat's hospital, comforting girlfriends who'd set themselves on fire to escape the despair of their lives. Homeira could never forget their names, their screams, and the putrid smells of burned flesh and iodine.

When the Taliban banned television and all books except the Quran, Homeira's father wrapped his books in plastic, stuffed them in an iron chest, and buried them by a mulberry tree in their yard. Homeira snuck out Pushkin's novel of romance and war, *The Captain's Daughter.* As she read under her covers by kerosene lantern, Homeira savored the story of a teenage girl free to dance and love. The book transported her from a reality in which a girl might be torn apart by her brother's dogs for disobedience, or throw herself down a well to avoid being stoned, or be forced to become the fourth wife of a Taliban fighter.

At her mother's urging, Homeira wrote her own stories as an escape. A male professor agreed to secretly teach storytelling techniques to her and several other girls, under the pretense of training them in tailoring. They called the literary lessons the Golden Needle Sewing Class.

On the way to one meeting, Homeira suffered a sexual assault by the same man from the mosque whom she'd reported years earlier for abusing a child. He'd returned to Herat as a gun-carrying Talib. When he put his hand to her mouth she bit his fingers and ran off. Another assault followed, by a bicycle repairman. "I wished that my burqa's folds would turn into the wings of a bird to fly me far, far away," she wrote of that attack.

Although she faced danger every time she left home, Homeira refused to quit the class. Her teacher was charmed by a short story she wrote about a hungry Afghan refugee boy refused service at an Iranian bakery. A local newspaper published it as "The Little Man with Empty Hands." Her grandmother couldn't read, but she begged to be shown Homeira's name in print. Tracing the letters on the page, the old woman said kindly, "God bless you, evil girl."

The happiness lasted barely a few hours. Her father heard local men whispering that if a woman's name appeared in a newspaper, it meant she had disavowed the Prophet Muhammad. Her punishment would be a public whipping. Wakil Ahmad ran through Herat buying up copies. He buried a few, set fire to the rest, and the threat passed. Later, Homeira learned that a friend named Lida whose poetry was published in Herat had committed suicide rather than face punishment. "None of my close friends has survived under the Taliban," she once wrote.

Not long after, the Taliban sent fighters to search houses in Herat for hidden weapons. When Talibs entered Homeira's home, she and her sister Zahra hid under blankets. Someone pulled them off, and Homeira saw two Talibs standing beside her father, grandfather, and uncles.

"Allahu Akbar!" one Talib said.

Homeira braced for a sword on her neck.

"For the love of God," her grandfather shouted, "they are both children!"

The blankets dropped over them. As Homeira relaxed, she realized Zahra had wet herself.

Later, one of the Talibs, known as Commander Moosa, told her brother Mushtaq he'd soon return to their home. Mushtaq understood the commander wouldn't be looking for guns. Moosa arrived the next day to announce he was going to Kabul, but when he returned he would take Homeira as a wife. "Marrying a girl will dignify her," the Talib told her grandfather.

Two anxious months passed but he didn't return. "I hope that soil has filled his eyes," her mother said. Homeira prayed she might avoid a forced or arranged marriage altogether, but a family from Herat approached her father seeking a wife for their son. Homeira's family agreed without consulting her, in line with tradition.

While her father and grandfather negotiated a steep bride price, Homeira caught a glimpse of her betrothed through a window. At seventeen, on the morning of her wedding, she seethed as she swept the courtyard. "If I had no choice in the matter," she thought, "what difference did it make whether it was Commander Moosa or this man?" Homeira wished she could live up to her rebel nickname and flee, but she suffered through the ceremony in silence.

"With a few short verses . . . I became the property of the groom," she wrote.

Her new husband's father had moved to Iran with his two wives and fifteen children, so the newlyweds crossed the border to live with them.

To Homeira's delight, Tehran at the turn of the twenty-first century was a liberal paradise compared with Afghanistan. Homeira cast off her burqa and roamed the bookstores of Revolution Boulevard in a headscarf. Women worked, went to school, drove cars, swam in public pools, and walked alongside their husbands. Sometimes they walked ahead of them.

Homeira enjoyed small acts of independence, like joining a volley-ball team that practiced in a public park. She graduated to bigger re-bellions, above all vowing not to get pregnant until she earned a university degree. Her husband was in school, too, and didn't object. At twenty-one, Homeira earned a bachelor's degree. A master's degree followed. She began studying for a PhD in Persian literature at Tehran University.

In the meantime, the 9/11 attacks plunged Afghanistan into the third war of her lifetime.

For nearly a decade after the Taliban fell, Homeira and her husband remained in Iran, although she returned to Herat often to visit her family. Over that time, Homeira warmed to her husband, even feeling something like love. She immersed herself in literature and published several novels, while he studied political science. By 2010, Homeira's husband wanted to return to Afghanistan to work in government, teach at a university, and build a political career. Homeira had hoped to finish her PhD in Tehran, but she didn't object to her husband's plan. The Iranian government also wanted her to leave: she'd joined her university friends at political protests, in violation of her status as a foreign student.

The couple moved to Kabul, where Homeira advised a government ministry focused on support for widows and orphans. She published another novel and several children's books, pursued a PhD at Jawaha-rlal Nehru University in India, and taught literature at Kabul Univer-sity. By age thirty, she'd achieved goals she could barely dream of as a girl, including a marriage she considered solid and successful.

In 2013, Homeira gave birth to Siawash. Almost immediately, her marriage soured. In Homeira's eyes, their son's arrival, her growing acclaim as an author, and their return to Afghanistan reawakened her husband's patriarchal impulses. He forbade her from driving or at-tending social events. He refused to attend the launch of her sixth book, a petulance Homeira attributed to his embarrassment for having such an accomplished wife.

During the same period, the Taliban reasserted itself. In 2015, the insurgents seized the city of Kunduz for two weeks before U.S. troops and the Afghan Army regained control. The United Nations declared nearly half the country's thirty-four provinces at high or extreme risk of Taliban violence. Parliamentary elections were postponed, and more than one million Afghans were displaced from their homes. That summer, Homeira avoided the streets of Kabul to protect herself and her toddler Siawash from the daily threat of suicide bombings.

One night during that period, Homeira's husband exploded her world: he declared that she was no longer his ideal wife, so he would take one of his students as a second wife. He expected her to follow ancient custom and meekly greet guests at the wedding. Heartbroken, Homeira concluded that the man with whom she'd spent half her life had become a Talib.

Several nights later, she dressed in a gown, polished her nails, and styled her hair. When her husband came home, she screwed up her courage and told him, "You have no right to bring another woman to this house. . . . I am not allowing it."

He ridiculed her. "My right has been decided by my religion and the Prophet, not by you," he replied.

When she didn't back down, he loomed over her and demanded: "Who are you?" Still she wouldn't relent. His yells woke Siawash, whose cries interrupted the confrontation.

Several days later, as Homeira taught a class, her phone vibrated with a text message: "Divorce. Divorce. Divorce." With those three words, her husband ended their marriage, under a practice known as *talaq-e-biddah or "triple talaq."* Another text informed Homeira that their son belonged to him. He told Siawash, who was not yet two years old, that his mother was dead.

Although Homeira had grown independent in many ways, the teachings of her mother and grandmother remained deeply ingrained.

Feeling like a failure as a woman and a mother, Homeira at first saw no way to fight back. She accepted a residency at the International Writers Program at the University of Iowa, lived for a time in California, and wrote her memoir as a form of therapy. Slowly, as months then years passed, she regained her confidence.

Threaded throughout *Dancing in the Mosque* are letters to Siawash from that period that express her sorrow and her pledge to seek his return. In one, she explained her decision to defy his father: "I always have and always will want to be a mother for you, but I also need to remain Homeira for myself. . . . I could not sacrifice my freedom or my dignity. I could not become just another humiliated woman, banished to the supposed sanctuary of our home."

Eventually Homeira found the strength she needed. She returned to Kabul, waged a bruising court fight, and regained custody. By the summer of 2021, she and Siawash had been together again for more than two years.

Now Homeira worried that if the Taliban regained power, the fundamentalists wouldn't accept a custody ruling in a woman's favor, particularly one that benefited a high-profile author and activist who wrote of dancing in a mosque. Homeira knew that a second Taliban regime would endanger her life, her family, her career, and everything else she held dear.

ON THE SAME night Homeira and Siawash took part in the *Allahu Akbar!* protest, the Taliban demonstrated in its own way.

Around 8 P.M., insurgents carried out their largest and deadliest attack in Kabul in nearly a year. They targeted a top military official in one of the supposedly safest areas of the city, a posh neighborhood less than three miles from Homeira's apartment.

The attack began with a car bomb outside the home of Afghanistan's acting defense minister. Gunmen stormed the building and exchanged fire with security forces who fought to rescue people trapped inside. The minister survived, but eight people were killed and more than twenty were wounded. Among the dead were two police officers and an employee of the Afghan Ministry of Refugees and Repatriation, along with his child.

The Taliban bragged of the results. Spokesman Zabihullah Mujahid called it "the beginning of retaliatory attacks."

He also threatened the *Allahu Akbar* protesters. "This is our motto," he tweeted. "This is not the motto of American slaves and secularists. We will hold the slaves accountable for Allah."

THREE DAYS LATER, on Friday, August 6, the Taliban captured the city of Zaranj, capital of the southern Nimruz province, its biggest military prize in five years. Afghan troops fled with barely a fight, shedding their uniforms and crossing into Iran. Sieges of Herat and Kandahar continued.

For Homeira, more bad news came the next day, August 7. In court that morning, she learned a judge had dismissed her financial support claims, declaring her evidence insufficient. The house her then-husband bought with her wages and the proceeds of her pawned jewelry belonged only to him. Afterward, he texted her a message as dismissive as their divorce: "You won't get anything no matter how hard you try. Don't waste your energy."

After their split, Homeira's ex-husband had pursued his political ambitions, placing a distant fifth in Afghanistan's 2019 presidential election. His new mother-in-law was chair of the country's election commission, which named Ashraf Ghani the new president. Homeira believed that her ex-husband's rising profile multiplied his advantages in court. In fact, seeking office probably wasn't necessary. Afghan law is so tilted against women that upon a married man's death, his widow receives only one-eighth of her husband's estate, while seven-eighths is split among his children. In a divorce, a woman is entitled to nothing. "When he kicked me out of his life," Homeira said, "I was left with only my clothes."

She cried over the judge's decision, went home, and showered. Then Homeira let anger take over. She resolved to start her court case over from scratch, no matter how long it took. "I failed," she'd say, "but that doesn't mean I will give up on this fight."

Thinking about the people of Herat made Homeira tearful again. She wept as she stroked the shell of Siawash's palm-sized turtle, which he called Sangi, or "made of stone."

While Siawash was at school, Homeira attended an emergency summit of prominent Heratis in Kabul. They called themselves the Council of Cohesion and Support for Popular Resistance in Herat. She arrived early for the meeting at the Afghanistan Institute for Strategic Studies, a progressive research organization based on the estate-like grounds of an old castle. Sitting among the women, Homeira listened as several men explained that they'd asked the Ghani government to send two thousand guns to the resistance in Herat.

A successful female lawyer offered to drive Homeira home. On the way, Homeira learned the woman had appealed to multiple foreign embassies to get her and her son out of Afghanistan. The woman shocked Homeira further by saying several others in their circle had already left.

When Homeira reached her apartment building, Siawash was waiting at her uncle Abo Ismael's apartment. Homeira told her uncle the situation was worse than they thought.

"No jan," Abo Ismael said. "We're not going to fall that quickly. This country has built and prepared a military for twenty years."

Upstairs, Homeira visited her brother Jaber. He, too, told her not to worry. "We are fighting," he said. "We believe in a free Afghanistan. Who will hand the country to the Taliban? The world is with us. The U.S. is with us."

She nodded but returned to her apartment with Siawash, unconvinced.

BEFORE SCHOOL THE next morning, August 8, Siawash asked Homeira how she planned to spend the day. She told him she would return to court and attend another meeting at the institute.

"Isn't the war over?" he asked.

"War? There is no war," Homeira said. "I just go there and sit with friends."

Siawash frowned. "No, you talk about war there."

Surprised, she asked why he thought that. Siawash opened the institute's Facebook page.

"I saw your picture. They were talking about Taliban and war." Siawash locked eyes with his mother. "Mom, are you planning on going to war?"

"No, honey," she said. "I don't know how to use a gun. I don't know how to fight."

"It says you're going to Herat," he replied, "to support the people of Herat."

In fact, the previous day Homeira had offered to join a delegation planning to fly to Herat to rally anti-Taliban forces. Further details would be discussed at the meeting this afternoon.

Homeira sent him to school, returned to court, and again arrived early at the institute. She wandered through the lush gardens, sipping a glass of tea as a cool breeze ran through the pomegranate and apple trees. Sparrows picked the season's last blackberries.

Homeira collected seeds from fragrant, trumpet-shaped Marvel of Peru flowers to plant on her balcony. She looked up and saw the lawyer who drove her home a day earlier. Homeira opened her hand to display dark beads that would blossom the following summer into bushes bearing vibrant yellow, magenta, red, and white flowers.

"Take them," she told the lawyer. "Even one seed can grow big in a vase."

The woman shook her head. "Who knows where each of us will be next year."

As the meeting began, a former general declared that Homeira shouldn't join the delegation to Herat. He said the city's defense was in the hands of Mohammad Ismail Khan, known as Amir Saheb, a white-bearded former warlord in his seventies called the "Lion of Herat."

"Amir Saheb is a *mujahid* and doesn't have much contact with the women," the former general said. "They have no need for a woman."

Even in a supposedly progressive institute, amid a crisis against their shared enemy, the old ways persisted. Homeira swallowed her anger to answer as calmly as she could.

"I will go," she said. "If needed, I will go by myself and I will return by myself."

As the meeting wound down, a former Afghan national security advisor announced the trip to Herat was canceled altogether. Significant Taliban forces had reached Badghis, a neighboring province. By the time the delegation reached Herat, the Taliban might control the airports and prevent them from leaving.

Homeira felt like a patient hearing a grim prognosis. Her phone vibrated: a text from Siawash. Again he'd gone to her uncle's apartment after school, but now he was hungry and wanted her to cook him dinner. With nothing more to accomplish, she left for home.

Back at their building, Homeira's uncle Abo Ismael continued to insist Herat wouldn't fall. She didn't have the heart to tell him he was wrong.

The only question was what the Taliban would take next.

2

SAM

THAT SAME DAY, nearly seven thousand miles away, Sam Aronson woke up hungover at a friend's beach house on Martha's Vineyard.

Sam was thirty-one, five foot ten, with a solid build and an olive complexion. A Roman nose anchored his handsome face. Normally his short, dark hair was neat enough for a job interview and his brown eyes scanned like searchlights. But on this morning his hair was tousled and his eyes were bleary from a night of drinking around a bonfire with his old college crew. The smell of wood smoke clung to the rumpled shorts and T-shirt he pulled back on when he rose.

Requiring coffee, Sam and his friends rolled up to a little café on Main Street in the quaint harbor village of Vineyard Haven. Notable people were common on the island in summertime, and Sam spotted Harvard legal scholar and former White House official Cass Sunstein reading that morning's Sunday *New York Times*. The front page on August 8 had stories on the pandemic, infrastructure, and the Olympics. Nothing on Afghanistan.

Sam did a double take when a woman with piercing green eyes and strawberry blond hair sat across from Sunstein with her own copy of the newspaper: Sunstein's wife, Samantha Power, newly confirmed head of the U.S. Agency for International Development.

During the Obama administration, Power was the United States' ambassador to the United Nations. In what felt like a previous life, Sam served as one of her bodyguards, as part of his then job as a special agent for the U.S. Diplomatic Security Service.

Sam's heart pounded as he walked to their table.

"Ambassador Power?"

She looked up, surprised.

"It's Sam Aronson. I was on your protective detail—"

"Oh right, right, Sam! How are you?"

The adrenaline caught in his throat and made his voice rattle.

"It's . . . it's so funny to see you," Sam said. "I'm just on the Vineyard hanging out with friends. What are you doing here?"

"We had a party to go to last night," she said discreetly. Power and Sunstein were among the select guests at Barack Obama's sixtieth birthday party at the former president's island estate.

She reintroduced Sam to Sunstein, whom Sam had met when he shadowed the couple on weekend outings in Manhattan. Then she asked, "Remind me what you're doing?"

Sam understood Power wanted to know where he was posted in his new job, as a Foreign Service Officer with the U.S. State Department.

Two years earlier, Sam sent Power an email saying he'd quit being a bodyguard. His experience protecting her at the United Nations—being tantalizingly close but strictly outside the decision-making realm of U.S. foreign policy—had played a major role in his choice to trade his gun, badge, and bulletproof vest for a suit-and-tie career as a junior U.S. diplomat.

At the time, Power replied by email: "This is such wonderful news! Yay! Boy does the FS [Foreign Service] need great people!"

Now, standing beside her, wishing he'd combed his hair, Sam updated Power on his professional life.

"I just got back from Nigeria and I'll be going to Erbil next. I'm about to start language training" in Arabic, he explained.

"Iraq, very cool," Power said. "I'm hoping to make a trip there"— she glanced at her husband—"if Cass will let me." Sunstein chuckled.

"That would be great," Sam said. "Maybe I'll see you there."

"Definitely," Power said. "It's such a small world."

AS A BOY, Sam's greatest fear was getting stuck in a small world.

Born in London, where his family lived briefly, Sam grew up in Tenafly, New Jersey, a privileged suburb fifteen miles from Manhattan, across the Hudson River. The second of four children, Sam watched his mother pivot from homemaker to high school history teacher, and his father climb from accountant to international executive with the National Basketball Association.

Both sides of Sam's family descended from Eastern European Jews who immigrated to the United States in the early twentieth century seeking opportunity and escape from persecution. His mother's great-uncle remained in Poland and was murdered along with his wife and children in a Nazi death camp. Sam's public schools in Tenafly regularly hosted talks by Holocaust survivors, wizened men and women who shared stories of loss and pain, cruelty and fortitude. Above all, survival. They'd roll up their sleeves to display wrinkled forearms tattooed a half century earlier with concentration camp identification numbers. Sam never forgot them.

Another boyhood memory came on 9/11, when windblown ash from the Twin Towers of the World Trade Center coated lawns, cars, and streets in Tenafly. Four of the town's residents were killed that day in the attacks by al-Qaeda hijackers. Eleven-year-old Sam felt a vague burden to do something in response. Later he learned the terrorists in the planes considered him an enemy, too, because of his religion.

As a boy Sam took Judaism for granted, or worse, rebelling against the demands of religious education classes and Hebrew lessons for his bar mitzvah. Like many assimilated Jews, the Aronson family adhered more to cultural identity than spiritual practice. Holiday dinners focused less on prayer than on current events. Even during Passover, the holiday celebrating Jews' deliverance from oppressive rulers in ancient Egypt, the Aronsons skipped scripture for discussions of ethics and politics, pinballing from social justice to global warming.

Among the four Aronson children, the family star was Sam's older brother Jacob, a gifted concert pianist by middle school, captain of the track and cross-country teams, a stellar student headed to Princeton. Sixteen months younger than Jacob, Sam loved his brother even as he felt "second tier" by comparison.

Jacob knew Sam felt overshadowed, but he viewed things differently: "I was very much the obedient child," Jacob explained, "doing whatever I was told. Sam thought critically much earlier in life. I think he was more mature about it than I was. More questioning of authority, questioning my parents and their authority, and wanting to have more independence."

Still, Sam's teenage self-assessment was ruthless: scrawny, awkward, shy, and nerdy. Difficult on their parents. Unmemorable, untalented, uncool, and unmotivated.

With one exception.

At fifteen, Sam felt an intense drive to become an emergency medical technician. Maybe the impulse was born of his father Mark's emphasis on doing meaningful work. Or maybe it came from his mother, Judy, who frequently clashed with Sam's strong will but impressed him by teaching in a low-income school district. Maybe Sam wanted to thrive outside Jacob's shadow. Or maybe it was simpler: helping people spoke to Sam in a way he couldn't explain.

New Jersey required EMTs to be sixteen, but Sam discovered that a nearby town allowed volunteer observers to start at fifteen and a half. Sam signed up the day he hit that milestone. He spent most Friday and Saturday nights in the back of ambulances, answering calls at crime scenes and car wrecks, medical emergencies and domestic disputes. When he turned sixteen Sam began formal EMT training several nights a week, then joined the ambulance squads in both Tenafly and neighboring Teaneck.

When his pager went off during school he bolted from class, running a half mile past ball fields and playgrounds to the Tenafly Volunteer Ambulance Corps station. After treating heart attack victims, mangled motorists, and whatever else presented itself, he completed his paperwork then returned to school hours later. It didn't improve his grades.

Sam loved the work, but he didn't see a career in it, and he worried he might get stuck forever in Tenafly. He shuddered at the thought of a future as an unpaid townie EMT wearing a self-bought uniform and driving a tricked-out car with flashing lights and fancy decals.

A pathway out, and an awareness of the wider world, came courtesy of his father's job with the NBA. As senior vice president of content and business affairs, Mark Aronson worked to extend the basketball league's global reach. At sixteen, Sam accompanied his father on a business trip to Moscow and Saint Petersburg. Next came China, Senegal, South Africa, India, and elsewhere. Occasionally NBA players joined these trips, but Sam found other contacts more fascinating.

The high profile of the NBA often meant U.S. diplomats abroad would host the league's representatives at their embassies or consulates. As a teenage boy, Sam was less interested in the ambassadors and their aides, with their binders and briefing notes, than in the earpiece-wearing, pistol-carrying Americans who protected them. Those were the special agents of the U.S. Diplomatic Security Service. When Sam got home, he began focusing hard enough on his grades to consider a career as a government agent.

When a high school classmate expressed surprise that he'd been accepted at Northeastern University in Boston, where she'd been rejected, Sam took it as an insult to his intelligence and resolved to prove her wrong. He stopped screwing around, chose criminology as a major, and became a serious college student.

AT NORTHEASTERN, ABSORBED in his studies and making friends, Sam became fixated on transnational crime, terrorism, illegal arms sales, and human trafficking. He grew curious about how the United States funds law enforcement efforts abroad. As a sophomore he took advantage of the university's co-op program, which emphasizes professional experiences, to wrangle an internship in Washington, D.C., in the international fugitive division of the U.S. office of Interpol, the International Criminal Police Organization.

Sam did low-level work on worldwide arrest warrants called Red Notices and helped roll out Interpol's Stolen and Lost Travel Document program. One day, a special agent from the U.S. Diplomatic Security Service came to work temporarily in Sam's office. The agent had an air of mystery and movie star looks. Sam peppered him with questions about his work in Senegal, Baghdad, Algiers, and beyond. Nineteen-year-old Sam told himself, "This is the coolest job in the world. How do I sign up?"

Back in Boston, Sam devoted himself to study of Kenya, Somalia, and other countries in the Horn of Africa. He published two research papers in a serious academic journal before he turned twenty-one. He won his professors' approval to create a minor in international affairs and African studies, then spent eight weeks during the summer between sophomore and junior years in Kenya, working on a global health study with a professor who taught him Swahili. With a deep tan and a couple weeks of stubble, Sam put on a Muslim skullcap and a local soccer jersey to pass as Middle Eastern, as a disguise to interview Somali refugees in a Nairobi neighborhood believed to be a breeding ground for terrorism. Locals chased him out when they realized he was American.

During junior year Sam returned to Washington, this time as an intern in the State Department's Bureau of Diplomatic Security, in the Criminal Investigative Liaison Branch. A bonus was the top secret security clearance that came with the internship. He spent part of his senior year studying at the University of London's School of Oriental and African Studies.

No longer a scrawny, awkward nerd, Sam had filled out physically, socially, and intellectually. As graduation neared, the question was what to do next.

Apply to PhD programs and become an academic? Too much research and not enough action. The FBI? He'd need to work for more than a decade in the United States before vying for an international posting. The CIA? Intriguing, but he had no idea what its staff actually did. Only the Diplomatic Security Service seemed a match for his skills and interests.

To keep his options open, Sam applied for a master's degree program in comparative politics at the London School of Economics. Then he promptly forgot about it and returned to his job search.

Sam accepted a low-level position at the Diplomatic Security Service criminal branch where he'd interned a year earlier. A week into the job, shortly after graduating with honors from Northeastern, turning twenty-two, and uprooting to Washington, Sam opened an acceptance letter inviting him to start grad school in London. He tossed it aside. Weeks later he mentioned it to his new boss.

"Are you nuts?" the boss asked. "London School of Economics? Quit this job now and go."

"I can't do that," Sam said.

"Government jobs will always be there for you. This opportunity will not. Quit. This. Job."

Sam understood that a supportive family and no debt gave him breaks most people lacked. Repayment for a silver spoon could be, in his words, "to make a positive difference, to do good things in this world." Sam gave two weeks' notice and repacked his bags.

In London, he grew intrigued by illicit finance in Somalia and took night classes to learn Somali. His language teacher mentioned an opportunity to serve as an election monitor in northern Somalia, so Sam petitioned his grad school professors to let him go there for two weeks and keep a journal on his work. More travel followed, including a three-week hitchhiking trip with two friends through the dangerous Tigray region of Ethiopia.

He wrote more scholarly papers, including one on U.S. counterterrorism aid to Kenya before and after 9/11. Again approaching graduation without a job, Sam leaned toward becoming a Foreign Service Officer at the State Department, where he could do policy work in an embassy or consulate in one of the countries he'd studied and visited. When he learned the hiring process might take two years, he contacted the boss who'd told him to quit and study in London.

Sam returned to Washington and the State Department, this time doing work he didn't enjoy among co-workers he disliked: giving security advice to private companies about West Africa despite knowing almost nothing about that part of the continent. He left that position to become an analyst with the U.S. Defense Intelligence Agency, which focuses on foreign military missions. There he gathered information to help the national intelligence community and the White House decide how to target suspected terrorists in the region he knew best, the Horn of Africa.

Eager to get back on track at the State Department, Sam sat for exams and interviews to become a Foreign Service Officer. To be safe, he also took tests to become a special agent with the Diplomatic Security Service. He passed the agent exams but failed the diplomat tests.

It made no sense. Sam's academic and work experiences fit the mold of an entry-level diplomat. By contrast, nearly all Diplomatic Security agents had experience in the military, law enforcement, or both. Sam had neither. He'd never even fired a gun.

Yet at the start of 2015 Sam joined the ranks of the State Department bodyguards who fascinated him a decade earlier when he traveled the world with his father.

AT TWENTY-FOUR, SAM was the youngest Diplomatic Security special agent trainee in his class. Most were in their midthirties and one was forty-two. Some had served in war zones. All except Sam were adept with firearms.

After a month in classrooms, the group moved to the Federal Law Enforcement Training Center in Georgia for three months of weapons training and hand-to-hand combat. They learned driving techniques and surveillance, courtroom testimony and search warrant procedures. Sam's more experienced classmates took him under their wing.

Other agencies also sent trainees to the center, and one weekend Sam got an ugly lesson in racial profiling. As team leader on a practice undercover operation, Sam's job was to surveil a laundromat on the training base being used for a mock informant meeting. As Sam photographed the building, two beefy white trainees from Customs and Border Protection demanded his ID. They detained him until a colleague verified that Sam was a State Department trainee.

"I have dark hair. I have a big nose. I look Middle Eastern, or you could say Israeli, but I don't look white," Sam said later. "I'd bet you big money if I had blond hair and Oakley sunglasses and an American flag T-shirt, they wouldn't have said anything." Sam's classmates urged him to point out the pair to deliver a lesson of their own. He declined, but it felt good to know he'd earned their loyalty.

After months of specialized training in protecting diplomats, Sam's initial post was a heartbreaker: the New York area field office, across the river from Manhattan in Fort Lee, New Jersey. "I took this job because I want to be in exotic places," he'd say. "I can't believe I'm going to be seven minutes from where I grew up."

Equipped with a gun, a badge, and a government-issued Chevy

Impala he could park anywhere, twenty-five-year-old Sam moved to Chelsea in Lower Manhattan.

His work was split between protecting dignitaries and investigating federal crimes. While working on a case of identity theft involving a Nigerian national, Sam woke after midnight to a call on his cellphone. A man with a Nigerian accent warned, "Mr. Aronson, I'm going to find you and I'm going to fucking kill you." The only personal information about Sam on the internet was the address where he grew up. Afraid, he called the Tenafly Police Department: "There's a suspect who has threatened me. I think he might be going to my parents' house." Without alarming Sam's parents, who were already skeptical about his career choice, Tenafly police stationed a car outside the Aronson home the rest of the night. The next morning, Sam and a squad of New York City police, U.S. marshals, and federal immigration agents burst into the man's apartment and arrested him on multiple charges.

Much of Sam's time in the New York office was spent protecting U.S. diplomats at the United Nations headquarters, above all Ambassador Samantha Power. The work confirmed his suspicion that he was in the wrong career. "I didn't want to be the fly on the wall taking the bullet for the diplomats," he said later. "I would have taken a bullet for her in a heartbeat, no question about it. But I wanted to be on her staff."

In an elevator one day, Power asked Sam about his career goals. He told her he wanted to get overseas as soon as possible, even though he was supposed to be stationed domestically for at least another year.

"There's this job in West Africa that's been open for eighteen months," he told her, "and nobody else wants it."

"Where is it?" she asked.

"Niger."

Agents tended to seek foreign postings in glamorous locations. Not Sam. He'd named the world's poorest nation, a mostly barren land dominated by the Sahara Desert. Niger's twenty-two million people ranked near the bottom of most global measures of economic well-being, life expectancy, and education. Terrorists waged a relentless insurgency.

"You'd really want to go there?" Power asked.

"Yes. I think it would be super cool."

Power told Sam to send his résumé to her chief of staff. Weeks later he got a call from his assignments officer: "I don't know what you did or how you did it, but you're going to Niger."

BECAUSE NIGER WAS considered a high-threat post, Sam needed to undergo added training. That necessity became especially apparent after the September 11, 2012, attack in Benghazi, Libya, when radical Islamists overran the U.S. compound there and killed Ambassador Chris Stevens, State Department information officer Sean Smith, and two CIA security contractors, former Navy SEALs Glen Doherty and Tyrone Woods.

The three-month high-threat training course, taught by former Special Operations Forces members, included advanced firearm instruction, navigation courses, combat emergency medicine, high-speed driving techniques, and intense close-quarter fighting skills. "If you're going hand-to-hand with someone in Iraq, or in Algeria, or Yemen, you're not there to arrest them," Sam explained. "You are learning how to kill them before they kill you."

When working abroad, special agents of the Diplomatic Security Service are called Regional Security Officers. Sam arrived in Niger in February 2017. Six weeks later, the only other Regional Security Officer left. At twenty-six, on his first overseas assignment, Sam spent months as the senior diplomatic security official at a U.S. embassy in a country tormented by terror groups. "Holy shit," Sam thought. "I don't know what I'm doing, and I'm alone."

In April 2017, Sam joined a team of FBI agents, Green Berets, and other U.S. government agents inside Niger's notorious Koutoukalé prison. Their job was to biometrically scan thirteen hundred of the jihadists and militants held there, from Boko Haram, ISIS-West Africa, and al-Qaeda in the Islamic Maghreb, to connect them to DNA found at previous attacks and to keep track of them after they left prison.

As Sam provided security, a Special Forces operator searched an al-Qaeda bomb maker. Fifteen feet away, Sam studied the prisoner, noticing several missing fingers.

The Special Forces operator felt a bulge at the bomb maker's waistband.

"What's this?" he demanded.

The prisoner reached toward the bulge.

"Grab your shirt from the middle and slowly raise it!"

As the prisoner lifted his shirt, Sam saw red and black wires.

Everything happened at once. The searcher yelled, "Don't fucking move!" A second Special Forces operator tackled the prisoner. Sam drew his gun and looked for a clean shot.

No explosion went off.

With his gun trained and his heart pounding, Sam saw the bulge was only a bundle of wires the size of an egg, with no bomb to detonate. Sam never knew if the terrorist hoped the dummy bomb would enable him to bluff his way to escape, if he was testing their security, or if he had some other motive. But Sam knew he didn't want to do security work anymore.

"There's a rush that comes with that, but not the kind that I wanted," Sam said later. "I wanted the rush of convincing the governor of the Tillabéri Region of Niger to agree to a weapons abatement plan, where we provided them a stipend each month and equipment to find surface-to-air missiles that were coming out of Libya." The work of a young diplomat.

Six months later, in October 2017, an ISIS affiliate ambushed four U.S. Special Forces soldiers in northern Niger. Sam was thirty miles away, negotiating the surface-to-air missile program. Initial reports suggested that one of the four, an army sergeant, remained alive. Sam and others worked relentlessly to find him, only to learn he'd also been killed.

Overcome by grief, Sam went to his rented house near the embassy and collapsed on the floor beside his bed. Mature beyond his teenage rebellions against faith, Sam found solace in a hymn he'd last heard at his grandparents' funerals. Normally spoken in unison by at least ten members of a congregation, the Mourner's Kaddish is a reminder that no one grieves alone.

Soon after, Sam finished his two-year stint in Niger and applied for a program that gives non-diplomat State Department employees an inside track to becoming Foreign Service Officers.

While awaiting word, he sought his next special agent posting, as an investigator working on kidnappings, hostage negotiations, and other crimes in a place arguably even more dangerous than Niger: Karachi, Pakistan. One lure was Sam's intense interest in journalist Daniel Pearl of *The Wall Street Journal,* who was abducted in Karachi in 2002 and beheaded by Islamist militants. Sam identified with Pearl's complex relationship with his heritage. It didn't define him, but it was indelibly part of him.

Sam returned to Washington to study Urdu, a requirement to be posted in Pakistan, even as he moved forward with tests and interviews to pursue his dream of diplomacy. In February 2019, Sam learned he'd been accepted for training as a State Department political officer. He gave his notice to the Diplomatic Security Service to begin a new life as a U.S. Foreign Service Officer.

IN THE MIDST of that transition, a college friend invited Sam to a party in Washington, D.C., to meet a young woman involved in government service who, like Sam, was fascinated by the cultures and people she'd encountered in Africa. Sam wasn't looking for a relationship but he tagged along.

Despite his experience in danger zones, Sam initially felt too scared to talk with Liana Cramer. Three years younger than Sam, Liana was lithe and beautiful, with dark hair, deep dimples, and a warm smile. When Sam finally approached her, he discovered Liana was smart, kind, and quick to laugh. They exchanged stories about favorite haunts in Senegal and bonded over their fandom of a bluesy singer from Niger named Bombino.

The longer they talked, the more they discovered shared values, interests, and ambitions. Liana liked Sam's passion and sense of adventure, and also how he seemed at once easygoing and highly motivated. They began dating steadily, even as Liana prepared to accept a new job on the diplomatic staff at the U.S. embassy in Bamako, Mali.

Over dinner two months after they met, Sam opened the Notes app on his iPhone. He clicked on a document whose title befit the mindset of a junior diplomat: "Define the Relationship Bilateral Meeting." Sam ran through talking points about how they could deepen their relationship, even as they pursued international careers that might force them apart for long stretches. Liana found the list charming.

As Sam completed Foreign Service orientation, he bypassed applying for open U.S. embassy jobs in desirable destinations including London, Singapore, and Rio de Janeiro. Instead, hoping to find relatively short flights to visit Liana in Mali, Sam chose Abuja, Nigeria.

Sam reached his new post in July 2019, accompanied by his miniature Australian shepherd, Stella. He'd been hired on the political affairs track of the U.S. Foreign Service, the most competitive of the five Foreign Service Officer tracks and the one that produces the most ambassadors. Sam began working the long days of a consular official, reviewing visa applications by Nigerians who wanted to visit or study in the United States.

Listening to thousands of people's stories gave Sam a discerning ear for the countless shades of gray between outright lies and unvarnished truth. He sought above all to protect the United States, while also showing compassion for the yearnings of people whose background and circumstances were far different from his own. Meeting so many Nigerians face-to-face changed Sam, especially after the Trump administration added Nigeria to the "Muslim ban" list of nations forbidden from sending prospective immigrants.

"I take on these matters and make them very personal," Sam said. "It's to the point where it's all I think about. Say I'm going for a run or I'm driving somewhere or I'm sitting in a movie, I end up thinking about these things because I feel like I have the ability to help people's lives."

He reflected often on an American diplomat in the 1930s and '40s whose story Sam learned during State Department training.

Like Sam, Hiram "Harry" Bingham IV was the privileged second son of a globe-trotting father. In his twenties, Bingham joined the State Department and was sent to Marseille, France. After Germany invaded France in 1940, thousands of refugees streamed toward Marseille. The State Department had a de facto policy of denying or delaying visa applications by European Jews, even if they met legal requirements. Bingham defied his superiors by issuing visas, hiding refugees, and providing false documents. Among those he helped were Jewish philosopher Hannah Arendt and artists Marc Chagall and Max Ernst, but most were unknown men, women, and children. In 2002, Bingham was posthumously honored for having "risked his life and his career . . . to help over 2,500 Jews and others who were on Nazi death lists to leave France for America in 1940 and 1941," in the words of then–Secretary of State Colin Powell.

Bingham's story echoed the tales of Holocaust heroes Sam heard as a boy, people like Swedish diplomat Raoul Wallenberg, who prevented the deportation of thousands of Hungarian Jews; Miep Gies, who hid Anne Frank and her family in Amsterdam; and German factory owner Oskar Schindler, who falsified records, bribed the Gestapo, and listed children as expert mechanics to shield Jewish workers in Poland.

The State Department hailed Bingham as a paragon of humanitarian virtue, but Sam learned a darker side of the story. When Bingham refused to stop saving Jewish refugees, his superiors derailed his career. They transferred him to Portugal then Argentina, and quashed his dream of an ambassadorship. Bingham resigned from the Foreign Service, ran through his inheritance, and died before his heroism was widely known.

Sam understood that independence like Bingham's could be viewed as career-ending insubordination. "It's one of those motivating factors for me. When you hear stories like that, you think, 'What would I do in that situation?'"

When he wasn't processing visa applications in Abuja, Sam spent as much time as possible with Liana. Sometimes that meant video "dates" during which they'd simultaneously watch a movie 1,400 miles apart. In March 2020, Sam and Liana went on safari in South Africa, where Sam enlisted their guides to help him arrange a sunset proposal on a hilltop under a painted sky. They married seven months later. Although Liana was raised Catholic and graduated from Notre Dame, they were wed by a rabbi at Sam's request.

When the engagement safari ended, Sam returned to Nigeria and Liana to Mali as Covid-19 spread around the globe. The State Department rushed to repatriate its officers, so Sam helped to coordinate flights and travel arrangements. His title changed from consular officer to staff aide, his desk moved to the ambassador's suite, and he managed a torrent of cables, memos, requests, and embassy correspondence. He took on special projects including delivery of a secret planeload of Covid vaccines to embassy staff and workers. He worked with others to build a case to the Department of Homeland Security to remove Nigeria from the "Muslim ban."

It was arguably the least exciting work of Sam's young career. But it felt the most meaningful. All his experiences had jelled. He applied what the Diplomatic Security Service calls the "deliberative planning process" to his judgments and actions as a diplomat.

In late 2018, when Sam first sought to join the diplomatic corps, he contacted the only other person he could find who'd made the leap from special agent to Foreign Service Officer: a State Department official with deep ties to Afghanistan named J.P. Feldmayer. Their phone call remained seared in Sam's memory.

"J.P. said, 'I was sick of standing outside the door. I wanted to be inside the room.' I was like, 'Oh my God, that is everything I've ever felt about this job. I don't want to be the bodyguard standing outside the door.'"

By the summer of 2021, the door was open and Sam was inside the room of American foreign policy.

WHEN SAM'S TWO-YEAR posting in Nigeria ended in July 2021, Liana joined him for a vacation in Washington and New York. After she returned to Mali, Sam had several weeks before he started Arabic classes and other training prior to his posting in Iraq.

That's how he ended up unwinding with friends on Martha's Vineyard during the first weekend of August 2021, and how that led to a chance reunion with Samantha Power, who'd played a major role in redirecting his career trajectory.

After Power's comments about the "small world" and possibly seeing Sam in Iraq, he said goodbye to her and Sunstein and returned to his friends.

As Sam drank his coffee, he still wished that he'd combed his hair and worn fresh clothes that morning. But he felt good, confident he had a bright future as a diplomat and that his days of risking his life for others were in the past.

3

KABUL

HOMEIRA AWOKE ON Monday, August 9, plagued by the twin crises of her life: the derailed financial support case against her ex-husband and the Taliban's menace to her home city of Herat. Sometimes they blended in her mind to form a single depressing, all-consuming threat.

After sending Siawash to school, Homeira welcomed a new lawyer into her apartment to discuss restarting her lawsuit. Over tea with milk, he delivered the bad news.

"It's a long journey," the lawyer said.

"What are the chances of me winning?"

Slim to none, he said. It wasn't clear they could convince a court to reopen the case. Even if they did, it was likely a waste of time and money. The laws overwhelmingly favored her ex-husband, and divorced women like Homeira might soon have even less standing in court.

"The Taliban is approaching from four corners," the lawyer said. "If they reach Kabul, they might not accept our legal system."

Those changes might be retroactive, he added. The Taliban might declare court decisions from the "republic era" of the previous twenty years illegal under its version of sharia. That meant Homeira had reason to worry not only about being denied her financial claims, but also losing custody of Siawash. If the Taliban took power, he said, secular lawyers like him and women like her would be cast aside: "Only God knows what will happen to you and I."

THE LAWYER'S WARNING rattled Homeira. The anguish of her sudden divorce and bitter custody battle remained fresh, ready to darken her mood and disrupt her thoughts. While they finished their tea, Homeira silently spun through a familiar cycle of rage, fear, and despair. Her first loss of Siawash nearly destroyed her. Losing him again might finish the job.

Homeira described the moment of separation in one of the letters she wrote to Siawash while they were apart, not knowing if he would ever read them. "You were snatched out of my arms while you were asleep and placed in your father's arms. I wanted you to wake up and fight the whole city—for your sake and for mine. But you were only nineteen months old and that was too much to expect of you." She passed out. Later she awoke in the care of a female friend, then imagined she heard Siawash wailing for her.

In the immediate aftermath, guilt compounded her grief. In the West, there would be little question that her ex-husband had selfishly triggered the crisis by discarding Homeira and denying Siawash his mother. But in male-dominated Afghan culture, the widely held view—even among some of her own family members—was that Homeira should have accepted her husband's authority and his right to polygamy, as generations of women had done before her. That way,

Homeira could have continued to raise Siawash, at the cost of her dignity. During the dark period when she was alone, Homeira sometimes wondered if she'd chosen wrong.

"Every day, I regret my decision to leave you," she wrote in one letter, begging his forgiveness. "I spend most of my nights crying in the corner of this room that has kept me so far from you."

Even as she suffered and second-guessed, deep down Homeira knew she couldn't have done otherwise. In one letter to Siawash, she urged him to view her actions as part of a larger struggle for women's rights. "Losing you was the most severe pain I have ever suffered," she wrote, "and I know you must be very, very angry. But I felt that I had to make a choice, not just for myself, but also for my country and ultimately for you. I don't want either of us to belong to a society that degrades women the way the Afghan society does."

Setbacks plagued her custody efforts, including one judge's cruel pronouncement: "This woman is no longer a mother. There is no need for the mother and child to know each other." She persevered, overcame her depression, and returned to Kabul from the United States to assert her maternal rights under Islamic law. She endured withering stares and harsh comments as she spent day after day in court. She refuted false accusations from her ex-husband about her fitness as a mother, eventually winning custody in a case that established a precedent for other Afghan women. That is, as long as the Taliban didn't return to impose its draconian form of "justice."

Once they reunited, Homeira appeared frequently on television to promote women's rights and her books, sometimes with Siawash at her side. He often seemed old beyond his years. Homeira called her son's emotional intelligence his "boldest and most beautiful characteristic." As they rebuilt their relationship, they formed a powerful bond around their shared sensitivity. "He is a boy who is never ashamed of expressing his emotions," she'd say. "When he's upset, he talks about why he's upset. When he's angry, he talks about his anger. When he's kind, he talks about his love and kindness with so much freedom and comfort."

By the summer of 2021, mother and son glowed in each other's presence. They danced, shared secrets, told private jokes, and watched movies. They bickered and made up, hugged with abandon, and dried each other's tears. At a small grocery store across from their apartment building, Siawash bought whatever he wanted and supplied friends with cans of Pepsi, all on her account, knowing she would never object. Yet scars remained. At night, mother and son each awoke multiple times to make sure the other was nearby.

AFTER THE LAWYER left, with hours until Siawash returned from school, Homeira set off for a place in Kabul she'd never been.

She'd always avoided the Shahr-e Naw Park, or "New City Park," where homeless male heroin addicts roamed barren fields. But in recent weeks hundreds of families from outside Kabul had flocked there, most of them women and children who'd abandoned homes and farms to escape the resurgent Taliban. Images she saw on social media reminded Homeira of the refugee children she taught in the mosque tent in Herat more than two decades earlier.

She took a taxi to the park carrying black garbage bags filled with packets of acetaminophen pills and sanitary napkins, based on her suspicion that male aid workers would overlook the needs of women. When she arrived, a male supervisor asked what she'd brought.

"Nothing much," Homeira said. "I need to talk to a woman." The migrant women gratefully snatched up her supplies. Homeira wished she'd purchased more.

Homeira learned that some of the women had husbands in the Afghan Army. They told her they'd fled with their children to Kabul to give the men peace of mind as they fought the Taliban. As she walked among them, Homeira became entranced by a girl perhaps five years old, running through a dusty field in a tattered red-and-yellow tunic. Homeira felt transported to her own childhood, when her family escaped the Soviet-Afghan War by fleeing to Iran. She could still taste the weak tea, hard bread, and salty cheese distributed in the refugee camps.

Back home, Homeira posted a photo of the girl on her Facebook page. "This girl is me, in a distant time," she wrote. "Those days, only God knows how much I missed home." She ended the post with a wish the girl would return home safely.

When Siawash returned from school, he told her many of his classmates had stayed away. "They're scared," he said. "They're saying the Taliban is coming to occupy the city."

Homeira exploded. "These are lies! No one is coming to occupy anywhere. The Taliban is not coming."

Seeking reassurance, she called her father. Again she heard gunfire as she urged Wakil Ahmad to bring their family to Kabul.

"What difference does it make where in this country we fall?" he asked.

What about the "people's uprising" led by Mohammad Ismail Khan, the "Lion of Herat"?

"Homeira-jan," her father said, "they can't fight with empty hands. They can't fight with axes and saws. No one is helping. Even the people's uprising is hopeless."

A DAY LATER, August 10, Homeira told her new lawyer she wouldn't try to reopen her financial support case. It felt heartbreaking, a capitulation to her ex-husband's spite and a surrender to the system that empowered him. To ease her regret, she told herself she'd reconsider as soon as the Taliban was defeated.

Homeira cleaned the apartment, played records on her gramophone, and scolded Siawash's turtle for sleeping late. "You are the lazy member of the family," she told Sangi. The turtle followed her to her office, its nails clicking against the floor as she worked on a collection of short stories for an Iranian publisher. The stories shared a common theme: the plight of women in Afghanistan and the changes that needed to occur.

As afternoon approached, she made plans to return to the Institute of Strategic Studies, for a news conference to call attention to the new Council of Cohesion and Support for Popular Resistance in Herat. She texted Siawash to remind him to go to her uncle's house after school while she was at the institute.

"What do you do there?" he texted back in frustration.

"I go there to fight with the Taliban," she said, half joking.

He replied with a screen filled with crying-face emojis.

At the news conference, the lone woman among ten men at a long table, Homeira wore a bright yellow dress and a matching lace headscarf. Facing a handful of reporters, Homeira listened as one man after another called on the central government in Kabul to support Herat. With each new speaker, the more pointless the words seemed. Her father's message sunk in. They were too late to save Herat. Their delegation trip had been canceled, and they lacked the power to persuade President Ashraf Ghani to send guns to their home city.

Yet Homeira wasn't ready to share her pessimism, at least not publicly. Even if she couldn't go to Herat or deliver weapons to its defenders, she could boost morale. That night, during an interview on Iranian television, Homeira denounced a suggestion by a political analyst that most Afghans had mentally surrendered to the Taliban. She insisted the resistance in Herat was gaining strength.

"If needed," she said, "we will fight to the last drop of blood."

Siawash always watched her television appearances.

Before he went to sleep, he asked, "Mom, you say the Taliban won't win?"

"No, honey. As long as we're here, the Taliban won't succeed. Sleep well."

HOMEIRA ROSE THE next morning, Wednesday, August 11, anxious to do something more meaningful than posting on social media and arguing with television analysts. She called her publisher to ask if two hundred copies of her new children's picture book could be distributed free to the refugee girls and boys in Shahr-e Naw Park. The publisher agreed and promised to supply juice and cookies, too.

Dressed in a cheery teal blazer and a headscarf with colorful stripes, Homeira squatted on the dirt as children crowded around her. She stayed at the park for hours, listening to one child after another read her words about a little brown bear who lived in a happy jungle and didn't want to go to school. One girl, perhaps nine years old, read with such passion Homeira fantasized about adopting her. She pulled the girl close and kissed her head. Each child who proved her or his reading ability received a book.

Many of the children, some as old as twelve, couldn't read. They worked in the fields or in stores, and they weren't allowed to attend school. Homeira grew emotional as she heard their stories. Tears streamed down her cheeks and saturated the striped mask she wore intermittently amid the ongoing pandemic. "How much these children understand pain," she thought.

As she read aloud to them, Homeira choked up at the thought that so many were illiterate, with no prospects for more schooling. As they waited for her next word, her audience sat still and silent. After more than a minute, her voice returned and she finished the book. She wished she'd brought a blackboard like the one her father carried each day to the mosque tent. Before she left the park, Homeira told children who could read to teach the rest.

Homeira hailed a taxi to Siawash's school and took him home early. She called her mother, Ansari, who worried about the gunfire at night but seemed most upset about not being able to stroll around Herat. "We're waiting for the whole Taliban and war issue to be done with, so we can go for walks again in a few days," her mother said.

Her father, who habitually staked out an opposing position from her mother, took a bleaker view. "This city will fall today or tomorrow," Wakil Ahmad told Homeira.

"I wish I could come to Herat," she said.

"Even the generals can't do anything," he replied. "What do you want to do here?"

Homeira's dark humor returned.

"I miss the Taliban," she said. "I want to see them."

"You will see them," her father said. "You will see them in your city."

That night, Homeira posted photos on Facebook from the book giveaway, with the message: "In war with the Taliban, everyone has a method. Everyone has a weapon. My weapon is my pen." A feminist magazine in Kabul published a story about the event, and one commenter wrote: "Kind lady, may you live a long life. May you become a thousand years old."

But Homeira also received troubling private messages from friends.

"From this moment, people like you are on their list," one wrote. "Your kind will get hurt. Taliban will remove you people first from the society, especially because you're a woman. Stay quiet for a while."

Most had good intentions, but it angered Homeira that Afghans were already prepared to return to the submission they endured under the previous Taliban regime.

"We lived under the tyranny of the Taliban for five years, and society was silent," she thought. "So much so that even the world became silent. The world thought we had surrendered to the Taliban and we were fine."

A migraine brewing for days hit full force. Homeira tried to ignore it as she scrolled sites on her laptop. News of defeat dominated her social media feed.

Hundreds of Afghan troops had surrendered to the Taliban in Kunduz. Reports circulated that U.S. intelligence officials believed the Afghan government could fall within ninety days, perhaps sooner. Commenters on Homeira's social media pages condemned President Biden's remark to reporters a day earlier that he had no plans to slow the withdrawal of U.S. troops.

"Look," Biden said, "we spent over a trillion dollars over twenty years. We trained and equipped with modern equipment over 300,000 Afghan forces. And Afghan leaders have to come together. We lost thousands—lost to death and injury—thousands of American personnel. They've got to fight for themselves, fight for their nation."

"Who says we don't fight for ourselves?" Homeira wondered bitterly.

Unable to sleep, she rose after 2 A.M. and went to an open window overlooking the nearby mosque. Homeira wasn't religious, but she knelt to say a prayer: "God, don't take this bed, these stars, the Sakhi Shrine, and Kabul University from me. This small geography is where my child and I are fortunate and happy. Don't take away Kabul and Afghanistan from us."

AWAKE AGAIN BY 6 A.M., on Thursday, August 12, Homeira stared at her reflection in the bathroom mirror. Her face looked swollen. She had bags under both eyes, and her cheeks were chapped from rubbing away tears in her sleep. Her migraine pounded behind her left eye. "I've never seen myself this ugly before," she thought.

She turned on the cold faucet and dunked her head under the water. Feeling slightly better, Homeira looked at the clock and saw she had another half hour before she needed to wake Siawash for school. She lay on a couch outside the bathroom. Staring into space, she spotted Sangi in the living room and realized she forgot to feed it again. She thanked God she hadn't stepped on it. After filling the turtle's plate with lettuce Homeira returned to the couch.

Lying there, she noticed a thin layer of dirt covering her wood floor. She hadn't closed the window after her late-night prayer, and all the grit of Kabul seemed to have blown in overnight. She rolled off the couch and drew lazy lines in the dirt with her fingers.

Homeira closed the window and found her phone. She read a text from her youngest sibling, her brother Khalid, a journalist and poet who worked for a radio station in Herat: "Everything is messed up over here." Other messages echoed the sentiment.

Typically grouchy upon waking, Siawash was grumpier than usual when she roused him. Homeira wanted to keep him home from school and try to enjoy the day together. She imagined hugging and talking with him for hours, as though the Taliban didn't exist. But she fought the urge and helped him dress. With the electricity out again, they walked downstairs to the waiting school van. As she dragged herself back upstairs, Homeira searched the faces of schoolgirls on their way down, trying to see if they had fear in their eyes.

Back in her apartment, Homeira put water on the stove for tea then returned to her bed. She awoke forty minutes later to a home filled with smoke. Coughing, she grabbed the scorched tea kettle to put it outside on the balcony, but on the way it brushed against a curtain and burned a large hole. She tossed the kettle onto the balcony and went to the kitchen to rinse smoke from her mouth.

Exasperated, fighting despair, Homeira threw herself back onto her bed.

Eventually she rose and made herself milk tea. She brought her laptop to bed, to distract herself by working on her story collection. Words swam before her eyes. She felt sick, closed her laptop, and flopped onto her back.

Returning to her phone, Homeira opened a group email inviting her to another meeting at the Institute for Strategic Studies. She noticed that every invited man with a PhD was called "Doctor," but she was addressed as "Ms." She wrote a scathing reply to the man who sent it.

Trying to remain constructive, Homeira poured out her feelings in an email to poet Christopher Merrill, director of the International Writing Program at the University of Iowa, where she took refuge after her divorce. Homeira asked for his help editing a letter she wrote asking the writers of the world to support the people of Afghanistan.

"My whole country is burning in the fire of war with the Taliban. We went back exactly to the point of twenty years ago. Our schools are destroyed and our women give birth on the streets. Our captives are killed and our people emigrate again. . . . This war belongs to the whole world. We do not have enough weapons, we do not have enough forces with such a big war. This war will soon reach all over the world in the form of small and large suicides. We are too few to resist this rapid terrorist current, although we will do this even to the last person."

Near the end of the email, Homeira turned the focus briefly to herself: "I know that if Talib reaches Kabul, they will kill me too. But before I die, I must do something."

HOURS PASSED. HER throat ached and she wondered if she'd caught Covid-19. The pandemic had slid far down her list of worries, and she'd lowered her mask among the refugee children at the park. She took acetaminophen and decided the kitchen smoke caused her scratchy throat.

Homeira texted her brother Khalid, "What news?"

His upbeat reply gave her the jolt she needed: "No news. I'm ready to go to work. All chic and handsome. I've shaved my beard"—a protest against the bearded Talibs—"put on my suit, and I'm going to work. To hell with the Taliban."

Homeira got off the bed and began her day anew. She forced herself to prepare for an online writing course she taught every Thursday. This week's lesson focused on the classic short story "The Lottery" by Shirley Jackson, about the cost of blind adherence to deadly traditions.

Afterward, Homeira returned to the kitchen to prepare her favorite meal, *ghormeh sabzi,* a savory Persian herb stew. As she cooked, she played a pop ballad on her laptop called "*Az To Dooram*" ("Away From You").

Her brother's text, the song, and the savory smells lifted Homeira's mood.

"When there is romantic music playing in my house," she'd say, "it makes me feel everything is normal and I am a normal, natural woman who can be in love but doesn't want to be. It makes me feel blessed and that there is nothing bad happening beyond the walls."

But quickly she returned to what she called "a thousand and one sorrows."

Homeira worried how her neighbors would react if they heard a love song playing in the apartment of a divorced woman. She wished she could banish feelings of shame about the judgments of traditional Afghan women, but her nanah-jan's warning that women should neither be seen nor heard went bone-deep. Homeira turned the volume low, so anyone outside her apartment would only hear the crackling of onions frying on the stove.

Her phone rang. She saw it was Khalid, and she didn't pick up. She worried that the bravado of her brother's earlier text would be replaced by terrible news from Herat. He followed with a text demanding that she look at the video he'd sent. In it, Homeira saw Taliban fighters carrying rifles and rocket-propelled grenade launchers as they ran past Herat's central mosque. She heard them shouting to passersby, demanding to know where to find the police department.

Homeira called Khalid.

"Did you see them?" he asked, weeping. "They were the Taliban."

Hearing her brother say the name devastated her. Twenty-six years after hollow-eyed Talibs first arrived in Herat with their medieval rules, they were back. Exactly as her father predicted.

"Herat has fallen," Khalid said. "The Taliban have captured the whole city."

Homeira cursed herself for not traveling there days earlier, to be with her family. If she'd gone, she also could have supported the girls of her home city who would soon be shackled in burqas and stripped of their freedoms and their futures.

Homeira felt sick. She told Khalid to go home.

"This city is home," he cried. "Where do I go from here?"

She urged him to come to Kabul, where she thought he'd be safe.

Soon, news reports would announce that Mohammad Ismail Khan had surrendered. Taliban fighters posted selfies with the "Lion of Herat" on social media, to lionize themselves and ridicule him. Also on Thursday, August 12, the Taliban seized Kandahar, the country's second-largest city, along with Lashkar Gah in the southwest, and the strategically important city of Ghazni. In little more than a week, over half of Afghanistan's thirty-four provincial capitals had fallen, with more teetering. Taliban fighters grew closer to Kabul by the hour.

WHEN HOMEIRA ROUSED Siawash the next morning, Friday, August 13, the sleepy boy reached up and rubbed the skin under her eyes. "You didn't wash your eye makeup," he said.

She told him her dark circles weren't from makeup. She'd barely slept.

"I understand," Siawash said. "It's because of the Taliban."

Homeira fought back tears.

Sitting up, stretching, Siawash said he needed to make a confession.

Homeira brightened. "You ate chocolate and cookies without my permission?"

"No." Siawash laughed. "If I eat those I won't tell you."

He grew serious. "Do you remember I always said that I and Danial always get the best grades in the class, and Marveh is always the last?"

Homeira said she remembered. She knew Danial was Siawash's best male friend at school, and Marveh was a tall girl with a ponytail who was born in Russia. Homeira spoke some Russian and occasionally talked with Marveh in her native tongue, which frustrated Siawash. From watching online classes, Homeira also knew that Siawash and Danial teased Marveh that they were smarter than she.

"Mom, I lied to you. Marveh gets the best grades."

She hugged him. "Siawash-jan, I knew that Marveh is a very good student." She asked why he spoke poorly of her.

"Because she would learn fast," he said.

"It's okay, but don't lie again," Homeira said.

"I wasn't lying," he insisted. "I didn't want you to know that Marveh knows more than I do."

Homeira was ready to move on. "Siawash-jan, you can skip school today. I have a couple of things to do outside. We can do them together."

Normally thrilled to spend a day with his mother, Siawash refused.

"Now that the Taliban is here, they might not allow the schools to stay open. They might not allow Marveh to come to our class. I might not see Marveh again. These are the last days. Let me go."

Homeira felt like she'd been struck. Her son had surrendered to the idea that a Taliban takeover was inevitable. And he knew the gravest cost would be borne by women and girls.

Homeira composed herself. Days earlier, she'd promised the head of Siawash's school she would send copies of her books for his daughter Asal, who was in third grade. Now, Homeira gathered the books in a plastic bag and gave them to Siawash.

"Go to the third grade class and ask who Asal is," she said. "Give her the books as a gift."

As they prepared to leave, Siawash asked, "Will you give Marveh a book, too?"

Homeira tucked two more into his backpack.

Outside, men and some women hurried to work. Children went to school. It looked as though nothing had changed, but Homeira felt heaviness in the morning air.

Back in the apartment, Homeira found an online link to an interview she gave days earlier to a publication at the International Writing Program at the University of Iowa. In the interview, Homeira blasted the Taliban and condemned the past forty years of wars as "monsters that have eaten two generations of Afghans." She insisted she had no plans to leave the country. "How can I leave my father at his age? My sister? My mother?" Yet she acknowledged feeling torn. "I am also responsible for my child. He is entitled to live in a peaceful and safe environment. My child is too young to die on the battlefield."

As a final question, the interviewer asked, "What is your utopia?"

Homeira could have said her apartment and her neighborhood, where Siawash shopped on her credit at the grocery store; where a pushcart boy sold lettuce they fed Sangi; where trees hung heavy with apricots; where red and white flowers decorated Kabul University; where docile stray dogs in the alleys bothered no one. The "small geography" of her rebuilt life.

Instead she answered with a global perspective: "I want the world to be a place where women are treated and respected equal to men. Really equal. I want children in Afghan schools to have time to tell stories—should there be any schools left standing. I want the world to be a place where people are more powerful than bullets."

She spent hours scrolling social media and reading sorrowful messages from friends and acquaintances. She remembered a line from the novel *A Time to Love and a Time to Die*, about a German soldier in World War II who returns home to find his house in ruins and his parents missing. She tweeted out the line: "I wish I could go to sleep and wake up in another time."

HOMEIRA BEGAN SATURDAY, August 14, with the realization that she had, in fact, woken up in another time. Afghanistan had turned back the calendar to the Taliban's September 1995 capture of Herat.

Even as she dreaded what would happen next, Homeira held no false illusions about the two decades that followed the Taliban's 2001 defeat. She believed the groundwork was laid for the extremists' return during the charismatic, chaotic, and frequently corrupt presidency of Hamid Karzai, from 2001 to 2014. Racial, ethnic, and gender-based discrimination ran rampant, she thought, as politically dominant Pashtuns hoarded Western financial support and handed out jobs and promotions to their kinsmen and political cronies.

Homeira insisted she had firsthand experience that non-Pashto speakers like herself were treated as inferior. A year earlier, when she worked at the Ministry of Education, the minister who was her boss spoke Farsi, just as she did. When he was replaced by a woman who spoke Pashto, Homeira said, she was barred from meetings and forced out of the job.

Her criticisms of the republic era extended more broadly to the absence of widespread improvements in infrastructure, education, and living standards. Under the Afghan republic, she said, the five million people who lived in Kabul generally enjoyed increased freedoms and better lives. But millions of Afghans in rural areas remained impoverished, with few if any advances for women and girls. Homeira believed the Taliban's resurgence reflected anger among people in the countryside.

"Being ready for the Taliban doesn't mean people would pick up their guns and join the Taliban," she thought. "It means if the Taliban comes, some people would support them."

Still, Homeira had no plans to join the crowds of Kabul residents who formed long lines around passport offices. She envisioned Kabul remaining independent, a fortified island surrounded by Taliban-captured territory. Maybe the Afghan Army would even regroup and repel them. The Ministry of Defense was in Kabul, as was the president himself. Kabul was also home to powerful warlords like Abdul Rashid Dostum, whose past brutalities and alleged war crimes were overlooked in favor of his anti-Taliban credentials. American troops remained, too, even if only temporarily. Homeira believed it might take the Taliban several months to breach Kabul's defenses, if ever. She felt certain that she'd have time to reassess her decision to stay in Afghanistan.

Homeira's analysis alarmed friends outside the country.

The translator of her memoir, Zaman Stanizai, a professor of Islamic studies who lived in California, insisted that she try to leave immediately with Siawash. She replied that being forced out of Afghanistan would feel like being evicted from her apartment. "I was meant to live my old age in Kabul," she told him. "I was meant to stay with my friends and family."

Other international friends tried to scare Homeira by describing how the Taliban would target her, as an example to others who might oppose them. She already knew.

"There's no doubt the Taliban would settle things with me if they show up," she'd say. "For twenty years, I fought against the Taliban in the world media. I wrote against them. . . . The Taliban had two enemies: enemies who had guns and enemies who had pens. They had to get rid of both of them."

Worried for her safety, her father sided with her far-flung friends.

"You are one of those people who need to leave the country," he told her by phone. "I wish you had a Turkish visa."

"What have I done?" she replied. "What crimes have I committed?"

Wakil Ahmad told Homeira that people were lined up at the newly occupied Herat municipal buildings, begging Taliban officials for letters of safe conduct attesting they shouldn't be harmed. Also known as amnesty letters, the documents might or might not protect a person who crossed paths with a Talib in the mood to commit violence against civilians.

"None of these people have committed a crime," her father said. "Also, none of them have a book like you've written about dancing in a mosque. Yet those people are standing in line. You have written against them for twenty years. Either they will force you to get a letter of safe conduct and then kill you, or they won't deem you worthy of even a letter of safe conduct."

She understood that he meant summary execution.

"I haven't committed murder," she said. "They have committed murders. They have committed suicide bombings. And I should receive a letter of safe conduct?"

Even as she argued with her father, Homeira knew that logic carried no weight. She sounded like Siawash suggesting they could defeat the Taliban by inviting them to learn the difference between right and wrong at his school.

"Homeira-jan," her father said. "I was much younger than you when I picked up a gun. At some point in Afghanistan's politics, I realized there is no use fighting, so I put down my weapon. If you stay here, you'll also have to put down your weapon. And if you put down your weapon, you'll have no identity. You are Homeira Qaderi, the writer whose voice people need to hear. If you get a letter of safe conduct and remain silent, who will you be?"

After the call, Homeira imagined Siawash as a grown man living an impoverished life in the ruins he'd sung about as a boy: "You damned Talibs. One day you will burn this country to the ground." If that happened, he'd have a right to ask why they hadn't fled.

She'd answer: "My child, I loved my country and I had to fight."

Homeira went for an afternoon walk around Kabul University, where an attack nine months earlier by three ISIS gunmen killed thirty-five people and wounded dozens.

The weather was good, not too hot, and normally Homeira would enjoy watching students talking and laughing near vendors selling *bolani*, a fried flatbread stuffed with leeks, pumpkin, or potatoes. But the tree-lined campus was empty.

As she walked, and again after she returned home, she considered the pleas by her father and her friends that she leave. She also thought about how much she loved living in Kabul, how tied she felt to the country, and how her apartment represented all she'd achieved and nearly everything she owned. She recalled how her mother explained being a refugee: "It means becoming a stranger in a foreign country. It means dying alone."

Homeira thought, "Running from my problems won't give me

peace."

She announced her decision to her family and international friends: "From this moment, no one is allowed to talk about me emigrating."

Siawash tested that edict immediately upon his return from school. Two of his classmates had fled the country with their families.

"When are we leaving this place?" he asked.

"We're going nowhere," she said. "This is our home. This is our life."

"What should I do if the Taliban kills you?"

The question reminded Homeira how large and frightening the world can seem to a child. She remembered wondering as a girl what would happen if the Soviets killed her father. But as much as she sympathized with Siawash, she felt tired of defending her position.

"We're not leaving!"

When she calmed down, Homeira grew unsettled by doubts about Siawash's future if something terrible happened to her.

Several days earlier, her ex-husband had texted: "Whoever leaves Afghanistan sooner has to take the child." Initially she dismissed the idea. Now she reconsidered it.

Her migraine worsened. Her stomach churned. The thought of losing Siawash again felt like too much to bear. But Homeira decided that Siawash's safety and future had to take precedence. If his father found a way out, Homeira resolved, she would allow Siawash to go with him, his new wife, and their young son, Siawash's half brother.

"What bad nights we have," she tweeted before going to sleep. "What a miserable time has befallen this nation. How disappointed . . . how lonely we are."

THE SAME DAY, Saturday, August 14, Taliban fighters captured Mazar-i-Sharif, the country's fourth-largest city, as well as six more provincial capitals: Gardez, Sharana, Asadabad, Maymana, Mihtarlam, and Nili. The lightning advance gave the Taliban control of much

of the north, west, and south. With a few exceptions where the Afghan Army fought fiercely, government soldiers and their allies generally offered little resistance. Two legendary warlords, Abdul Rashid
Dostum and Atta Muhammad Nur, fled to Uzbekistan.

By day's end, Taliban fighters encircled Kabul.

In a televised address, his first public comments in a week, a subdued Ashraf Ghani said he was focused on "preventing further instability, violence, and displacement of my people." Yet his own finance
minister had fled the country. Ghani didn't address a Taliban demand
that he resign the presidency as a condition of cease-fire talks. Criticism of the former World Bank anthropologist intensified after the
speech, based largely on Ghani's role in bringing the country to the
precipice and refusing to take advice on military matters beyond his
expertise.

As the crisis intensified, Biden told reporters in Washington he
would increase the number of U.S. troops to approximately five thousand, roughly one thousand more than previously announced. Still,
they wouldn't fight the Taliban. American forces would only ensure
"an orderly and safe drawdown of U.S. personnel and other allied
personnel, and an orderly and safe evacuation of Afghans who helped
our troops during our mission and those at special risk from the Taliban advance."

AT 10 A.M. on Sunday, August 15, Homeira was home alone, having
sent Siawash to school. Her puffy face and bloodshot eyes displayed
her anguish. Days had passed since she'd last cleaned the apartment,
so the dust that blew in through open windows hung like a veil on
every surface.

Her ringing phone roused her from a daze.

"The Taliban is behind the gates of Kabul!" her brother Jaber
shouted when Homeira answered. Jaber said Ashraf Ghani had fled
the country, perhaps recalling a disemboweled previous president who

was hung from a lamppost the last time the Taliban seized power. Afghanistan had no government. The republic was dead.

In danger of being branded a collaborator, Jaber set off walking across the fallen city toward their building.

The sudden collapse of Kabul defied nearly unanimous predictions by international diplomatic, military, intelligence, academic, and media experts, who expected a monthslong siege and a stout defense of the capital.

A Taliban spokesman would explain that the insurgents hadn't planned to take the city that day, but Ghani's unexpected departure left no alternative. A hasty agreement was reached between U.S. and Taliban officials: Kabul would be under Taliban rule, but American troops and diplomats would control the airport for a massive evacuation until August 31.

After Jaber's call, Homeira fell deeper into shock. She stared at her laptop screen and watched images of her Kabul-jan unraveling around her, in real time.

Siawash rushed through the door around 11:30 A.M.

"Mom," he announced, "they have taken the city! My teacher sent us home so we would be safe." He explained the situation to Sangi the turtle: "Yeah, Taliban have reached Kabul, too. It's over. Running around is over. Going to school is over."

Jaber arrived home around 1 P.M., his eyes red, his clothes caked in dust after the four-mile walk from the presidential palace.

"People were running around in every direction," he told Homeira. "There were no cars. No one was willing to open their car doors." Jaber said Afghan Army soldiers streamed toward the airport. Exhausted, his shoulders slumped, he went to his apartment to shower.

Homeira's ex-husband called to talk with Siawash.

"Don't go outside," he warned. "There are Taliban members outside your house."

Determined to show Siawash she wasn't afraid, she put on a black-and-white-striped dress that almost touched the floor. She picked out a long black headscarf large enough to drape around her body, if necessary.

She left the building and walked directly to a neighborhood bank. No Taliban marauders in sight.

Homeira navigated lines of panicky customers to get inside, where she emptied her savings account of the equivalent of about two thousand U.S. dollars. She anticipated the Taliban would prevent her from working outside her home, so she intended to ration the money to keep herself and Siawash fed. The bank manager knew Homeira and presumed she had powerful connections. As he handed her the cash, he begged, "Please help me leave Afghanistan."

Until then, Homeira thought the other customers were like her, gathering money to survive in the Taliban's new Kabul. Now she realized many were withdrawing money before rushing to the airport.

Homeira saw no sign of the Taliban as she returned home. Inside the apartment, she tried to calm the fears of her Facebook followers. She posted a photo of herself kneeling on the balcony with a hint of a smile as she watered her plants. "Sweet land," she wrote as a caption. Thousands of "likes" poured in. But even that image held pain. One vase held a pumpkin plant Siawash nurtured from a seed for a school project. Homeira suspected he would never return to his international school.

She walked Siawash downstairs to her uncle's apartment to play with Abo Ismael's sons. Siawash darkly joked, "I'm going there to talk about politics."

Homeira left the building and took her usual route toward Kabul University, a few hundred meters away. She crossed a road parallel to the campus and approached the high walls surrounding the school. Dark green government cars bearing the insignia of the Ministry of the Interior sped past. Taliban fighters filled each one.

Homeira felt light-headed. They really had arrived.

Losing her balance, Homeira leaned against the university's wall to keep from falling. She stood there like a butterfly pinned to a board.

Unable to regain her bearings, she slumped to the ground. She spread her black scarf over herself like a tent. Homeira thought she must resemble a homeless beggar. More Talib-filled cars raced by. They looked the same as when she last saw them in person, more than two decades earlier: bearded killers, hungry and hard.

Homeira felt jolted back to her teenage self. She recalled the day her students danced inside the mosque. How they cowered when two Talib guards came to investigate the joyful sounds of clapping. How she lied her way out of trouble from under her burqa. She remembered the friends who set themselves on fire. She recalled her father burning newspapers to save her from a public whipping. She remembered Commander Moosa's threat to take her for a wife, and how she'd been forced into an arranged marriage to avoid that fate. She felt overwhelmed, suffocating, as her past and present collided.

Beneath a smoldering summer sun, her back against a wall, hidden under her scarf, Homeira blacked out.

WHEN SHE WOKE, Homeira didn't know how long she'd been unconscious.

The street was quiet. The sun sunk toward the horizon. Her bones creaked with complaint as she rose to stand in the shade of the university wall. She wondered if she could muster the energy for the short walk home.

Stumbling forward, she moved by memory toward her building, her eyes seeing only darkness and the imagined faces of Talibs. Homeira took a step, then another.

She reached her apartment and crumpled onto the couch. Until this moment, Homeira thought nothing could be worse than her divorce, the custody battle, and the failed financial support case. No longer. She'd call those hardships "a small blow." The Taliban's return and the fall of Kabul were "a hard blow that has beheaded me."

Homeira burst into tears, wailing until her lungs and throat ached.

She didn't care if the neighbors heard her. They should be crying, too.

Thinking of her neighbors snapped Homeira back to the present. She remembered she'd been invited to an engagement party that afternoon for a young woman in the building. She couldn't contemplate a celebration. Later she'd learn the family had turned the event into a rushed wedding. It lasted fifteen minutes and no one touched the food.

When she stopped weeping, Homeira tweeted: "I walked the streets of Kabul as much as I could. I do not hide that for many minutes I cried for my country, my homeland." Privately, she wrote a friend: "I feel sorry for my eyes that I had to see the Taliban twice in my short life."

She saw that a different friend had posted a video of herself screaming, "The Taliban have reached Kabul!" Homeira sent her a private message: "These people, these little girls, are already afraid enough. Don't do this. You have a foreign passport and you can easily leave, but millions of people here don't have passports. We are staying here. Don't make our fears worse."

She spoke by phone with a cousin in the Afghan Army. He said his commander ordered their unit not to fight. "Put down your guns and get yourselves home as soon as possible if you don't want to get killed," he quoted the officer as saying. Her cousin and his comrades stripped off their uniforms and sprinted home in their underwear, humiliated but alive.

Homeira's father called.

"My girl, don't be scared," Wakil Ahmad said.

"It's not about being scared," she said. "I'm sad."

She walked downstairs to get Siawash. Clusters of children huddled in the stairwell on each floor, forbidden or afraid to play outside. Homeira saw one of her uncle's sons wearing a little white hat that resembled a Taliban turban.

"It's so that when the Taliban sees me they won't kill me," the boy explained. "They'll think I'm one of them."

4

VOLUNTEER

O N THAT SAME Sunday, August 15, a week after returning from Martha's Vineyard, Sam sat in his small Washington, D.C., apartment and watched grim news reports about the collapse of Afghanistan's government and military.

He saw images of Taliban fighters parading through the presidential palace and celebrating with gunfire in the streets of Kabul. American Chinook transport helicopters churned through the sky bearing U.S. diplomats fleeing the embassy and the fortified Green Zone for the relative safety of Hamid Karzai International Airport, better known as Kabul International. Soon he'd learn that, before leaving, the diplomats filled incinerators, disintegrators, and "burn bins" with classified documents, American flags, and other items the Taliban would value for intelligence and propaganda. Commentators spread blame between the Trump and Biden administrations, and likened the scene to the fall of Saigon at the end of the Vietnam War.

Sam's boss, Secretary of State Tony Blinken, had spent the morning making the rounds of Sunday news shows. He tried to downplay the Taliban's lightning takeover, the resulting rush of frightened Afghans and international citizens to the airport, and the rapid reinsertion of thousands of American troops. On ABC's *This Week*, Blinken described the U.S. embassy evacuation as a routine step in a long-planned withdrawal.

"This is being done in a very deliberate way," he said. "It's being done in an orderly way. And it's being done with American forces there to make sure we can do it in a safe way."

Anchor Jonathan Karl objected: "Respectfully, not much about what we're seeing seems too orderly or standard operating procedure. . . . Just last month, President Biden said that under no circumstance, and those were his words, under no circumstance, would U.S. personnel, embassy personnel, be airlifted out of Kabul in a replay of the scenes that we saw in Saigon in 1975. So, isn't that exactly what we're seeing now?"

"Let's take a step back," Blinken replied. "This is manifestly not Saigon."

Blinken insisted that the United States had succeeded in its original mission to punish Osama bin Laden for 9/11 and to remove the threat of terrorism by al-Qaeda against the United States and its allies. He emphasized those accomplishments came at a cost of more than 2,300 American lives and a trillion U.S. dollars. He asserted that the time had come to leave: "In terms of what we set out to do in Afghanistan, we've done it."

Even as Blinken pushed back, he somberly conceded a harsh truth about the Taliban's return to power: "When we consider women and girls, all those who've had their lives advanced, this is searing. It is hard stuff." On behalf of those twenty million Afghan women and girls, the U.S. secretary of state could only make a tepid appeal to the Taliban's self-interest.

"[I]f they truly seek acceptance, international recognition, if they want support, if they want sanctions lifted. All of that will require them to uphold basic rights, fundamental rights. If they don't . . . then I think Afghanistan will become a pariah state."

THAT NIGHT, AS Sam readied for bed, his phone pinged with a text from his father.

"Did you know anyone who was evacuated from Kabul?" Mark Aronson asked.

As Sam read the text, Afghanistan seemed nearly as remote to him as it did to his father. Some of his former Diplomatic Security colleagues worked there, he thought, but Sam wasn't in regular contact with them.

"I know a few people there," Sam texted back, "but not sure if they've been evacuated yet."

As a young diplomat, particularly one new to the job who'd served under two vastly different presidents, Sam didn't publicly express opinions about the conduct or rationale of American foreign policy. Even in private, he possessed no special knowledge or strongly held beliefs about the end of the United States' presence in Afghanistan.

In fact, in the summer of 2021, Sam's familiarity with Afghanistan reflected the detached awareness of many Americans who lacked first-hand experience of the country. He understood why the United States was there. He knew the names of its major cities, a handful of significant historical events, and the main languages spoken by its people. He could find it on a map but knew little of its geography or climate. He had no Afghan friends. He knew what he read in newspapers, and what he heard or saw on television, radio, and the internet.

Yet also like most Americans, Sam understood that Afghanistan had suddenly flared into the biggest news story in the world. Attention focused on the danger to Americans and U.S. Green Card holders trapped in a country suddenly controlled by the Taliban, as well as

Afghans who'd worked with the United States and NATO or served in the democratic government. Plus untold at-risk Afghan activists who'd opposed the Taliban and now feared death. Tens of thousands of them—some eligible for evacuation, some not—streamed toward the gates of Kabul International with their families to seek seats aboard outgoing flights.

On Monday, August 16, the day after Sam exchanged texts with his father, he watched President Biden defend the U.S. withdrawal in a televised address.

Biden acknowledged being surprised by events on the ground. "The truth is, this did unfold more quickly than we had anticipated. So what's happened? Afghanistan political leaders gave up and fled the country. The Afghan military collapsed, sometimes without trying to fight."

He insisted that the United States made the right decision.

"I'm left again to ask of those who argue that we should stay: How many more generations of America's daughters and sons would you have me send to fight Afghans—Afghanistan's civil war—when Afghan troops will not?" the president asked. "How many more lives—American lives—is it worth? How many endless rows of headstones at Arlington National Cemetery?"

The mission ahead, Biden said, "will be short in time, limited in scope, and focused in its objectives: Get our people and our allies to safety as quickly as possible."

That meant somehow assembling, screening, safeguarding, searching, and evacuating an estimated 120,000 people from Kabul International in little more than ten days. That timeline would allow several additional days for thousands of U.S. servicemen and women to leave before August 31. Biden initially set a final withdrawal date of September 11, for the symmetry of ending the war twenty years after its start, but he moved up the deadline when Kabul fell.

Two hours after Biden's speech, Sam read a text from The Squad, four friends from his Foreign Service orientation class he maintained a group chat with. One, a consular official who examined visa applications in Monterrey, Mexico, told the group he'd volunteered to go to Doha, Qatar, to help with the evacuation. If selected, he'd process the paperwork of Afghan nationals who held or had sought Special Immigrant Visas, or SIVs, a program created in 2009 to help people who'd worked on behalf of the United States.

At 6:16 P.M., Sam responded in the chat: "Whoa, super cool."

For the next half hour, Sam's mind whirred with possibilities. With Liana back in Mali and his Arabic classes not starting until after Labor Day, Sam had few plans for the next three weeks other than a dentist appointment and a vet visit for Stella. Allergic to inactivity, repelled by boredom, impulsive when it came to opportunity and adventure, Sam's beach weekend on Martha's Vineyard was all the idle time he could stomach.

At 6:48 P.M., Sam asked in the group chat: "How do I volunteer?"

Even if he wasn't sent to Doha or Kabul, which seemed unlikely, maybe Sam could get assigned to night shifts answering emails for the Afghanistan Task Force at State Department headquarters, a few blocks from his apartment. Or maybe he'd be sent to a U.S. military base receiving Afghan refugees. Anything would be better than nothing. He resolved to mount a campaign the next morning to be chosen as a volunteer.

AS SAM TRIED to sleep, he vacillated, not about the mission but about his eligibility for it. He recalled an incident in September 2018, when he volunteered for an emergency Diplomatic Security assignment in Syria in the midst of a crisis there. After being chosen, with his flights confirmed and his hopes high, Sam ran into a buzz saw of bureaucracy from the State Department's human resources bureau. Someone noticed that Sam hadn't completed the mandatory twenty days of home leave after his Niger posting. Feathers were ruffled, his flights were canceled, and his hopes were crushed.

Three years later, Sam remained bitter. Gun-shy, too. He worried he might be denied even a minor role in the Afghanistan evacuation for another bureaucratic reason: although he'd been a State Department employee for seven years, he hadn't yet completed five years as a Foreign Service Officer, the time needed for tenure as a "career" U.S. diplomat. No clear policy prevented junior diplomats from temporary assignments, but Sam understood the system might not allow it. He also feared he might not be home for the start of his mandatory language classes.

The next morning, Tuesday, August 17, Sam's friend in Mexico asked if Sam took the plunge and volunteered. Sam didn't mention his Syria setback, responding by text: "I decided against it because I realized I don't have as much time as I thought before language [class] begins, so I didn't reach out."

His friend commiserated, then added: "They told us today it would be like only short assignments, probably three or four weeks, but to expect 70-plus hour weeks, probably."

A short-term commitment and brutally long days? Sam jumped back in. He'd accept the risk of disappointment and try to finesse his lack of career-diplomat status.

Sam emailed the State Department bureau that oversees passports, visas, and travel by foreigners to the United States, touting his experience as a consular officer who reviewed visa applications in Nigeria and also as a former special agent for Diplomatic Security. He acknowledged his lack of five-year career status and signed off: "I am willing to work long/irregular hours."

A reply arrived twenty minutes later, along with a request for more information. With it came an encouraging note: the department "may still be looking for people to go to Doha and possibly a few other locations to help with our effort there." Energized, Sam swung into high gear, emailing his career development supervisor and making repeated calls, unanswered, to a senior State Department official who'd become a mentor after they worked together in Nigeria.

Anxious for answers, Sam emailed the mentor: "I figure you're in the know with high-level Department things. Any idea how to get my name on the list of volunteers for this urgent [temporary assignment]?" The mentor replied quickly and added the email addresses of top officials in the department's Middle East bureau.

To settle his nerves, Sam pulled on running clothes and a backward ball cap. He left his apartment for the nearby National Mall, where he jogged mile-long loops in the liquid heat between the U.S. Capitol and the Washington Monument. He stopped repeatedly to check his phone.

At 1:01 P.M., standing on the Mall between the National Gallery of Art and the Smithsonian National Air and Space Museum, Sam received a one-line email. The executive director of the State Department's Joint Executive Office for Near Eastern Affairs and South and Central Asian Affairs had a single exhilarating question: "Sam—can you leave tonight?"

After a quick phone call with her to talk logistics, Sam called his father, who put the call on speaker so Sam's mother could hear, too. He told them, "I think I'm going to Doha tonight."

His parents' reaction was equal parts pride and worry.

"Is there a chance that you're going to Afghanistan?" his mother asked. Judy Aronson had never been comfortable with the dangers of Sam's bodyguard work, and she only relaxed a little when he switched to diplomacy.

"I can't believe you'd ask me that," Sam snapped. "They're pulling people *out* of Afghanistan. They're not sending people *in*!" An exchange of texts followed, during which Sam apologized for letting stress get the best of him.

Dripping sweat, Sam rushed home and updated his career development supervisor by email. Nearly an hour later, she replied coolly: "I just talked to my leadership, and at this time the decision has been made to not allow [junior officers] to go to Doha or Kabul for the task force." Despite an urgent need to evacuate tens of thousands of American citizens, Special Immigrant Visa holders, their families, and other at-risk Afghans, the bureaucracy shut Sam down.

Gut-punched, Sam felt déjà vu from his Syria experience. He shared the news with his mentor and the State Department official who initially gave him the green light. Sam followed those contacts with a flurry of calls and emails seeking an appeal. In the meantime, his friend in Mexico also was denied, ostensibly because he was too busy with his regular duties.

Sam wasn't sure how or why, but his request was kicked up the chain of authority for reconsideration. Sam imagined the conversation: "Here we have a guy. He's a warm body. He's an officer [of the diplomatic corps]. He's volunteering to be on an airplane tonight. Why did we turn him down? Because of some bullshit decision that isn't even a regulation?"

However the actual conversation went, whether influenced by his mentor's support, Sam's unusual background as a Diplomatic Security Agent, simple need, or a combination of factors, by late afternoon the denial was reversed. Sam took a moment to celebrate.

Then reality dawned about what he'd gotten himself into.

The delay made it too late to catch his original flight on Qatar Airlines, so he was told to get a Covid test the next morning and fly out at night. As he reread long chains of emails, Sam began to question whether he'd end up in Doha, Qatar, to process paperwork for refugees airlifted from Kabul, or would be sent onward to the cauldron of Kabul itself. Some emails were vague and some mentioned both places. Even if he were sent to the relative calm of Doha, Sam felt rising self-doubt. Less about personal safety than about whether he had the right knowledge and skills. Despite his pitch to be chosen, maybe his bosses' original denial made sense.

"I can't believe they selected me," he thought. "I'm probably the least qualified person for this. What do I know about refugees? Nothing. What do I know about visas? Very little. I did nonimmigrant visas like tourist visas, student visas, that kind of stuff in Nigeria for a few months. SIVs? I don't know anything about SIVs. I can't believe they're sending me."

His doubts grew worse when his mind drifted to the possibility that he'd be assigned to the front lines of the evacuation: Kabul's besieged airport. Every television channel seemed to be replaying images of hundreds of Afghans chasing a gray U.S. Air Force C-17 as it taxied down a runway with a dozen men clinging to its side. When the huge cargo plane took flight several people plunged to their deaths and others were crushed inside the wheel wells by the landing gear.

Sam had dealt with crises, but he'd never leapt into the middle of one. He'd worked abroad in embassies, but the U.S. embassy in Kabul was empty after being evacuated under siege. The remaining State Department presence in the Afghan capital was a handful of diplomats at Kabul International overseeing a massive human airlift and staffing a shadow embassy that existed mainly online.

"Oh my God," Sam thought. "I've never been to a war zone before."

He'd spoken earlier by phone to Liana, and now he needed to talk with her again. But Mali's time zone was five hours ahead of Washington's, and he knew she'd be asleep. He tried calling his brother Jacob but got no answer. Sam's closest friend, whose family owned the beach house on Martha's Vineyard, was living in London, so it was too late to call him.

Sam met a friend for drinks, called another, then ended up on the couch of the friend who introduced him to Liana. They drank beers, didn't talk much, and Sam went home to sleep.

THE NEXT MORNING, Wednesday, August 18, Sam's Covid test came back negative. He arranged for Liana's parents to watch their dog Stella, who'd grown increasingly anxious at the sight of Sam's open suitcase on his bed.

Sam called Liana just as his email traffic suggested he might in fact be headed to Kabul.

No one in Sam's life was more attuned to the work he did or what he might encounter than his wife of ten months. Sam admired Liana's high tolerance for danger and discomfort. She often worked sixteen-plus-hour days at the embassy in Bamako, Mali, where two military coups made it the world's deadliest mission for United Nations peace-keepers and only slightly less dangerous for U.S. officials. Electricity was hit-or-miss in her rundown rental house, and empty store shelves meant she endured regular meals of canned beans and rice.

Sam loved how they balanced each other emotionally, too. When one grew flustered, the other knew how to have a calming effect. This was Liana's turn.

Sam paced around his cramped living room while talking to Liana via WhatsApp. She couldn't completely hide her concerns, but mostly she expressed encouragement and excitement. She knew how elusive it could be for a government employee to make an impact. Sam had a chance to make a big one.

Liana also settled Sam's fears about whether he could do the job. Liana told him that his unusual combination of high-threat security skills and diplomatic experience made him ideal for the task. She amused him by saying he'd finally be "in the room where it happens," quoting Sam's favorite line from the show *Hamilton*.

Liana's reassurances felt especially meaningful because Sam knew her embassy job gave her access to situation reports from Afghanistan, even if she couldn't share details.

"Once you arrive in Doha or Kabul, you'll be living in it," Liana said. "You'll understand what's happening."

Sam told Liana he wanted their parents to think he was going no farther than Doha, regardless of where he ultimately landed.

Knowing that Sam could be headstrong, with an abundance of confidence and a potent sense of justice, Liana asked for three prom-ises in case he was sent to Kabul:

"Don't leave the airport."

"Don't do anything unnecessarily dangerous."

"Don't be a hero."

Sam gave his word on all three, even as he told Liana her concerns were unwarranted.

"I'm probably not even going to Kabul. If I were to go, it's probably just for a few days, and I'm sure it's going to be very secure." He was trying to reassure himself, too.

Next Sam called Jacob. He trusted his lawyer brother would make steady judgments in an emergency: "I'm sure nothing will happen. But if anything does happen all my important documents"—his will and a living will—"are in mom and dad's safe deposit box."

Jacob said he understood. He promised to handle everything if disaster struck and wished his younger brother well.

Knowing that Kabul or Doha would be even steamier than Washington, Sam took an Uber to an REI store to buy summer hiking clothes: two pairs of pants, three moisture-wicking shirts, and a gray ballcap designed for hot weather. At checkout, Sam stewed when the clerk crashed the computer trying to enlist him in a rewards program. "I don't have time for this," Sam said. "I have to be on a plane to Afghanistan in a couple of hours." It was the first time he'd said those words aloud, dropping the self-delusion of a trip to Doha.

An hour later, on the ride to Dulles Airport, Sam told his Uber driver, an Ethiopian immigrant named Samuel, their destination was the terminal for Qatar Airways.

"Oh, going to the Middle East?" Samuel asked.

"Yes, I'm going to Doha," Sam answered.

"At least you're not going to Afghanistan. That place is a shithole right now."

Sam's pandemic mask hid a wry smile. He and Liana shared a laugh about it when he called her from the airport.

As Sam checked in for his flight, he scanned his fellow passengers for subtle signs—certain clothing choices, or government-issued protective carriers for vaccine documents—that might reveal fellow State

Department employees. He spotted one and helped her get a printout to prove she'd tested negative that morning for Covid.

Once on board, Sam bought himself a glass of champagne to relax. He got comfortable and tried to bank as much sleep as he could on the thirteen-hour flight.

WHEN SAM LANDED in Doha late Thursday afternoon, August 19, he opened an email telling him to find someone holding a sign with the name Jim DeHart. A Google search informed Sam that James "Jim" DeHart was their group's VIP, a senior diplomat with nearly three decades at the State Department, currently serving as U.S. Coordinator for the Arctic Region.

Bearded and avuncular, with a self-deprecating sense of humor, DeHart was twice previously posted to Afghanistan, most recently as assistant chief of mission from 2018 to '19 at the U.S. embassy in Kabul. A decade earlier he was director of a U.S. reconstruction team in Panjshir Province, northeast of Kabul. Between those assignments, DeHart spent three years as deputy chief of mission, or deputy ambassador, in Oslo, Norway.

Days earlier, DeHart volunteered to return to Kabul to serve as the top deputy to John Bass, U.S. ambassador to Afghanistan from 2017 to 2020, whom President Biden chose to oversee the emergency evacuation. The previous month, Biden had nominated Bass to be an undersecretary of state, but that was before Kabul imploded.

The same email directing Sam to find DeHart removed any lingering doubt about his ultimate destination: upon connecting with DeHart, as well as a Consular Affairs officer and two information technology experts, they'd be driven to a nearby U.S. military base for Sam's first flight aboard a military C-17. His mother's worried premonition proved correct.

"I'm going to Kabul," Sam told himself.

At the Qatari base, a State Department Regional Security Officer guided Sam, DeHart, and the three other new arrivals to an armory. Sam wandered among huge cardboard boxes filled with used body armor and helmets, picking out protective gear reminiscent of his bodyguard days that he thought he'd never wear again. He chose a thirty-pound dun-colored body armor vest with steel plates front and rear, plus bullet-resistant Kevlar on the sides, for a combination of safety and ease of movement. Sam's colleagues snatched helmets with ear guards, but he picked a sleeker model that looked like a bicycle helmet, which left his ears exposed for a radio set. The helmet also had a mount for night-vision goggles that Sam didn't expect he'd need.

Their security escort went person-to-person adjusting the vests, only to find Sam already squared away in full kit. Sam attached a first aid pack to his vest, but pockets meant for ammunition remained empty. As a diplomat, Sam wouldn't be issued a firearm.

Outside the armory, Sam saw dozens of troops from the army's 82nd Airborne Division, part of the sudden influx of U.S. service members, wilting in the heat even before they reached Kabul. Sam noticed how young they looked, most in their early twenties, men and women who'd been babies on 9/11. Sam spotted one soldier, small in stature, with a big M249 machine gun, too green to know he should hide his fear. Sam realized he felt scared, too. His hand shook as he handed his State Department ID to an airman who checked him onto the C-17.

As he found a seat across from DeHart, Sam noticed a half dozen long-haired, disheveled men who looked like surfers in civilian clothing. Sam learned they were Swedish special forces operators, Nordic equivalents of a U.S. Navy SEAL team. Foam earplugs handed out by the C-17 crew did little to defeat the deafening engines, so Sam copied one of the Swedes and used the noise cancellation mode on his Air-Pods. He walked around inside the plane to burn off anxiety then returned to his jump seat. He pulled off his body armor, strapped in, leaned back, and fell asleep.

Near the end of the four-hour flight, Sam startled to a tap on his shoulder. The consular officer beside him mouthed the words: "Put the vest on!" The plane plunged several thousand feet. Sam's stomach dropped. His head swiveled to other passengers, but only he and the consular officer seemed worried. Next thing Sam knew they landed, arriving at a location that countless thousands wanted to flee: Kabul International Airport, the United States' last stand in Afghanistan.

On the ground, shortly after 5 A.M., Friday, August 20, Sam learned he'd experienced his first combat landing, the safest approach in a war zone to evade surface-to-air missiles. He also learned that his suitcase missed the flight; for now, he'd have to live out of his backpack.

DESIGNED AND BUILT by Soviet engineers in 1960, Kabul International possesses all the charm of a Cold War military installation.

Shaped like an enormous garden spade, the airport is four miles long, a mile and a half at its widest point. Its spine is a single runway that divides it lengthwise. Before the collapse, the airport's southern half served civilian flights to and from Dubai, India, Turkey, Pakistan, Iran, China, and elsewhere. The northern half was effectively a military base under U.S. control, with barracks, hangars, supply depots, and a hardened State Department outpost called Camp Alvarado. Concrete perimeter walls, tagged by graffiti and topped by coils of concertina wire, defined the airport's two-thousand-acre footprint.

From the heart of the city, a three-mile drive north along Airport Road led to the main entrance, also known as South Gate, where bumper-to-bumper bus convoys of evacuees sought deliverance. By the time Sam arrived, the dusty road was already choked with vehicles, bicycles, and thousands of suitcase-toting pedestrians. Countless Afghans waited for days in the heat, and at least four people had been crushed to death in the overwhelming crowds.

Roaring plane engines alternated with the thrum of helicopter blades, drowning out shouts, cries, and pleas by men, women, and children. Taliban fighters with Kalashnikov rifles patrolled at checkpoints outside the gates, allowing most foreigners and visa holders to pass, while threatening, whipping, and beating back Afghans without travel documents.

Throngs of people with their most precious possessions also sought escape through secondary airport entrances—Abbey Gate, East Gate, North Gate, and other passageways—with mixed results. American troops feared the sustained crush could overwhelm their numbers, force open one of the gates, and trigger a riot.

During the first few days of what was officially known as the Non-combatant Evacuation Operation, several thousand Afghans gained entry to the airport, to undergo searches, questioning, and document reviews. If their papers and stories checked out, they received prized seats on outgoing flights. Otherwise they were ejected from the airport. Thousands of American citizens and Afghans had departed in the previous week, their numbers swelling after the August 15 fall of Kabul.

But the clock ticked toward the U.S. withdrawal deadline, with several thousand more Americans and well over 100,000 qualified Afghans still seeking airport entry and evacuation.

SAM AND HIS State Department colleagues followed the 82nd Airborne troops and the special ops Swedes off the C-17 and onto the tarmac, directly in line of sight of a modest sign: "Welcome to Kabul."

The rising sun beat down on them, casting a harsh glare on mounds of trash coated in khaki dust. More than a dozen other C-17s and smaller planes crowded the apron. U.S. Marines used yellow police tape to corral groups of Afghans seeking deliverance in makeshift holding areas before they were processed for departure or expulsion.

Unsure where to go, a member of Sam's group sought directions from a young Marine, who pointed them toward an old passenger terminal on the military side of the base being used as a clearinghouse for evacuees. They walked up an outdoor staircase and entered the building's second floor, where they found two large waiting rooms with scores of worn gray benches with thin leatherette cushions.

Nearly every seat was occupied, mostly by women and children, with some older men mixed in. Marines sat at tables behind computers at one end of each waiting room, recording the soon-to-be refugees' biographic information and distributing hospital-like plastic wristbands with barcodes that tracked identities and destinations. A smaller room held unaccompanied children overseen by an older State Department official and a young Marine sergeant.

Sam's group spotted two Americans wearing ill-fitting body armor, a sure giveaway they were diplomats not soldiers. The pair led Sam, Jim DeHart, and the other three new arrivals down an airless rear staircase lined with bulging black garbage bags that reeked from rotten food, used diapers, and filth of unknown provenance.

Back outside in the morning heat, Sam's group walked past a ragged line of roughly four hundred Afghans awaiting screening. Frustrated Marines held back two hundred more, shouting orders in English to the uncomprehending or uncooperative crowd. Sam saw dozens of families lying on cardboard, the women in dark abayas and colorful hijabs, most men and boys in Western clothing. Some slept on beds of trash. The air smelled of waste from discarded bags of military rations known as Meals Ready to Eat, or MREs. Glass littered the ground from the smashed windows of two disabled blue-and-white airport buses. At the edge of the scene, a roundabout twenty meters in diameter displayed flags of the allied countries of NATO. The flags hung limp from their poles in the absence of wind.

A block from the terminal, Sam's group arrived at a barn-shaped building being used as the U.S. Joint Operations Center, or JOC, pronounced to rhyme with sock. Guarded by Marines, ringed with razor wire, and equipped with rocket bunkers, the JOC had served the U.S. military even before the collapse, so the fortified building already had communications and security equipment needed by the State Department evacuation team.

To the immediate right upon entering the JOC was the office of Brigadier General Farrell Sullivan, who served multiple tours in Afghanistan and was now one of two generals leading the military element of the evacuation. Nearby were American drone operators, intelligence officers, medical staffers, flight logistics supervisors, and officers from the British, Australian, and Canadian militaries.

Sam's group walked through a double set of glass doors that separated the military JOC from a nondescript area being used as the headquarters for U.S. State Department evacuation operations.

Bathed in harsh fluorescent light, with a high ceiling and cheap tile floors, the room contained a dozen banged-up desks. A wall of flatscreen televisions displayed live footage of Kabul on a constant feed from drones overhead, satellite imagery, and news programs. A horizontal row of clocks showed the time in Washington and in cities around the world. Cases of bottled water and boxes of MREs teetered beside worn couches. With thin walls like a tar paper shack beside a rail line, the building shook with each C-17 takeoff.

Inside the JOC, small teams of State Department officers alternated twelve-hour shifts overseeing the frenetic job of logistical management and evacuee processing. The room also served several dozen State Department security officers and private security contractors who'd spent long years in the world's deadliest corners. Signs warned: "Before you leave sanitize your area." It was a demand to shred or secure sensitive documents. Almost no one took pandemic precautions, and several American diplomatic team members caught the virus.

The overnight shift was ending when the newcomers arrived in the JOC around 6 A.M.

Sam still didn't know what he was supposed to do. He hoped for an assignment as a political officer or staff aide to the ambassador, as opposed to consular work checking visas and other documents held by would-be evacuees.

"Go ask Bass," someone told him, pointing up a narrow spiral staircase to an office that overlooked the main floor of the JOC. He climbed upstairs and spotted Jim DeHart talking with an unassuming man with a Vandyke beard whom Sam didn't recognize.

"Oh hey, sir, Mr. DeHart. I'm wondering what work I should be doing," Sam said.

"Where do they need you?" DeHart answered.

From their introduction in Doha, DeHart took an instant liking to Sam. He got the impression Sam was hungry in a good way, with the kind of energy they'd need.

Sam took his shot: "Well, consular said they need me, but if there's something you'd rather have me doing, staff work, something like that, I could definitely do that because I wasn't sent by Consular Affairs. I'm not technically here as a consular officer."

DeHart wanted to accommodate Sam, but the greatest need was to screen as many qualified evacuees as possible, as quickly as possible. Fewer than forty State Department officials were in Kabul to do that work, while tens of thousands of Afghans surged through the surrounding streets and pressed against the airport walls.

DeHart batted away Sam's pitch: "Do you have a consular commission?"

Sam knew where this was headed. He still held the status of vice consul from his days adjudicating visa applications in Nigeria.

"It's still valid as far as I know."

"If they need your help," DeHart said, "that's probably where we should put you right now."

Sam pretended to be excited as he descended the spiral staircase.

He returned to the garbage-strewn area outside the passenger terminal with another new State Department arrival. They joined fifteen Marines overseeing the intake screening process for hundreds of Afghans who'd spent more than twenty-four hours in the hot sun and the cold night.

Soon after they arrived, one of Sam's colleagues tossed plastic water bottles to the waiting Afghans, nearly causing a stampede. Afghans rushed forward as irritated Marines pushed back and screamed in pidgin Pashto and Dari, "Sit down!"

Some Afghans kept moving forward, breaching a line of low concrete barriers. A few rushed onto the waiting line to the terminal. Sam understood they'd be turned away because they hadn't gone through the initial screening. Afghans who proved especially unruly faced the worst penalty: a Marine would yell "Red!" and a security team would evict them from the airport.

Standing beneath a shaded area alongside a more experienced consular officer, Sam worked with an Afghan interpreter who'd been a U.S. embassy employee. Sam quickly learned the priority order for evacuation: American citizens, Green Card holders who were legal permanent residents of the United States, local embassy staff, plus the immediate families of each category. Next came anyone entitled to a Special Immigrant Visa, Afghans at demonstrable risk from the Taliban, then any Afghan holding a valid U.S. visa. Women and children received added benefit of the doubt, at least when Sam did the screening.

He fell into a rapid-fire rhythm, requesting passports or Afghan identity documents called *tazkira*, and questioning would-be evacuees through the translator to confirm identifications. Most met the evacuation rules, which wasn't surprising because they had already cleared several checkpoints and gained entry through an airport gate. In his role as traffic cop, Sam waved those people ahead to the terminal, declaring them "Green." Perhaps one group out of every ten hit a snag.

"Okay, you're the dad," Sam said after collecting identification documents. "All right, so where's your wife? Okay, you're the mom. Mom, how many kids do you have? Okay, point to each of your kids. All right. This one, how old is he? What's his name?" Even the youngest children had *tazkira*, so Sam checked to see if the parents' answers matched the documents.

"Okay, Dad, what do you do for work? Okay. Mom, what do you do? Do you stay at home? Okay, then who's this guy over here? That's your cousin? Okay. How is your cousin related to you? Oh, he's not a blood relative? He's a family friend. He's a neighbor? Okay."

Neighbors didn't count. The rules applied only to nuclear families. Knowing what it must have taken to get this far, Sam tried to determine if the neighbor somehow qualified.

"All right, sir, let me see your passport or *tazkira*. Where's your wife? Oh, you're not married? What do you do for work? Oh, you're a shoe cobbler?"

At that point Sam made a quick mental calculation: "So he's a single, military-age male. No family, not related to them." No SIV, no apparent qualification for evacuation. Maybe harmless, but maybe Taliban or ISIS-K, shorthand for Islamic State Khorasan, a terror group that was the Taliban's enemy.

He sent the family inside the terminal then returned his focus to the neighbor.

"Sir, can you wait out here while I ask you a few more questions? Actually, do me a favor, go sit on that bench. I'm going to take another family, and then I'm going to ask you a few more questions."

Sam motioned to a nearby Marine and said quietly, "We have one Red." The Marine led the man to a waiting area to be driven by van outside the airport walls.

In one case, a man made Sam's decision easy by openly admitting ties to the Taliban.

Several said they burned their work records or U.S. embassy staff identification cards in fear of the Taliban. Having never been to the Kabul embassy, Sam improvised. "What section did you work in? Who was your American supervisor? Tell me the procedures to get into the embassy." Sam trusted his gut and hoped if he somehow sent an unqualified person onto a C-17, officials from the Department of Homeland Security would conduct a more thorough review and reverse the decision when the person landed.

For the most part, Sam overcame his fears of being unqualified. Yet new doubts arose, too. He knew he'd never forget the faces of several people he'd declared Red, uncertain whether he'd made the right call in a potentially life-and-death situation.

Complicating matters, speed was paramount. With the civilian departure deadline in little more than a week, and with a relentless flood of Afghans clamoring to enter the airport, Sam knew his first order of business was to fill plane seats as quickly and safely as possible.

AS SAM WORKED, he noticed a thin young woman in a dark-blue abaya sitting cross-legged on a piece of cardboard, her back against the terminal building. Something about her reminded him of Liana. In her arms she held an infant boy wrapped in a dirty blanket.

Sam brought the woman a bottle of water. He noticed blood on the baby's neck from angry, fresh scratches. The woman spoke no English, so he called to several waiting Afghans.

"Who speaks good English? Who can translate?"

A man joined them, spoke with the woman, and explained to Sam she was waiting for her husband. This didn't make sense to Sam, so he asked more questions but got no clearer answers. "That's weird," Sam thought. "The Marines let her and the baby go through but kept him behind?"

Sam directed the young mother to a shaded area and told her to keep trying to call her husband. He asked an interpreter who'd worked at the U.S. embassy to figure out the woman's story. She gave the same explanation about waiting for her husband.

"How old is the baby?" Sam asked. About two weeks, she said through the translator.

The more questions Sam asked, the more certain he became that the woman's husband wouldn't be allowed to join her.

"I'd like to get you on a plane today," Sam said through the translator, "but that means leaving your husband and hoping that he makes it out, and you reconnect somewhere else."

She refused. Sam asked her to call her husband again. When they connected, Sam delivered a stern message through the translator: "Convince your wife to get on the plane. You and I both know you're not making it in anytime soon. I hope, sir, for your benefit, you get in. But she's got a baby. She's been in the hot sun. You've got to let her get out of here."

The interpreter handed the phone back to the young mother. She burst into tears as she listened to her husband. She ended the call and agreed to leave.

As Sam escorted her into the terminal, an irate Marine sergeant joined them.

"You know the story here? Bro, she threw her baby over fucking concertina wire out at East Gate," said the Marine, who told Sam he had a baby of his own back home. "They ended up letting her in, too. The Marines had to catch the baby. I hate her for what she did." Reports soon spread of multiple Afghan women who threw or passed young children over or through the barbed wire atop airport walls.

Sam's revulsion quickly turned to pity. Now he understood why the woman was let inside without her husband. Sam took the mother and child to a room in the terminal where military doctors treated refugees. A pediatrician told Sam she'd treated the baby earlier.

"Can you just let me know if the baby is clear to fly?" Sam asked.

The doctor cleaned the wound, affixed a bandage, and said the infant was good to go.

Sam guided them past scores of other Afghans to the front of the line to be processed for a flight; the woman's identification band went on her wrist, the baby's around its ankle. Sam asked a Marine at the processing station for a piece of paper, then led the woman and child to a bench to await their places on a C-17. Sam handed the woman the paper and a pen, then called over an English-speaking Afghan.

"Tell her 'Write down your husband's phone number,'" Sam said.

When she did so, he told her to fold the paper and tuck it safely in her bag. That would be a safeguard if her phone was lost or broken.

"You're going to be very flustered for the next few days," he told her through the translator. "I want you to call your husband when you arrive safely."

When Sam returned to the terminal several hours later, the mother and child were gone.

BACK AT THE JOC for the night shift changeover, Sam filed into the room with the entire State Department evacuation team in Afghanistan: about forty diplomats who needed to oversee the exodus of three thousand times that number, plus government agents and private contractors providing security.

Sam cringed when he saw everyone focused on the man with the Vandyke beard whom Sam had ignored earlier when he went up the spiral stairs to see Jim DeHart.

"You're doing incredible work," said the man, who turned out to be Ambassador John Bass. "This is being briefed to the secretary [Blinken] on almost an hourly basis."

Outside, Sam looked for a ride to his assigned sleeping quarters. Hundreds of vehicles had been abandoned at the airport without keys, but someone on the State Department team had hot-wired an armored van formerly used by U.S. intelligence operatives for snatch-and-grab missions against terrorists. It seemed a fitting passenger shuttle for Kabul International.

On the ten-minute ride, Sam soaked up the scene of thousands of troops and Afghans inside the airport walls. The van drove past dozens of planes, most of them American military transports but also British, Australian, Hungarian, South Korean, and Japanese. He saw scores of vehicles, from Land Cruisers to school buses to fire trucks, spray-painted with markings of the military, intelligence, and Special Operations units that had hot-wired and claimed them. Some vehicles had sprayed-over markings from being "stolen" multiple times by different outfits from different countries.

Sam jumped out at a hardened facility at the southwestern edge of the airport, on the former civilian side. He walked through a cafeteria, grabbed an MRE bag for dinner, and passed a small room where a skeleton crew from the evacuated embassy maintained what was left of the U.S. diplomatic operation in Afghanistan. They had ironically chosen as their headquarters the compound's MWR room, for Morale, Welfare, and Recreation.

Once among the largest U.S. missions in the world, with fourteen-hundred American staffers and thousands of local Afghan employees, fewer than a dozen U.S. diplomats from the abandoned embassy remained. Part of their job involved issuing warnings to anyone still hoping to escape. The latest ones came with a disclaimer in bold: **"The U.S. government cannot ensure safe passage to the airport."**

Sam found his way through cinder block halls to his quarters, a windowless room the size of a prison cell with a thin mattress, a television, and a small bathroom. At least it was clean.

He stripped off his body armor and filthy clothes for a hot shower that washed away a coat of caked dust and dried sweat. Sam set his alarm for 4:40 A.M. and fell hard asleep at the end of his first day in Kabul.

5

TALIBAN

I N THE STILLNESS of her apartment on the morning of Monday, August 16, Homeira spent the first hours of the first full day of the new Taliban regime trapped between disbelief and despair. Sleep wouldn't come. Her migraine wouldn't leave.

As dawn approached, she sought comfort and commiseration in the insomniac Facebook community that gathered online to mourn the Afghan republic. It didn't help. She scrolled past countless posts, each one more bleak than the next. She resisted impulses to type comments in reply, to avoid compounding the collective misery. Some of Homeira's thousands of social media followers seemed to yearn for her reassurance. She had none to give, so she lurked in digital silence, her tear-streaked face lit by the glow of her laptop screen.

At 5 A.M., Homeira sat by a window and watched the sun rise. The unobstructed view north from her apartment extended to the horizon, so Homeira watched as one evacuation flight after the next rose from the airport and soared out of sight over the mist-covered mountains.

Normally Kabul sprang to life at first light, but on this day the streets were empty. The quiet made it possible to imagine the Taliban remained far away. But the quiet was worse in a way. Homeira couldn't fathom how Kabul had fallen without a fight, with no resistance from the Afghan Army and none of the gunfire she'd heard on her phone calls to Herat.

As 6 A.M. neared, Homeira wished for the normalcy of needing to rouse Siawash for school. But he had no reason to wake so she left him to the innocence of sleep.

Her laptop and cellphone batteries were nearly drained, so she charged them to be ready for the next electrical outage. She fed Sangi the turtle then returned to her lonely post at the window.

At 6:30, Siawash woke by habit.

"Mom," he called drowsily, "do I go to school today or not?"

"No, jan. Let's see what happens. It's better you stay home today."

Homeira knew the Taliban couldn't impose its tyranny overnight, so she resolved to defend her apartment from the new reality for as long as possible. She played a happy song on her gramophone as she made coffee in the kitchen. The volume was low, but her brother Jaber heard the cheerful notes through the shared wall between their apartments.

He entered unannounced with an accusation: "You're playing music?"

"So what?" she snapped. "Can't I play music in my own house?"

She realized she wasn't arguing with her brother, but with an imaginary Talib who would call music haram, or forbidden. Homeira softened when she noticed Jaber's red, puffy eyes. He'd been grieving most of the night, too. He left, then returned carrying a backpack.

"I'm getting out of Afghanistan," he declared.

Surprised, Homeira thought Jaber had somehow made arrangements for a seat on an evacuation flight. She asked how he'd done it and who was going with him.

He admitted he had no real plan.

"I'm headed to the square. My friends are all there. No one has promised us anything, we're doing it ourselves." His destination, Shahid Square, was a major traffic circle about two miles from the main entrance to Kabul International Airport. Homeira's social media feeds were filled with photos of teeming crowds there and beyond, on the treacherous route to the airport.

"Jaber," she said, "it's chaos over there. People are getting trampled."

"I can't tolerate that they're pulling down our flag and raising the white Taliban flag. I want to get out of the country before all this happens."

Homeira understood Jaber's fear that his work for the swiftly departed President Ghani marked him as a Taliban enemy. But she urged him to be rational. Without proper documents, such as a stamped exit visa, or a confirmed place on an evacuation list, a single, military-age Afghan man would be turned away by the Americans who controlled the airport. He'd get stuck, beaten, or worse by the Taliban fighters doing crowd control at checkpoints.

"I don't care," he said as he left. "I can't stay here and grow a beard the length of a Talib's hand."

SEVERAL INTERNATIONAL MEDIA organizations contacted Homeira that morning seeking interviews. She declined them all, feeling angry that most of the planet ignored the suffering of Afghans or saw their pain as a fleeting headline, only to be forgotten by the next news cycle.

She replied to worried messages from female friends in Iran and elsewhere. To one, she wrote, "I feel as if the entire city of Kabul has shattered on my chest." Her inbox filled with new pleas from friends and colleagues urging her to flee. Some tried to alarm her with disturbing, graphic predictions about how the Taliban would punish or kill her.

Homeira teetered on the precipice of depression, but she felt determined to present a defiant face to the world as she returned to social media.

"I'm not afraid," she wrote, never mentioning that she'd blacked out a day earlier at the sight of Taliban fighters near Kabul University. "Why should I be afraid when my whole goal is science and literacy? I have not been a thief, I have not betrayed, I love/loved my country."

She sought to calm recriminations against Afghans who'd found a way out: "Let those who are gone go. Everyone has the right to decide for themselves. . . . Do not break each other's hearts. Control our anger and frustration."

Her posts prompted a stream of supportive comments that reinforced her decision to remain in Afghanistan, regardless of the risks. Yet sprinkled among the positive replies were threats, some veiled, some not. One commenter who described himself as a business student in Kabul wrote: "With your evil thoughts, this land is not your place. You deserve to be executed."

Homeira refused to be intimidated, and she wanted to teach Siawash not to let fear of the Taliban rule his life. After breakfast, she announced that they needed to brave the streets together, to pay their internet bill.

"I'm not going," Siawash insisted. He parroted his father's warning from a day earlier: "It's far away and there are Taliban around."

She compromised by suggesting a shorter walk to a second bank where she kept an account. Homeira planned to withdraw about eighty thousand Afghanis, or about nine hundred American dollars.

Siawash relented, on one condition.

"I'll only go out with Afghani clothes," he said. "I won't leave with my jeans on."

Less than two weeks earlier, Siawash wore a white *shalwar kameez* to stand out in the dark during the *Allahu Akbar!* protest. Now he wanted to wear traditional clothes to be invisible.

Homeira told him to wear whatever he wanted. To show she wasn't frightened, she wore a typical long-sleeved blouse and a simple headscarf.

Five minutes from their apartment, they saw a throng of people outside the bank. A harried manager shouted for everyone to leave.

"We have no money! This bank is closed!" The crowd ignored him.

Homeira steered Siawash past the bank, pointing them farther from their apartment.

"You're lying!" Siawash cried. "You've just gotten me out of the house. I want to go back home. Take me home now!"

Homeira grabbed his shoulders. "You cannot go home. This is our city. This is your city and my city. Why should the Taliban be here and we stay back? I want to be here. I want to go out and you have to come with me."

He shuffled behind her, one hand gripping the back of her skirt. Homeira led him through an alley toward an entrance to the park-like grounds of the Ministry of Agriculture, Irrigation, and Livestock, near Kabul University. Ahead she spotted several dozen people watching at a safe distance as a group of Taliban fighters crowded around a green police car. Walking in front of Siawash, Homeira guided him closer. A few steps farther, Siawash caught sight of the Talibs, the first he'd seen in person, and began to cry.

"Where are the police officers?" he wept. "If this is their car, where are they?"

She kept walking. He clutched at her, begging, "Let's get back home. We have to get back home." Several boys recognized Siawash and tried to comfort him. One older boy who'd also been crying said, "Don't worry. Everything will be okay."

Homeira worried she'd pushed Siawash too far. She turned them back toward home. Several boys fell in step, sharing their sadness on the way. The talk reminded Homeira that Taliban rules wouldn't affect only women. The imposition of extreme sharia law would be awful in its own way to boys like these and to young men like her brothers, who might be whipped for small perceived infractions like shaving their beards. They'd suffer in larger ways, too, in a system that destroyed individual freedoms and devalued their mothers and sisters.

Back inside their building, Siawash stamped his foot. "You cannot get me to go outside again!"

They went to her uncle's apartment, where Homeira tried to make Siawash's brief proximity to the Taliban seem heroic to the other children. He glared at her.

"I won't live in this country," he said, his arms crossed on his chest.

She left him there and returned to her apartment for a long, tearful call with her mother.

DESPITE HOMEIRA'S INSISTENCE she wouldn't leave, the fall of Kabul triggered an intense campaign among her international friends to change her mind and find a way out for her and Siawash. Similar efforts were under way for thousands of other at-risk Afghans, some of whom had worked with Americans and NATO forces during the previous twenty years.

Aware of Homeira's refusal, her friends organized behind her back. At the center were Homeira's translator, Zaman Stanizai, and her literary agent, Marly Rusoff, whose own family history featured a flight from terror.

At three years old, Marly's father fled Ukraine with his family in the early 1900s to escape murderous Russian pogroms. They landed in Winnipeg, Manitoba, and eventually he moved to Minneapolis, where he met and married Marly's mother. They opened a book bindery where Marly worked as a teen. In love with stories, Marly felt intoxicated by the words on the pages and the bindery's perfume of glue and ink. After college she opened a small bookstore near the University of Minnesota campus that became a hangout for local writers.

Later, in New York, she enjoyed two decades as a publishing executive until 2001, when she launched the Marly Rusoff Literary Agency. Drawn to tales of courage, Marly represented Homeira for the sale of *Dancing in the Mosque* to publishers in the United States and the United Kingdom.

Marly had spent the past few weeks nursing her husband Mihai Radulescu through a bout with Covid, while also worrying about her client in Afghanistan. Three days before the Taliban reached the capital, unable to reach Homeira, Marly wrote to Homeira's translator, Zaman: "Please tell me Homeira is out of Kabul somewhere safe."

"Sorry to tell you this," he replied, "but Homeira is stuck in Kabul with a totally unpredictable future awaiting her. . . . Homeira doesn't know I am writing to you, and I would like to keep it that way. But this is a real emergency because if the Taliban take over as predicted, she will be in very serious trouble."

That exchange sparked a flurry of emails to enlist other friends and colleagues, including Christopher Merrill at the International Writing Program at the University of Iowa and Sara Nelson, Homeira's editor at HarperCollins Publishers. Individually and collectively, they pled Homeira's case to corporate leaders and politicians, including U.S. Sen. Chuck Schumer of New York, the Senate majority leader. They gained little traction, as they competed with a deluge of similar requests, many on behalf of people who—unlike Homeira—had been directly involved with assisting the American war effort.

On Monday, August 16, the same day Homeira showed Siawash she wasn't intimidated by Taliban fighters outside the agriculture ministry, Marly asked Zaman for an update. When Zaman called Homeira to check in, translator and author fell into an argument.

"Your agent is doing all she can to contact someone to help you with this," he said.

"Marly shouldn't do anything," Homeira replied. "I'm not leaving the country."

"You have to leave there!" Zaman insisted. "What point is there in you staying quiet and not being able to talk? These are their first days. These people will slowly find their civil enemies. They've already destroyed their armed enemies. They will find you."

They hung up at odds.

In his reply to Marly, Zaman brushed past Homeira's refusal: "Threats against Homeira's life are now turning into a campaign against her on social media, where even individual extremists are threatening her life. . . . Homeira is in an extremely dangerous situation."

JABER RETURNED HOME around dinnertime. Normally dapper and neatly groomed, he arrived disheveled and covered in dust. He showed Homeira terrifying photos on his phone of a mob scene that stretched nearly two miles from the airport. The photos triggered Homeira's memories of massive protests in 2015 after a street mob killed Farkhunda Malikzada, a twenty-seven-year-old woman falsely accused of burning a Quran. Even then Kabul's streets weren't this crowded.

"Stop going there," she told him. "You and I can't get away from this."

"I won't stay in Afghanistan even if they kill me," Jaber said. "If I couldn't do it today, I'll do it tomorrow. If I can't tomorrow, I'll do it the day after. . . . I'll get out and fight from outside of this country."

Later that night, their brother Khalid, a radio journalist and poet, called Homeira from Herat with the same message.

"I won't stay in this country even if it means my life," he said. "I'm coming toward Kabul."

She discouraged him, insisting that without travel documents he'd be denied and possibly beaten by the Taliban.

"I'm coming and I'm leaving," Khalid replied.

He posted a photo of himself online with the caption: "Either I will get killed, or I will kill, or I will leave this country." Homeira implored their father to order Khalid to delete it.

Unable to sleep, Homeira drank coffee and surfed Facebook. She discovered some of her activist friends had already left Afghanistan. Others who remained had deactivated their accounts or changed their online names, to make it harder for the Taliban to find them.

Seeking a distraction, Homeira watched an episode from *The Handmaid's Tale*, the television adaptation of Margaret Atwood's dystopian novel of female subjugation. She flinched when a male boss told women working in an office they could no longer hold jobs.

"It's the law," he said.

She turned it off.

"I WANT TO tell you something. I couldn't tell your father this. I was afraid of making your mother worried. I just want to tell you."

The caller the next morning, Tuesday, August 17, was Homeira's aunt Azizeh, one of her father's younger sisters in Herat. Homeira and Azizeh were close but hadn't spoken in days.

Between sobs, Azizeh struggled to continue. The longer she hesitated, the more anxious Homeira became.

"Leave the country if you can," Azizeh said finally. "Your life is in much more danger than ours. We haven't done anything. You, on the other hand, have been against the Taliban all this time. And during these last few days you wouldn't stop being stubborn and wrote against them."

Homeira relaxed. Azizeh sounded like everyone else trying to frighten her into leaving. She answered with nonchalance.

"Auntie, I'll get killed if we all get killed. Why would I get killed in a special way?"

"You'll get killed in a special way because you're a special enemy to them!"

Homeira heard something ominous in Azizeh's certainty. She pressed for more.

Through tears, Azizeh described a visit the previous day to the home of another relative, Homeira's aunt Hajar, whose husband's family included several men who'd become Taliban fighters. One young Talib in the family came to the house and told Azizeh and Hajar, "Your niece is a target for the Taliban and we can't do anything about it."

Homeira stiffened but pushed back. "I won't leave the country over the words of a baby Taliban relying on his gun and feeling proud of himself that he's in charge. It's the Taliban who commit suicide bombings, so why should I be the one to flee?"

Azizeh cried harder. "Your lack of fear means you don't know them very well! It's better you lay low and stay away from the Taliban." At least deactivate your Facebook page, Azizeh said. Homeira agreed to consider it but doubted she'd do so.

In desperation, Azizeh pleaded to Homeira's father. Wakil Ahmad called Homeira with a different tack.

"This Taliban is not the same Taliban you knew twenty years ago," he said. "The old Taliban came straight in and nobody fought against them. The new Taliban have been fighting for over twenty years and have lost a lot of fighters. These Taliban are angry. They will take revenge on everyone."

Wakil Ahmad warned Homeira to be wary: "You don't know who is your friend and who is your enemy in revolutionary times."

"I will be a little more careful," she promised.

That wasn't enough. Take your son to the airport immediately, he said.

"The airport is not a place for me to go," she replied.

Jaber walked into Homeira's apartment during the call. She could tell from his mournful expression and soiled clothes that for a second straight day he failed to reach the airport.

After the call, Jaber begged Homeira to ask her international friends to put her name on an evacuation list for at-risk Afghans. She could add his name as her *mahram*, a close male relative she lived with.

"Who will find out I wasn't living with you?" he pleaded. "Write my name on the list. I can't take it anymore."

Homeira had never heard so much pain in Jaber's voice.

"I'll message everyone I know," she assured him.

When Homeira spread word that she needed asylum, relieved friends and colleagues outside Afghanistan believed she'd wisely changed her mind. They leapt to the task.

Privately, her plans to remain in Kabul remained firm. If anything, her resolve had stiffened. Out of sympathy for Jaber, Homeira plotted a clever ruse: Once their names were added to a list of approved evacuees, Homeira intended to send her brother to the airport alone.

"How could I abandon the rest of my family and leave Afghanistan? Just to save myself?" she thought. "And how could I ever abandon my country? There are twenty million women here. If one million of us go to the streets, it's impossible for anyone to defeat this rebellion."

After reaching out to her international contacts, Homeira joined conversations on social media that raged at the Taliban. Almost as vitriolic in her online community were attacks on the U.S. government.

For two decades, Afghans heard American presidents and policymakers talk about freeing Afghanistan from the Taliban, protecting women and girls, and building the country into a stable democracy with a robust economy. Some gains were made, as Homeira's own successes proved. But overwhelmingly, the Afghans who filled Homeira's social network insisted the United States cared only for itself, particularly during the previous two years.

The hope among anti-Taliban Afghans for long-term stability and progress effectively ended in February 2020, when President Trump approved the withdrawal agreement with the Taliban in talks that excluded the Afghan government. Under the terms of the deal, the Taliban agreed to fight terrorist groups like al-Qaeda that might threaten the United States, to negotiate with the elected government, and to neither target U.S. soldiers nor mount "high-profile attacks." In exchange, the United States promised to draw down its troops toward withdrawal and press the Afghan government to free five thousand imprisoned Taliban fighters.

Almost immediately, questions arose about the Taliban's adherence to the agreement. Later it announced plans for an Islamic emirate even if that meant continued war against the elected Afghan government with whom they'd agreed to negotiate. Trump ignored the violations and stuck to the withdrawal plan. So did Biden, only pushing back the final exit date.

"America entered Afghanistan to secure its own interest," Homeira told friends, "and they got our soldiers and families killed for twenty years. Only God knows how many mothers in Afghanistan became bereaved in these twenty years. And the U.S. suddenly wanted to clear their image after all these major failures and defeats. They handed us over to the Taliban."

While Homeira focused her rage online, Siawash spent the day furious at her for refusing to leave. He passed most of his time playing with his cousins in Homeira's uncle's apartment.

Between trying to help Jaber, scrolling the internet, making calls with her family, and railing at the United States, Homeira began replying to journalists who beseeched her for interviews about the turmoil in Kabul. She realized that only two days since the Taliban's arrival, women had largely disappeared from television. It reminded her of her girlhood in Herat, when the only radio station played endless male voices discussing the Quran.

Homeira put on a gauzy white headscarf and caught a taxi to the studios of Tolo TV, Afghanistan's largest and most popular broadcaster. She appeared on a live news show, breaking her promise to her father to be careful and lie low. She delivered a powerful message built around the phrase "We need to talk." In a calm, steady tone, she urged women to leave their homes and raise their voices to preserve their hard-won rights. A video post from the appearance received more than ten thousand likes and a thousand positive remarks, although some commenters outside Afghanistan criticized her for not condemning the Taliban harder.

The positive responses buoyed her mood, but only briefly. On a call with her father, Homeira returned to despair. "The world has never disappointed us like this before."

Wakil Ahmad had no answer. Afterward, he told his wife Ansari he was concerned about Homeira's emotional state.

That night, Homeira wrote on Twitter: "I'm awake. Worried. I'm having a hard night."

SIAWASH WOKE ON Wednesday, August 18, itching for a fight with his mother.

"You don't think about me at all!" he yelled. "People are leaving and you're staying!"

Homeira suspected Siawash had heard from children in the building that the Taliban would come looking for her. They likely heard that message from their parents, who feared the Taliban would enter their building to search for her. Maybe Siawash heard the same warning in Homeira's uncle's house.

"Half the building is empty," Siawash said. "Half the building has gone to the U.S. because the Taliban would kill them."

Homeira wasn't surprised. She'd heard from the building's manager at least nine families had abandoned their apartments.

Siawash continued: "You are here and won't take me. If the Taliban kills you, they'll kill me, too, because I'm your child."

When Homeira wouldn't yield, Siawash broke the emotional glass that protected the mother-son bond they'd rebuilt: "If Dad leaves because his life is in danger, I'll leave with him."

Siawash stormed out the door. Homeira slumped in a chair. She thought about a call the previous day from her publisher in Iran, who urged her to leave for Siawash's sake if not for herself.

She dressed and went after Siawash. She wove through children who crowded the stairwells on every floor. Days earlier they flew kites, ran in the alley, and talked about soccer games. Now they scrunched together and discussed a child's version of politics. Many held toy guns and walkie-talkies. All wore traditional clothing, some with white hats, having abandoned shorts and T-shirts, which they now called "infidel clothes."

Homeira found Siawash playing in her uncle Abo Ismael's apartment. Instead of making a scene, she decided to resume their fight later.

Her uncle's wife Samrina brought Homeira green tea with cinnamon. The two women had regularly taken walks together, but now Samrina was too scared to leave her apartment.

Abo Ismael looked tired. He seemed to have aged a decade in a few days, his beard suddenly gone gray. He asked about her plans to leave. When Homeira said she was staying, her uncle's response removed any doubt about where Siawash heard of the dangers she faced.

"They won't show you mercy," Abo Ismael said. "At least have some mercy on yourself. Writers are dangerous because you can focus the perspective of the Afghan people. Taliban are afraid of you as much as they are afraid of a gun."

Samrina offered her a meal, but Homeira had no appetite.

She returned upstairs and knocked on Jaber's door. No answer. Homeira grabbed a long scarf and went downstairs. Siawash had joined his friends on the stairs.

"Where are you going?" he asked.

"I'm going outside."

"Don't go!" he cried. "The Taliban will kill you!"

"Siawash-jan, I'm going to walk around a little bit. I will be back."

"Taliban are here! Don't you understand politics?"

"Nothing will happen, jan."

Homeira walked along shaded pathways on the empty campus of Kabul University. She returned to the Tolo TV studios for another appearance. Choked with emotion, she defended women's right to work and attend school: "This land must not be turned into a big cage."

Afterward, Homeira hailed a taxi. The driver, an old man, struck up a conversation.

"My child, we survived the first Taliban period."

"I was there, too," she said. "I survived that, too."

He said he worried what would happen "if" the Taliban stayed in Kabul for a month. No one would have money for taxis, and he'd be unable to feed his family. It occurred to Homeira the driver was in denial, apparently believing the Taliban's return was temporary.

She directed him to Pole Sorkh, a lively neighborhood Homeira liked to call the Las Vegas of Kabul. The nickname would be accurate only if Las Vegas outlawed casinos, alcohol, and strip clubs. What Pole Sorkh did have in common with Sin City was restless energy. Writers, teachers, and intellectuals gathered in its bookstores and coffeehouses. A little girl sold flowers on the street. Young women clustered in groups without chaperones, enjoying one another's company, an occasional cigarette, and the attention of passing young men. Homeira and Siawash paid weekly visits to a shop called The Cup Cake, where they drank tea with honey, ginger, cinnamon, mint leaves, and lemon. Homeira would order a Napoleon, Siawash would choose cheesecake or chocolate cake, and they'd pass a few happy hours.

Now the storefronts were dark, the sidewalks empty.

"This was the place for all the book readers," the taxi driver said. He laughed darkly. "Who needs a book from now on? People won't have food to eat in a month."

Homeira fought tears. "Do you see how we lost everything so suddenly?" she asked.

"My child, it was not suddenly. We were sold to the Taliban two years ago. The blood of our soldiers was shed for nothing."

They drove aimlessly until Homeira directed him to her building. As Homeira entered her uncle's apartment, Siawash ran to her.

"You've been out for two hours! I thought the Taliban had taken you!"

"Honey," she said, "it's not that simple for the Taliban to take me."
Jaber walked in and overheard her.

"No," her brother said, "it *is* that simple."

Upstairs in their apartment, Homeira asked Siawash to feed Sangi
lettuce while she made dinner. He refused.

"You don't listen to me, so I won't listen to you," he said. "You're
staying here so the Taliban kills me. You worry about Sangi, but not
about me. You love Sangi more than me. You expect me to take care
of a turtle? I don't love you anymore."

A knock at the door interrupted their argument.

Siawash opened it to a welcome shock: Homeira's parents, his
grandparents, Wakil Ahmad and Ansari. With them were Homeira's
sister Zahra, a doctor, and her youngest brother Khalid. With airports
closed to domestic flights, they'd driven sixteen hours from Herat.

Homeira rushed to the door and into her parents' arms. They
hugged and cried, then laughed at the irony that after nine months
since their last visit, they'd been reunited by the Taliban.

Homeira texted Jaber. He raced home within a half hour. Abo Ismael and Samrina came upstairs with their children. Soon they were
joined by two cousins who lived in Kabul, Qasem and Basir, both of
whom Homeira viewed like brothers. Surrounded by family, Homeira
felt the happiest she'd been in weeks.

After a shower, Wakil Ahmad told Homeira they came to Kabul
because they feared for her safety and her emotional well-being.

"You'll do foolish things and get yourself in trouble."

Homeira was so glad to see him she didn't get angry.

WHEN THEY TURNED on the television, Homeira and her family
saw traumatic scenes from the airport. Horror stories circulated on
social media of children being crushed to death against airport walls.
Images of people plunging to their deaths from planes left Homeira in

disbelief.

"We've had all kinds of deaths in this country," she thought. "Deaths from dishonor, decapitations, dismemberments, stoning. But we never had a death where someone would hang on to an airplane and fall. It's like Afghanistan is breaking records in new types of deaths."

Early on Thursday, August 19, scenes of the crowds at the airport triggered an argument between her parents.

"Oh my God," Wakil Ahmad said, "what would happen if someone committed a suicide bombing among all these people."

His wife snapped at him: "You never talk about nice things!"

"And you've never had any patience with me!"

The two recycled four decades of marital disputes. Homeira tried to defuse the tension by urging her father to call her oldest brother, Mushtaq, to encourage him to bring his wife and son to Kabul. Ansari said the roads were too dangerous. Wakil Ahmad scoffed.

"The roads used to be dangerous because the Taliban would try to kill us left and right. Now the roads are theirs. Why would the roads be dangerous now?"

He called Mushtaq, who discussed it with his wife and agreed to make the trip. They'd arrive the next day. When Mushtaq and his family reached Kabul, four of Homeira's five siblings would be with her and their parents. The fifth, her brother Tariq, had no plans to join them. He'd held jobs he thought would expose the rest of the family to too much danger.

Other arguments between Homeira's parents cut deeper. When Ansari seemed depressed, Homeira tried to cheer her by suggesting her life wouldn't change much under the Taliban.

"They are going to take away our schools and jobs. You were always fine with staying home," Homeira said.

Ansari shook her head. "I see Talibs inside the house, and I see Talibs outside the house. I see them everywhere."

Wakil Ahmad exploded. "When were we ever Talibs in the house?

You had freedom in the house. You left whenever you wanted and came back whenever you wanted, and no one asked where you were going. Now you're saying there were Talibs at home?"

Ansari tried to explain. As a girl, she dreamed of becoming an artist. Instead she entered an arranged marriage, bore children, and did needlework at home between cooking meals.

"I don't know if you are Talib or not," she told her husband. "The fact that I couldn't go to university is enough to tell me that the whole of Afghanistan is Taliban."

6

ASAD

SAM WOKE IN his windowless room to the gentle alarm chimes of "Slow Rise." He looked at his phone: 4:40 A.M., Saturday, August 21. Forty minutes until sunrise, day two in Kabul.

Sam checked his messages and turned on the small television. Most of what he knew about the churn of tragedies, threats, and circumstances happening within a few kilometers of where he slept came from CNN and AFN, the U.S. military's American Forces Network. Clips aired that morning on CNN showed Taliban fighters cruising Kabul in abandoned American Humvees and brandishing M4 carbines and M16 rifles, weapons supplied by the United States to the Afghan Army before it dissolved on contact.

He showered, dressed, and walked to the compound's cafeteria, run by a chef who Sam decided was a badass if only for his uniform: white tunic, cargo shorts, Crocs, and a Glock 19 on his hip. Breakfast service hadn't begun, so Sam ducked into the improvised embassy quarters to grind beans for a quadruple espresso, then caught a ride to the Joint Operating Center.

At the JOC, Sam's supervisor assigned him to the front lines of the evacuation effort: North Gate, where he would screen Afghans and anyone else seeking entrance to the airport.

The gate, a volatile access point near the airport's northeast corner, was located on a main street called Tajikan Road, known to some as Russian Road, that ran along Kabul International's northern perimeter. Thousands of Afghans gathered there, and for several days Marines guarding the gate repeatedly fired warning shots, smoke, and flash-bangs or stun grenades to maintain control. Gunfire also erupted regularly from deep within the crowd, from a mix of Afghan Army soldiers and Taliban fighters who fired their weapons for no apparent reason or to subdue restless would-be evacuees. Some of those rogue rounds flew toward the airport walls.

Sam's assignment reflected an awareness among his State Department superiors that he'd traveled an unusual path to becoming a Foreign Service Officer. A few of his colleagues had military backgrounds, but young American diplomats generally considered a Brooks Brothers suit to be the only body armor they'd ever need.

Sweating in the morning heat, Sam and three experienced consular officers made the ten-minute walk from the JOC to North Gate. Their protective escorts were a Regional Security Officer and several private security contractors, including a paramedic, all colloquially known as "shooters." At the gate they looked over the wall, out to Tajikan Road, and saw a roiling sea of desperate Afghans waving documents and pleading to be let in.

But North Gate was closed, with no sign of opening. Concrete barriers pressed against the steel gate to prevent anyone from pushing through. Marines in desert camouflage stood atop the barriers and stacked wooden pallets to peer over the crowd, occasionally firing rounds from their M4 rifles.

Sam and others on the State Department team approached a Marine captain to ask about the barricaded gate, which made it impossible for them to do their work facilitating entry.

"It's been too unsafe the last couple of days," the Marine told them. "Our job now is to keep it secure, keep the crowds back."

Sam's group asked if the captain would make an exception if they saw passport-holding American citizens seeking evacuation.

"Yes," he replied, "if I see American citizens, and they're easy to spot, and they're right up here where we can pull them over the gate." Then he added, "But that's not going to happen."

Sam looked over the wall and understood. He could make out the faces of only thirty or forty people closest to the wall, a tiny fraction of a crowd he estimated at three thousand. They looked anxious, tired, hungry, surrounded by trash. Some called and waved, begging for the gate to be opened so they could flee their homeland.

Sam recognized that the Marines were exhausted, too, having spent multiple days at the gate, eating MREs, snacking on Cheetos, and sleeping amid garbage. Their conditions resembled those of the Afghans beyond the wall, but the Marines had ready access to three advantages: food, water, and latrines. Outside, an open ditch of human waste flowed past the airport walls.

Sam texted his bosses at the JOC a photo of the blocked gate and of the concertina-topped, garbage-filled concrete barriers. He wrote: "There would be no way to get anyone through this until Mil [the military] decided to bring a crane to remove it."

THAT SAME MORNING, Sam received an email from a former boss, the deputy chief of mission at the U.S. embassy in Nigeria, who'd heard about his trip to Kabul. Her email was among countless urgent messages sent by Americans in public and private life to anyone who might help evacuate family, friends, or colleagues before the clock ran out. Among them were numerous U.S. military veterans who mobilized to help secure visas for Afghans who served as interpreters, guides, and security contractors. One of those efforts, dubbed the Pineapple Express, reportedly helped as many as five hundred Afghans.

"We sure miss you!" the email from Sam's former boss began. "Do you have any thoughts on what a UN employee from Nigeria who was in [his native] Afghanistan on leave when the place fell apart should do? He is outside the airport trying to get out."

Sam tried to lower his old boss's expectations by noting how the situation remained "tenuous and fluid." He added: "I've never heard so much gunfire so close before." Sam briefed his supervisors about the UN program officer, then asked his former boss for the man's full identification and contact information. She sent them, and added that the man, named Mohammed, was with his wife, three children, and parents.

Sam texted Mohammed to gather more details.

Mohammed replied: "Last night I went to Airport with my family to go inside Airport because I am under security threat but unfortunately I spend all night in the East Gate. . . . There was a lot gunfire and my kids are so scared. . . . Sometimes back I received dead threat [*sic*] from Taliban from my Village . . . but I ignored because I am living Kabul. . . . I need urgent support for evacuation."

A series of text exchanges followed. Each new message read more discouraging than the last. The best Sam could offer was a recommendation from a supervisor that Mohammed travel to a UN compound eight kilometers outside the city. But Mohammed had already been told by the UN that only employees could be evacuated from there, without their families.

As the texts continued, Sam felt a growing connection with Mohammed that distinguished him from the countless strangers outside the airport walls. Sam knew those people were equally distressed and perhaps equally deserving. But Sam could read the fear in Mohammed's texts. With that knowledge came a sense of responsibility.

WITH NORTH GATE still closed and nothing else to do, Sam leaned against the wall with security officers and a State Department colleague named David Josar, a former *Detroit News* reporter who gave up journalism to become a Foreign Service Officer. As they rested, Sam heard noises that sounded like huge zippers being drawn up fast.

"What was that?" he asked.

"Oh shit," a security officer said. "They're shooting at us now." The gunfire sounded to him like Russian 7.62 millimeter rounds from AK-47s, the iconic weapon of the Taliban.

The bullets flew over the wall, well above their heads. The State Department team agreed the risk was too great and the Marines would be even less inclined to open the gate. They decided to return to the JOC to find other ways to be useful.

A few hundred meters into their walk, several Marines intercepted Sam's group and told them to take cover. A backpack believed to contain an improvised explosive device had sailed over the wall, not far from where Sam and the others stood minutes earlier.

Sam, David Josar, and a security contractor crouched behind a concrete wall to wait. They got to know one another, trading stories of previous postings, family, and life in general. Two female Marines who took cover nearby joined the conversation. Sam's group tried to radio the JOC to inform them of the IED, but the Marines had activated signal jammers to prevent a remote detonation. The all-clear came an hour later when an ordnance team safely detonated the backpack.

The day was still young, and Sam had endured his first experience of hostile gunfire and his first close call with an IED.

After an MRE lunch at the JOC, Sam, Josar, and the security team received a new assignment: screen potential evacuees at Abbey Gate, a major entrance on the airport's southeast side.

Two hundred meters outside Abbey Gate stood the Baron Hotel, which boasted high walls, American security contractors, and bomb-sniffing dogs. The hotel declared itself Kabul's "safest boarding for any tourists, travelers, officials, or employees." Four days earlier, 169

American citizens took refuge there on their way to the airport, but felt too unsafe to travel the short distance to Abbey Gate. Three U.S. military helicopters landed at the hotel and ferried them into the airport.

Abbey Gate was in full swing when Sam and the others arrived.

Marines waded into the crowd of imploring Afghans. After being searched for weapons and explosives outside the gate, the families entered to reach Sam, Josar, or another State Department screener, each with at least one shooter hovering protectively nearby. Sam tugged on disposable black nitrile gloves, knowing that many Afghans had slept outside for days in the oppressive heat. Nothing protected him from the noxious smells of human waste, rotten food, and body odor.

To speed the process, one of Sam's consular colleagues took the initiative, and the risk, of going outside Abbey Gate with security officers and Marines to pre-screen applicants.

Sam remained inside the airport walls and applied a similar approach to the one he'd used the previous day outside the passenger terminal. With a shooter close at his back and another nearby, he made rapid-fire connections between IDs and travel documents and the people standing before him with beseeching looks and stuffed suitcases. Men pressed close to Sam, as women and children hung back in the shade of a blast wall.

The day's code word for approval was "Right." A call of "Left" meant a Marine would lead the unqualified Afghans to the left side of the screening area, to be immediately hustled back through Abbey Gate into the crowds. Sam suspected some would make multiple tries to enter rather than give up and go home.

Only nuclear family members were allowed to be evacuated on a Special Immigrant Visa, so Sam repeatedly felt the anguish of dividing extended families, banishing uncles or cousins to the left, while granting rightward access to the rest.

One family arrived with seventeen members, but under the rules only a few could be allowed to pass. The process forced instant, painful decisions among the Afghans whether everyone would remain in Kabul or some would leave and some would stay behind. Many sobbed. Sometimes it happened so fast they had no time for goodbyes.

Sam ached as his rulings forced family separations. When he volunteered for the evacuation, he expected the physical toll of long days. He never imagined the emotional cost.

THE NEXT MORNING, Sunday, August 22, Sam's supervisor told him he'd be returning to Abbey Gate. Before he left the JOC, Sam learned at a briefing that his job had grown even harder: the window to freedom for Afghans had narrowed.

At-risk Afghans, even those in fear of their lives from the Taliban, no longer qualified automatically for evacuation. Neither did families with pending Special Immigrant Visa applications. Sam and other screeners were told to limit passage inside the airport to American citizens, Green Card holders, local embassy staff members with so-called yellow badge IDs, and Afghans who held approved SIVs, along with nuclear family members in each category.

That same day in Washington, President Biden gave an account of the evacuation that appeared to contradict the new guidelines being applied on the ground in Kabul.

In a televised address from the Roosevelt Room at the White House, Biden began his remarks by responding to thunderous criticism about the evacuation, and by quantifying the around-the-clock work at the airport. He said the United States had evacuated 28,000 people since August 14, including 11,000 in the previous thirty-six hours. Biden also said the Taliban was keeping its word not to attack U.S. forces or stop American citizens and qualified evacuees from reaching the airport.

Biden also acknowledged the terrible conditions and the humanitarian disaster outside the airport, where that day the British military reported seven Afghans were killed in a panicked crush, and others died from suffocation, trampling, or heart attacks. "There is no way to evacuate this many people without pain and loss," Biden said. He called the televised scenes at the airport "heartbreaking."

Biden made no mention of the new, tighter evacuation rules that Sam and others at Kabul International were told to enforce. To the contrary, the president pledged the United States would continue to evacuate at-risk Afghans.

"And as we do this," Biden said, "we're also working to move our Afghan allies, who stood with us side by side, and other vulnerable Afghans such as women leaders and journalists, out of the country."

The reason was unclear for the disconnect between Washington and Kabul International.

WHEN SAM REACHED Abbey Gate, he had no idea the president would be speaking that day about the evacuation rules he was supposed to enforce. What Sam did know was that he and his colleagues were expected to apply the instructions issued that morning at the JOC about who to allow inside and who to deny.

A text exchange between two other State Department officials clearly defined the stricter new rules as they applied on the ground.

"Want confirmation: at [A]bbey [G]ate we are told ONLY amcits [American citizens]. Is that correct? Only AMCITS?" one consular official wrote.

The reply: "AmCits and yellow badges and foreign passports, green-cards, visa holder including SIV."

"Roger that."

No mention of at-risk Afghans or SIV applicants still awaiting approval.

To speed the screening process, Sam applied the proactive, higher-risk approach he witnessed the previous day, when a State Department colleague went outside the gate into the crowd, flanked by Marines and security officers. By doing so, Sam broke the first of his three promises to Liana: "Don't leave the airport." Sam rationalized the decision as a technical violation because he was only a few meters beyond the wall. For the same reason, he decided he also hadn't broken the second promise: "Don't do anything unnecessarily dangerous."

Each time a security contractor ten feet farther into the crowd determined that a family had what looked like proper travel documents, he sent them forward to Sam. With another armed contractor at his side, Sam raced through formal screening. The denial code returned to "Red." Under the newly tightened rules, the number of denials rose significantly.

Anxious families pressed uncomfortably close to Sam, who grew concerned he might be pushed into a vulnerable position with his back literally against the wall. To create space, he applied his Diplomatic Security training, positioning himself in a nonconfrontational field interview stance: feet spread and left shoulder forward, like a boxer with his hands relaxed.

Sam's colleague David Josar vetted families about two meters to his right, which made Sam feel crowded. He moved even deeper into the throng of Afghans to stagger their positions.

The distance Sam created between screening stations outside the gate made it slightly easier to conduct interviews, but he still had to contend with deafening noise. Gunfire rang out repeatedly and flashbangs exploded intermittently. Roaring engines from takeoffs and landings became an incessant soundtrack. People on the far side of a concertina wire fence waved documents and shouted constantly—"Please help me!" . . . "Sir! Sir!"—to attract gatekeepers' attention.

One man held up paperwork in a plastic envelope and called "American! American!" Sam walked over and saw it was a printout of a form that said the man's SIV paperwork was submitted. Sam knew that a duplicate of the form had made the rounds on WhatsApp, and thousands of Afghans had bootleg copies.

Sam's approach of the man caused dozens of others to surge forward, some slicing their skin on the coils of concertina wire. Fearing a stampede, Sam decided not to go near the fence again.

Sam yelled—"Line up, single file!"—as much as he asked questions. The process picked up speed when two more State Department officers joined Sam and Josar for outside-the-gate screenings.

Family separations again proved the most wrenching part of the work. Weeping women clung to Sam. Men cried in his arms. Sam had to pry some away, into the custody of Marines. Each "Red" decision preyed on his conscience, the faces of the rejected burrowing into his memory. At the same time, Sam understood that for all his emotional distress, the Afghans he denied entry bore the true cost, including potential death sentences from the Taliban.

Seeking to minimize separations, Sam applied his best judgment to massage or stretch the rules. He allowed a widowed aunt to accompany her visa-holding family rather than be left behind alone. He permitted visa-holding parents to include their twenty-two-year-old son with severe learning disabilities, despite the fact that the man's age disqualified him as "a child of the nuclear family." Sam could only hope his exceptions wouldn't be overruled when the Afghans reached the passenger terminal.

Some denials were easier. Around midday Sam was approached by a lean, nervous-seeming forty-eight-year-old man with leathery skin and a black beard. He told Sam through an interpreter that he'd fought the Taliban as an officer with the Afghan intelligence agency, and he'd left his wife at home. His only ID was a frayed paper with a pasted-on photo at least fifteen years old. If the man's story were true, he had good reason to fear for his life, although Sam knew almost from the start the man didn't qualify for entry under the new rules.

Sam tried to give him a fair screening. A security officer urged Sam to pat him down and scroll through his Chinese-made smartphone. Without considering his own safety, Sam returned to special agent mode and did so. A body search produced no weapons. Sam and the interpreter found no texts or photos on the phone, which Sam considered suspicious.

The man claimed he had no other devices. Sam patted him down again and found a second phone, an old model terrorists sometimes used as remote detonators. Sam's normally polished vocabulary adapted to his surroundings.

"You fucking lied to me!" Sam said as the interpreter translated.

"Oh, I forgot," the man said.

"Get him out of here!" Sam called to nearby Marines.

Later Sam spotted the man watching them a short distance from Abbey Gate. Sam suspected he was Taliban or ISIS-K, sent to probe their system. And yet, Sam wondered if an Afghan intelligence officer who fought alongside Americans would act any differently upon the return of the Taliban. Sam had no way to know, but he wasn't about to admit the man.

Each individual or family designated Green was escorted inside the gate to await a bus to the terminal, where they'd receive wristbands and be logged in to computers. Then they'd wait, sometimes more than a day, for a flight to Doha or elsewhere to start hard new lives as refugees.

Sam and his colleagues turned away a majority of the families they interviewed that day at Abbey Gate, including many who likely would have been admitted a day earlier.

Late in the afternoon, a text message from the JOC sought specifics: "Can I get an update on a number of persons admitted at Abbey?"

Sam replied: "From Abbey—we've adjudicated 450-500. We approved approx. 90."

A whiteboard in the JOC meticulously recorded the number each day by category, starting with American citizens, then Afghans, then "other."

AS HE WORKED, Sam continued to exchange messages with Mohammed, trying to help the UN program officer who had a connection to Sam's former boss in Nigeria. Early in the day, Sam texted him: "[I]f you can make it to Abbey this morning I will be there and can try to see if the US Marines can find you."

Privately, Sam decided to bend the rules to the breaking point. Mohammed technically didn't fit the day's new guidelines for evacuations. But surely, Sam thought, there must be room on a plane for a UN employee, a man who'd been threatened by the Taliban and had support from a respected American diplomat. Knowing that Mohammed's family included his wife, three children, and his parents, Sam considered the chances of success slim. But if they reached an open airport gate, Sam intended to pull in all seven without explaining his actions to his State Department colleagues, the security team, or the U.S. troops nearby.

Sam texted Mohammed: "If I can get to you, I will need to move you very quickly. But remember—no promises. I cannot guarantee anything. . . . Abbey Gate is still very crowded but if you can get to the British military checkpoint, show your UN passport and say you spoke to [a] consular officer in Kabul who said you are good to get on a flight. British is the first check point. After that is American military."

Mohammed replied he would do as Sam instructed. But several hours later he texted again: "Actually it is really difficult it is so crowd [sic]. . . . I am in the way to back home because Taliban was everywhere and they may follow."

Sam told Mohammed he was sorry.

Soon the new screening system Sam helped to create proved too efficient. By early afternoon a State Department Regional Security Officer came outside Abbey Gate and told Sam: "You have to stop interviews. There haven't been enough buses. It's completely packed inside."

Sam passed back through the gate, where he found more than two hundred Afghan men, women, and children wilting in the heat. Some had been there for more than a day. Dozens more American citizens and Green Card holders fared slightly better, resting in the shade of a three-sided tent surrounded by rotten food and other waste. SIV holders in the sun complained they should be allowed inside the tent, while those inside the tent complained about the smell. All complained equally about the wait.

Sam appointed himself a logistics chief and bus dispatcher. He organized the refugees and hurried them aboard blue-and-white school buses driven by Marines. His State Department bosses emphasized Washington's relentless demand for numbers, so Sam kept track of each forty- or forty-five-person busload by marking his bare forearm with a black Sharpie. By the end of Sam's shift, the intake backlog at Abbey Gate had cleared, but larger and more frantic crowds kept surging toward the airport walls.

THE MORNING OF Monday, August 23, Sam's supervisors assigned him to East Gate, named for its location near the eastern edge of the airport. He'd again be working alongside his colleague David Josar.

Privately Sam grumbled: "Did I do something wrong? Why aren't they sending me back to Abbey Gate? That's what I'm good at."

Quickly Sam learned he had it backward. The streamlined, well-run intake system at Abbey Gate was the reason he and Josar were being sent to deal with the mess at East Gate.

Upon arrival, it seemed like a repeat of Sam's frustrating North Gate experience. Marines told them they'd been ordered not to allow anyone inside regardless of citizenship. Intelligence officials had gathered information about terrorist threats, and the huge crowd outside East Gate was volatile.

Sam climbed a dirt hill alongside several Marines and peered over the airport wall. He saw several thousand people, weary and wound up by fear and stress, their health and sanitary conditions deteriorating by the hour. He heard gunfire fifty meters from the gate. Several times each hour Marines set off smoke grenades and flash-bangs, the explosions echoing in Sam's ears.

Sam wandered over to three Afghan men who sat forlorn in the dirt, their hands zip-tied behind their backs. A Marine corporal stood guard as he waited for intelligence officers to interrogate them.

"What's up with these guys?" Sam asked.

"Wall jumpers," the corporal said.

Sam inspected their passports and thought the first two looked genuine. The third passport indicated the man was nineteen years old, but the passport was dated 2012. Sam peeled back the photo to find it had been pasted over a picture of someone else. Even if all three passports had been legitimate, Sam knew that as military-age men without travel documents, the trio wouldn't be allowed anywhere near an evacuation flight.

Soon after, a hot-wired silver Toyota Land Cruiser pulled up to East Gate. Out stepped two 82nd Airborne military intelligence officers who roamed the airport collecting information and working to help evacuate American citizens. Out of the back seat bounded a gregarious twenty-year-old Afghan man who spoke perfect English with a California surfer accent. Wearing body armor with an American flag patch, the young man could pass for Sam's younger brother.

His name was Asad, and Sam had met him briefly at the passenger terminal on his first day in Kabul, three days earlier. At the time, Sam was trying to help reconnect a lost child with his parents. Asad had volunteered to translate.

When they met, Asad had already been approved for an evacuation flight along with his mother and older brother, but he refused to leave. He'd spent days at the airport trying to arrange passage for his older sister, his brother-in-law, and their two children. After Asad helped Sam by translating for the lost child, he asked for Sam's cellphone number. Sam declined. Asad shrugged it off and went to help some nearby Marines. Watching Asad, Sam got a good feeling about him. He thought the young man's language skills might be useful in the coming days. Before leaving the terminal, Sam gave Asad his number.

Now at East Gate, Sam called out, "Asad?"

Asad shushed him.

"Don't call me that." He told Sam his nom de guerre: "Call me Ryan."

Asad explained that he'd been a translator for the U.S. Special Forces, and the Taliban's return made him a marked man. He didn't want his real name known by the wall jumpers or any other Afghans he didn't trust.

ASAD'S FULL NAME was Asadullah Durrani. Born seven months before 9/11, he had no memory of peacetime. The youngest of his family's three children, he grew up in Kandahar, in southern Afghanistan, the country's second-largest city and the birthplace of the Taliban.

Ten years old when his parents separated, Asad stayed with his mother, brother, and sister. As a precocious teenager Asad borrowed money from his sister for English classes. To repay her, he worked after school in a jewelry shop making necklaces and earrings. In addition to English, he spoke Pashto, Dari, Urdu, and a little Spanish.

As a high school senior, Asad received a scholarship from the U.S. government for a month of leadership and English language study in India. Upon his return he applied to be an interpreter at the Kandahar Airfield, a major NATO base that at its height was home to 26,000 U.S. and international troops. He got the job in 2019, only to discover he wouldn't be working for the airport, but as an interpreter for U.S. Special Forces. They renamed him Ryan.

For the final two years of the U.S. military presence in his country, Asad did work on behalf of the American military that he was forbidden to discuss. He had no formal training as a soldier, but his bosses in the Special Forces took him to gun ranges to be sure he could use an M4, an AK-47, or whatever other small arms were available when necessary.

In May, when the United States turned over Kandahar Airfield,

Asad went home to discover the Taliban had already taken near-total control of Kandahar city. He felt more afraid for his family than for himself.

"I didn't want them to pay for what I did," Asad said.

He convinced his mother, Horya Mohammadi, his older brother Rohullah, and his sister Taiba Noori to move to the presumably safer city of Kabul. They did so along with his sister's husband, Noorahmad Noori, a social worker for the U.S Agency for International Development, and their five-year-old son Sohail and three-year-old daughter Nisa. Asad's estranged father remained in Kandahar.

They rented an apartment in Kabul, and Asad returned to work as an interpreter for the U.S. military, first at Bagram Airfield until it closed in July, and then at Kabul International. When Kabul fell and the rushed evacuation began, Asad was at home, but a Special Forces captain texted him to go immediately to the airport. An initial attempt to bring him through North Gate failed, but he connected with a fellow interpreter who snuck him in another way. The U.S. embassy in Kabul contacted his mother and brother, and they got in, too.

Once inside Kabul International, Asad linked up with an army intelligence team that tried to gain entry for his sister, her husband, and their children. Repeated attempts failed, even as Asad helped to bring in more than four hundred American citizens in a matter of days. His sister and her family spent an entire night within two meters of a little-known entrance to the airport variously called Black Gate or Santa Cruz Gate. But the plan went awry when covert U.S. operatives decided to use the gate for American citizens and ordered Afghan paramilitary soldiers to clear the area. They used stun grenades and beat the Afghans assembled there.

When Asad wasn't working on the airport grounds with the army intelligence team, he lived the life of a man without a country. He grabbed food and water where he could and slept inside the passenger terminal, all the while strategizing a way to help his sister's family.

ASAD REMINDED SAM that his sister's family remained stuck in Kabul with no way into the airport. Asad said he wouldn't leave until time ran out or the rest of his family joined him. Sam told him to stay in touch. Sam thought if he returned to Abbey Gate, maybe he could help, even if Asad's sister's family didn't qualify under the new rules. Before they parted, Sam and Ryan/Asad took a photo together, both smiling, with Asad making the "hang loose" sign, his left thumb and pinkie extended.

At the Marines' insistence, East Gate remained closed.

Sam returned to the JOC with Josar, another State Department officer, and their security team. Sam's supervisors reassigned him again, this time to Camp Alvarado, the State Department base at the far western edge of the airport, for a mission Sam and his team called Operation Freedom Gate.

U.S. officials had quietly negotiated a deal with the Taliban: American citizens, Green Card holders, and their families were told to gather at the former headquarters of the Afghan Ministry of the Interior, located about a kilometer west of the airport. After screening by the Taliban, the evacuees would be allowed to walk down a closed-off road toward the airport's Camp Alvarado entrance, now dubbed Freedom Gate, where they'd be searched by members of the 82nd Airborne and screened by Sam and other State Department officials. Then they'd be bused to the passenger terminal for flights out. That was the plan, at least.

Sam and the others spent hours waiting for the Taliban to allow the American citizens and legal U.S. residents to leave the ministry building. As Sam killed time, a call came over the radio warning of an imminent rocket attack. A high-tech system at the JOC had picked up the heat signature of rockets about to be fired. Sam strapped on his helmet. With four other members of the State Department team, he squeezed into the most hardened structure they could find, a guard booth. Thirty or more 82nd Airborne troops hunkered down outside.

Trying not to show fear, Sam listened intently when someone asked what they should do.

"You'll hear it when it's about to impact," a security contractor said. He warned them of the blast pressure. "When you hear it, keep your mouth open or start singing so your lungs don't explode."

Then the contractor described their bigger worry, one that had no defense: "If it's a direct hit, well, you'll never know the difference because you'll be dead immediately."

They huddled in the guard booth for an hour, with Sam calculating the odds of a direct hit and hoping they'd be safe from shrapnel if it struck nearby. If they were killed, he worried that the deaths of five members of the American diplomatic corps would be a nightmare for the administration on top of the one it already faced. Later he realized he hadn't thought about the effects on Liana and his family.

When the threat passed, Sam hung out in a watchtower and befriended an army second lieutenant fresh out of West Point who'd also just endured his first rocket warning.

Sam's shift ended without the arrival of anyone from the Ministry of the Interior. He felt as though he'd accomplished next to nothing the entire day. Sam called his supervisor at the JOC to ask if he could stay at Camp Alvarado through the night to await the American citizens and Green Card holders. She declined, telling him he'd be replaced by the night shift, so he'd be fresh for another try the next morning.

THAT NIGHT SAM wrote Liana an email acknowledging the psychological toll of his first days in Kabul.

"We have strict orders on who we're allowed to bring in," Sam wrote. "I've even teared up a few times under my sunglasses when sending certain families away. I'm not emotionally processing it right now because there's no time to, but that's something for me to worry about once I get home."

He used an emoji for love, then gave her false reassurances about his physical well-being, not mentioning the IED and rocket warnings or the gunfire and stun grenades at the gates.

Sam invoked their dog to vouch for his claims: "Don't worry about me. I swear on Stella's life that I am very, very safe and well protected."

SAM WOKE TUESDAY, August 24, to an email from Secretary of State Tony Blinken. Addressed to "Team Kabul," it read in part:

> "We know that these past several days have been grueling, draining, and emotional—and the next several days will likely be just as hard. . . . You are saving lives and futures. You're all heroes to us, your grateful colleagues."

Buoyed by Blinken's note, Sam returned to Freedom Gate at Camp Alvarado eager to screen evacuees. But the Taliban proved no more cooperative than it had a day earlier.

When Sam arrived, he learned the first group of evacuees had been released from the former Ministry of the Interior building shortly after nine the previous night. Because that process went relatively smoothly, another five hundred or so American citizens and Green Card holders were told to assemble at the ministry building, with the expectation the Taliban would release them throughout the day.

Sam and other State Department diplomats stood ready to greet and screen the evacuees after they were searched by the 82nd Airborne. But hours passed with no sign of anyone walking along the road toward Camp Alvarado's Freedom Gate.

MEANWHILE, THE OVERALL pace of evacuations had increased sharply.

The White House reported the number of evacuees since August 14 had exceeded 70,000 Soon, Blinken would update that number to more than 82,000 On Tuesday afternoon, August 24, in Washington, President Biden struck an optimistic tone as he insisted his withdrawal deadline would be met. Still, he warned of ongoing threats.

"Every day we're on the ground is another day we know that ISIS-K is seeking to target the airport and attack both U.S. and Allied forces and innocent civilians," Biden said.

Meanwhile, during a press briefing a day earlier, State Department spokesman Ned Price faced withering questions from reporter Andrea Mitchell of NBC News about the fate of several thousand Afghans who worked at the U.S. embassy in Kabul.

"A memo was sent to Afghan staff at the embassy on Wednesday [August 18] inviting them to head to the airport," Mitchell told Price. "[T]he physical situation was simply impossible, and some staff reported being separated from children. They said, quote, 'It would be better to die under the Taliban's bullet than face the crowds again.' One staff member said they felt betrayed, that it undermined their sense of dignity, their loyalty."

Price acknowledged that the United States has "a sacrosanct obligation" to Afghans who served the United States. He explained that most of the embassy's local staff were working from home when the building emptied and military helicopters ferried diplomats to the airport. Price renewed the State Department's commitment to evacuating and relocating them and their families.

From a practical standpoint, that promise meant that several thousand yellow-badge-carrying Afghans who'd been employed by the U.S. embassy, including those who burned their ID cards in fear of the Taliban, became the responsibility of the State Department team and the troops at the airport.

TO PASS THE time at Camp Alvarado, Sam spotted an abandoned truck with a teal green Afghan license plate he thought would make a good souvenir. A young U.S. soldier pried it off in exchange for two

Diet Cokes that Sam grabbed that morning from the cafeteria.

Sam texted a college friend who was among the army pilots ferrying people into the airport aboard huge Chinook helicopters. The pilot detoured to Camp Alvarado so he and Sam could catch up and take a reunion photo of Northeastern University criminal justice majors on the far side of the world from Boston.

As hours passed with nothing else to do, a security contractor taught Sam how to hot-wire a bus. Sam used trial and error to touch wires under the steering column, overcoming unfounded fears of sparks flying in his face. When he connected the battery wires to the ignition wire and the engine turned over, Sam felt the pride of a potential car thief. He drove the bus around Camp Alvarado as his reward.

Sam returned to the watchtower and reconnected with the young army lieutenant he'd befriended the previous day. Staring out toward the Ministry of Interior building through binoculars, Sam saw white Taliban flags but no sign of Americans or Green Card holders. Again, it turned out, the Taliban preferred to release its detainees at night.

Sam ended the shift dour and dispirited, unaware that he'd spent his last quiet day in Kabul.

7

WHITE SCARVES

AFTER BREAKFAST ON Thursday, August 19, Homeira redoubled her efforts to build Siawash's confidence and acclimate him to their new reality under Taliban rule.

When he finished eating, she told him to get ready for a walk. Their overdue internet bill gave her the excuse she needed. Siawash resisted, but Homeira insisted.

The twenty-five-minute walk to the internet provider was uneventful. They headed toward home along a tree-lined street, with bright sunlight casting shadows onto their path. As they approached an abandoned government building, Homeira noticed two Talibs standing guard outside. One was heavy, in his midtwenties, with a thick beard and kohl-ringed eyes. The other was in his teens, skinny, not yet able to grow a beard. His Kalashnikov rifle looked too big for him.

Pulling Siawash behind her, Homeira walked over and said hello.

Siawash stood petrified. Neither Talib responded. Homeira repeated her greeting.

As he stared at his feet, the younger one said in Arabic, "Assalamu alaikum" ("Peace be upon you").

"My little boy is very afraid of you," Homeira said. "I want you to shake his hand so his fear goes away."

Looking down, refusing to make eye contact with a woman, the older Talib growled: "We're not allowed to give handshakes."

Homeira took a deep breath. She tapped into a reservoir of courage that ignored the possibility that the Talibs might recognize her and treat her as an enemy or an infidel.

"I'm not on the ground," she told the older Talib. "I'm not an ant. I'm standing here." Still he wouldn't look at her. It was possible he spoke only a little Farsi, so he didn't fully comprehend that he'd been scolded like a schoolboy.

Homeira knew a Talib would never touch the skin of a woman or girl other than his wife. Such behavior was haram, forbidden.

"I didn't ask you to shake my hand," she continued. "I said, 'Shake my child's hand.'" She added, "My child is a boy."

"No, no, no," the older Talib said. "We're not allowed to give hand-shakes to anyone."

She turned to the younger one: "At least put your hand on my child's chest and see how fast his heart is beating. He is afraid of you."

The younger Talib did as Homeira asked, placing his hand above Siawash's hummingbird heart.

"Everything will be okay," he said. "Everything will be peaceful."

Homeira suppressed a mocking laugh. She thought, "An armed child is telling an unarmed child that everything is peaceful and okay. If everything was okay in this country, that same child would be in school and not keeping watch with a gun in the street."

As they walked away, Siawash dug his fingers into his mother's leg.

"I'll never be friends with a Talib," he whispered.

Homeira explained she didn't want him to befriend or even accept the Taliban. She wanted to demystify them, so he didn't live in fear.

As they entered the alley that led to their building, Homeira saw a crowd watching several Taliban fighters trying to smash open an armored car that had belonged to a member of the Afghan foreign ministry. Children watched from balconies above.

Siawash scurried into their building, but Homeira stayed outside. Among the spectators was her building's manager.

"We keep telling them that even if they get in the car they can't drive it without the keys, but they won't listen," he said. "They say, 'We'll force it open and hot-wire it.'"

He begged Homeira to leave the scene: "The whole building will be in danger if you get recognized."

"Am I a criminal?" she asked. "What have I done? I'm just a writer." But she knew his fear was real, so she returned to the building.

Inside Homeira's apartment, her mother told Homeira that Siawash ran to the exercise room and slammed the door. She overheard him saying: "My mom is crazy. She takes me to be friends with the Taliban. I will never be friends with the Taliban."

Homeira explained that Siawash confided in Sangi when he was too mad to talk to her. She said sometimes she talked to the turtle, too.

FROM THEIR HOMES on opposite coasts, Homeira's literary agent Marly Rusoff in South Carolina and translator Zaman Stanizai in California continued their nonstop evacuation campaign. Despite dozens of emails, texts, and phone calls, they made little progress weakening Homeira's resolve to remain in Kabul or finding her a way out. So they made contingency plans.

During a phone call that day, Marly asked Zaman if Homeira might consent to a new title for the paperback edition of her memoir, as well as for yet-to-be-published foreign editions. Something perhaps less likely to get her killed by the Taliban than *Dancing in the Mosque*.

Marly jotted down the translator's reply: "Zaman says he asked Homeira, who said she would not back down and change her title for them."

BEFORE DAWN THE next morning, Homeira's requests to be placed on an evacuation list bore fruit. She told no one about her plot to remain behind and send only her brother Jaber.

At 2:30 A.M. on Friday, August 20, Homeira received a call from a woman in London involved with Vital Voices, a global nonprofit that supports the work of female leaders. Homeira had met the woman more than a decade earlier in Germany, at a conference on Afghan women.

"We're trying to list a group of women," the woman said. "Get ready for departure tomorrow."

"How many of us can be on the list?" Homeira asked.

"You and Siawash only, if you have his full custody."

Homeira wanted to scream at the absurdity. The Afghan government and the courts under which she won custody no longer existed, but someone outside Afghanistan might have a problem with a mother trying to save her son from the Taliban? She told the woman Siawash was legally hers.

"I won't go anywhere without my brother Jaber," Homeira added.

The woman said she'd check and call back within the hour.

Homeira texted Jaber: "They want me to go to the airport."

From his apartment, he texted back: "Go."

"I won't go without you."

"Don't worry about me. You go."

An hour passed and Homeira grew impatient. She called the woman, who said: "We'll put your brother on the list, too." She told Homeira to wear dark, loose clothing, so she wouldn't attract the Taliban's attention, and a white headscarf, as a sartorial password.

The urgent drive to rescue at-risk Afghan women and their families would come to be known as the White Scarves campaign. The effort was overseen by a coalition of civil society groups including the Georgetown Institute for Women, Peace and Security and numerous Afghan women's and human rights organizations. Homeira was one of the first twenty women whose names appeared on the White Scarves' target list, based on extreme risk of assassination by the Taliban. Eventually the list held more than three thousand names, including politicians, journalists, and activists, plus their families.

Homeira's contact in London said to expect a call later in the day telling her when to leave for the airport. Suddenly Homeira felt torn.

Now that the opportunity was real, she felt a powerful temptation to abandon her ruse and flee Afghanistan with Siawash as well as Jaber. She could save her own life, fulfill Siawash's desires, and relieve his fears. She also worried how he'd react if he eventually learned she rejected a chance to escape.

Yet Homeira still didn't want to leave. She wanted to fight for herself and other women to preserve the hard-won rights they'd gained during the previous two decades. She felt guilty about leaving her parents, her sister Zahra, and her other brothers and cousins. Homeira feared she might never be able to return to Afghanistan or see her family again.

"What if people who say I should leave are right?" she asked herself. "What use is my dead body?"

But then she thought: "Those who are leaving are leaving for the future. My future is now. I've been running all my life and now I want to be at peace in my home."

After hours of uncertainty, Homeira asked her father for advice. He was unequivocal.

"Do it," Wakil Ahmad said. "Go."

THE TAXI CARRYING Homeira, Siawash, and Jaber toward the airport crept through Kabul's packed streets. The temperature topped ninety degrees Fahrenheit, sending heat waves shimmering in the dusty air. The entire city seemed headed to the same destination. An hour into the trip, they still had far to go.

In the back seat, happy that his mother had finally listened to his pleas, Siawash rocked with nervous energy at the prospect of leaving the country. He'd heard about chaos at the airport, and he promised Homeira he wouldn't be afraid. Jaber talked nonstop by phone with a friend who was already among the crush of humanity outside Kabul International. Homeira sat quietly, nursing doubts about her decision behind dark sunglasses. She felt a strong premonition that their journey wouldn't go as planned.

The phone call from the woman in London telling them to go to the airport had come earlier that afternoon. Goodbyes were brief. Homeira's parents expressed joy and relief. Her brother Khalid was out visiting friends, but Homeira's other siblings and relatives embraced them and wished them safe travels. Several talked hopefully of following soon.

Homeira wore boot-cut jeans under a green dress, topped by a fashionable cloak. Her stylish outfit defied her London friend's order to wear loose, dark clothing. Homeira liked how she looked in clothes that flattered her curves, and she refused to wear a shapeless sack to appease the Taliban. Her headscarf was white, as instructed, with a green fringe.

Siawash dressed for a vacation: jeans, a red shirt, and black shoes. He insisted on a chic striped jacket two sizes too small. Jaber also rejected Afghani clothes, choosing tan pants and a brown-and-white plaid shirt. A white scarf hung loose across his shoulders.

Stuffed inside Homeira's small black suitcase were four pairs of pants, two blouses, sneakers, her MacBook, two watches, gold jewelry, eyeglasses, sunscreen, diplomas, several books, and her divorce and custody documents. She squeezed in a beloved photo of herself as a girl alongside her mother. Siawash's little red suitcase held his iPad, clothes, books, and his Superman watch. He hated to leave Sangi, but his grandmother promised to care for the turtle. Jaber carried a small black backpack with a few clothes and precious belongings.

The airport was less than five miles as the crow flies from Homeira's apartment, but the taxi driver took a roundabout route in a futile effort to avoid heavy traffic. They snaked through a residential area at the foot of a mountain, creeping down Qasaba Road toward busy Tajikan Road, which stretched along the airport's northern border.

As the taxi drew nearer to the airport, pops of gunfire became louder and more frequent. Blood drained from Siawash's face. He struggled to keep his promise of bravery.

In an area north of the airport where Homeira had never been, the driver stopped beside a large dirt field filled with hundreds of people, young and old, every one of them hoping for a seat on a plane. He refused to drive farther, and no amount of money could change his mind. In the stifling heat, Homeira, Siawash, and Jaber faced a three-mile walk around the airport's perimeter to reach the entrance where they were supposed to connect with other women on the White Scarves' list: Abbey Gate.

Jaber shared their location with his friend, who was nearby. The friend promised to find them and help guide them to the gate. Homeira suspected the friend's ulterior motive was to sneak into the airport with them. She didn't mind.

Moments after Homeira, Siawash, and Jaber stepped from the taxi, they were swept into a scrum of hundreds of their countrymen. Gunfire and belligerent orders screamed in Pashto drowned out the wails of men, women, and children. Homeira heard what sounded like manic laughter. She clung to Siawash as she fought to stay on her feet.

Disoriented, unsure where to go, Homeira tossed Jaber her suitcase. Shoved and shouldered, they ran across the barren field with the panicked mob to avoid being trampled underfoot. Homeira grabbed Siawash's shoulders with both hands from behind as she propelled him forward. He held up a hand to shield his face from swirling dust created by the human stampede. A layer of dirt coated his glasses.

Worried the lenses would be scratched or broken, Homeira yelled at him to give them to her. Siawash refused, fearing he'd be blind without them.

She leaned close to his ear: "Don't worry! I am by your side everywhere!"

His cheeks trembled. He squeezed her hand, to let her know he understood.

They reached an unpaved road where the mad rush ebbed. Jaber spotted his friend.

Before they caught their breath, Jaber saw a fresh wave of people roaring toward them from a different direction, fleeing ahead of Taliban fighters who whipped anyone within reach and fired semiautomatic rifles into the sky to herd the rest. A misstep inside the swarm meant injury or death. Bullets rained down around them as Jaber shouted for Homeira to get Siawash away from the oncoming crowd, pointing toward a sidewalk at the edge of the road.

Before Jaber could join them, a Talib with a horse whip struck him across the back and shoulders, then moved on to other victims. More shocked than hurt, Jaber looked to Homeira, his brows furrowed in an expression of sorrow and embarrassment.

Siawash burst into tears, yelling, "Let's go home!"

Jaber shouted, "Let's go forward!"

Homeira stood between the two, unsure what to do.

As she hugged Siawash on the sidewalk, Homeira realized this was the Taliban's violent idea of crowd control.

Everywhere outside the airport, extremist fighters prodded hundreds or thousands of people in one direction, creating room for hundreds or thousands of others to fill the space left behind. When Talibs returned to force away the newcomers, others moved in. The ebb and flow of groups rushing one way then another repeated like cycles of waves and undertow at the beach.

With help from Jaber's friend, they navigated away from the busiest and scariest areas, to continue their trek toward Abbey Gate.

Wherever she looked, Homeira saw hundreds of people covered in dust from days of trying and failing to convince the Americans to allow them inside the airport. Some of those turned away went home, while many more remained to try yet again, including those who'd traveled from outside Kabul and had nowhere else to go. More would-be refugees kept arriving, creating whirlpools of people that circulated and recirculated, seeking an opening at any known approach to the airport. No one could say how many were ordinary Afghans seeking new lives away from the Taliban and how many were on Taliban hit lists for helping the Americans, working in the republic government, serving in the Afghan Army, or like Homeira and other White Scarves, campaigning for a modern Afghanistan and living lives that offended the extremists.

Homeira noticed that the Taliban fighters patrolling outside the airport had developed an uneasy alliance with their longtime enemies, Afghan Army soldiers and paramilitary officers, who performed similar crowd control duties with similarly turbulent results. One big difference was motivation. The Talibs were victors, focused on their immediate future as rulers of Afghanistan. The sooner the Americans and their enablers were gone, the sooner the Taliban could consolidate control. The Afghan soldiers and paramilitary troops were helping to maintain order until they and their families could board evacuation flights to start new lives far away.

As Homeira's group neared Abbey Gate, the air reeked of expended ammo, sweaty people, human waste, and spoiled food. Crushed water bottles, plastic bags, and abandoned clothes carpeted their path. Bullet casings felt like pebbles underfoot.

Jaber, who stood nearly a foot taller than Homeira, was a magnet for the whips and sticks of Talibs. The beatings came whenever Jaber couldn't produce travel documents on demand.

"If you don't have documents," one shouted, "why are you here? Leave!"

Jaber kept his head down and walked on. Homeira could tell that he felt humiliated, reduced overnight from a presidential aide to a would-be refugee being beaten like a thief.

The sights and sounds of his uncle being lashed made Siawash cry more. He pleaded harder to go home. Homeira's hugs and comforting words didn't help. Tired, parched, with dust coating her mouth and eyes, she lost her temper. She shook Siawash by the shoulders.

"All these days you've been screaming to leave the country. Now that we're here, you're screaming to go back? Be a man and keep walking forward!"

He sniffled and complied.

More than two hours after they left the taxi, Homeira, Siawash, Jaber, and his friend approached the final pathway to Abbey Gate.

TO CONTROL THE flood of people approaching Abbey Gate, U.S. Marines placed truck-sized shipping containers at the far end of a road that led to the actual gate. Taliban fighters patrolled around the containers, making it a checkpoint for cursory document checks and crude interrogations. They beat back anyone they deemed unqualified, directing special fury toward military-age men without U.S. visas, passports, or Green Cards.

The Talib guards lashed Jaber and his friend, forcing them to take refuge with Homeira and Siawash inside a nearby car that belonged to an acquaintance. When the beatings and gunfire subsided, the foursome tried again.

Homeira hovered over Siawash to protect him from an errant blow. On their second try, they passed the Taliban's checkpoint and entered a half-kilometer straightaway packed with hundreds of people. High airport walls bordered one side of the entry road; lower walls topped by fences flanked the other. In the middle was an open canal with knee-deep raw sewage. To move forward more quickly or to avoid the body-to-body crush, some people waded through the fetid canal, carrying their children and luggage above the brown sludge.

American and British troops oversaw the entire length of the entry road from sniper and observation towers. At the far end of the road, just outside Abbey Gate, stood Marines who decided which people to bring inside the airport, where waiting U.S. State Department officers conducted final screenings.

A few meters beyond the shipping containers, Homeira held Siawash by the hand and approached an Afghan paramilitary soldier who belonged to a notorious, CIA-trained outfit known as Zero Unit One. Among the most feared commandos on the American side of the war, Zero Unit members now served their U.S. allies as airport gatekeepers, within shouting or shooting distance of their Taliban nemeses.

Pointing to the end of the entry road, toward a soldier near Abbey Gate, Homeira asked the Zero Unit fighter: "Can I talk to that American?"

The whip-toting commando looked Homeira up and down. She concluded he was assessing her appearance to calculate the likelihood that she had connections to the West that would make her eligible for evacuation.

"Do you have documents?" he asked.

"I'm a member of the White Scarves. All I have is my name, my son's name, and my brother's name on the list. I can cross the gate if you help me."

The Afghan commando nodded. Homeira felt a rush of satisfaction about her decision to ignore her London friend's orders to wear drab clothing.

The commando led them through the crowd as Homeira prodded Siawash forward, followed by Jaber and his friend. Even with the Zero Unit escort, Talibs continued to strike Jaber and his friend as they passed. As they moved farther down the entry road, Homeira recognized a popular comedian who appeared frequently on television. He noticed her commando escort and called to her: "Please do something for me so I can go to the gate! I have documents for leaving!"

Homeira asked the commando if the comedian could join them.

"Taking you there is enough," he answered. "Don't look for any others."

Homeira saw several other women with white scarves tied to their bags or worn as hijabs, including a friend named Najibah who worked on human rights issues. The same woman from London had called her. Normally vibrant, Najibah looked defeated, her face pale and dirty.

"When did you get here," Homeira asked.

"I've been here a long time," she said. "Homeira, I've never been so disrespected in my life."

"Me, too," Homeira said.

The commando kept them moving forward. Homeira lost sight of Najibah.

Finally they reached a U.S. Marine a short distance outside Abbey Gate. Over ceaseless noise from shouts and gunfire, Homeira heard the Marine's name as either Marcos or Lucas. He asked for their documents.

Homeira explained she didn't have official travel papers, but she, her son, and her brother were on the White Scarves' list. She tried to show him confirmation emails on her phone, including an electronic document that looked like a U.S. visa but didn't have her name on it.

"No," the Marine said.

He gave no indication he'd ever heard of the White Scarves. "Only Green Cards or American passports." He didn't explain further or inquire who had placed Homeira's name on a list of Afghan women at risk of death.

Homeira and the Marine went in circles, with the Afghan commando helping to translate. Each time Homeira mentioned the White Scarves, the Marine answered: passport, Green Card, or no entry.

Jaber yelled that Homeira should show him a California driver's license she obtained after her writing fellowship in Iowa. She ignored him and called the woman in London.

"They said no!" Homeira shouted into the phone.

"We've added your names to the list!" the woman insisted.

She told Homeira a female member of Parliament and a leader of the Afghan Women's Network had just passed through Abbey Gate as part of the White Scarves' effort. She said Homeira should keep trying.

"We can't do anything if the list is inside the airport!" Homeira yelled. "Someone has to let us through. We have no documents."

The woman said no one who'd passed through the gate could come back out to help.

Homeira hung up and turned to the Marine. She asked again. He gave the same answer.

All around, people with travel documents waved them in the air, shouting to catch the Marine's attention. The Zero Unit commando told Homeira they needed to leave.

"When this man tells you no, you better believe you can't get in," he said. "I fulfilled my duty and took you to the gate, but it's up to the Americans from here."

"I told them my name was on the list," Homeira said.

"These Americans don't care about lists," the commando said. "They are just standing here. They don't look at lists. They only accept Green Cards or passports."

Jaber and his friend were crushed. They'd tried repeatedly in previous days, and this looked like their last, best hope. Siawash looked to be in shock. Homeira felt oddly calm, upset mainly about the beatings Jaber suffered. Later it emerged that the White Scarves' list was one of several ad hoc evacuation efforts, with no central coordination or communication inside the airport. A single U.S. military official had the White Scarves' list, but he rotated among different airport gates and didn't share copies with others. If he wasn't at a gate when a White Scarf evacuee arrived, she was out of luck.

The commando steered them upstream against the current of people who surged toward the gate. Homeira realized some must have been turned away multiple times but refused to leave. She resolved not to be among them.

A thought dawned on her: "America has no plan for getting people out. They only have a deadline."

THE SUN BEGAN to set. More than four hours had passed since they left home. Out beyond the Taliban checkpoints, Homeira, Siawash, Jaber, and his friend hailed a taxi. Jaber hung his head in disappointment.

"Not long ago, the Taliban would have been flogging the Americans here," he said. "Now they're protecting the Americans and whipping us."

Homeira felt a swirl of emotions, above all relief.

Despite her doubts, she gave in to pressure from family and friends. She tried to satisfy the desires and demands of Siawash and Jaber. She didn't know why some White Scarves were allowed to enter Abbey Gate and others weren't, but that wasn't her fault. Now she could return without guilt to her apartment and her life in Kabul.

"I'm not indebted to anyone," she thought.

Secretly she wondered if she hadn't shown the Marine her expired California driver's license because she thought it might have helped them win passage through Abbey Gate.

When they returned to her apartment building, Homeira learned the young neighbor who'd turned her engagement party into a rushed wedding on the day Kabul fell had a strong motive: her new husband had an American passport, and the newlyweds immediately fled Afghanistan with the groom's mother and two sisters.

On her way upstairs, Homeira stopped at her uncle Abo Ismael's apartment. She couldn't hide her happiness to be home. She told him, "We went to the U.S. but now we're back."

When she saw her parents, her sister Zahra, and her brothers Khalid and Mushtaq, Homeira understood why she hadn't cried earlier when she left: she suspected she'd be back.

Khalid harbored hurt feelings that she went to the airport without him.

"Why would you leave us?" he asked.

"I won't leave again," Homeira answered.

Her mother returned her house keys. Homeira watered the plants and flowers on the balcony. She smiled at the sight of a tower of lettuce leaves her mother put out for Sangi.

When her father asked what happened, Homeira turned serious: "It's one thing to talk about the airport. It's another to actually see it."

Wakil Ahmad wanted her to try again for her own safety, as well as for Siawash and Jaber. "I was young when I supported you," he said. "I no longer have the ability to support you."

That night another one of her mother's brothers who lived in Kabul paid a visit. As he left, he said the strangest goodbye Homeira had ever heard: "I pray that none of us sees each other next time."

Before bed, Homeira learned that her friend Najibah had also been turned away from Abbey Gate. Feeling sorry for Najibah but finally at peace, Homeira stood by her window looking out at the Sakhi Shrine. Her migraine eased.

Whatever the future holds, she thought, I'm home.

8

GLORY GATE

THE BIDEN ADMINISTRATION'S pledge to rescue Afghans who worked for the U.S. embassy in Kabul turned into a giant logistical puzzle for Sam and his colleagues to solve.

Overnight between Tuesday, August 24, and Wednesday, August 25, an American diplomat in Kabul spent $60,000 in cash—delivered in stacks of hundred-dollar bills—to hire more than fifty tour buses from a private company. He dispatched their drivers to fan out to select street corners throughout the city. Local embassy employees were sent instructions with individual bus assignments, and senior Afghan embassy employees were appointed "captains" of each bus. Their job was to negotiate their way through Taliban checkpoints to reach the airport.

The key U.S. organizer for the bus captains was a bearded, bespectacled Foreign Service Officer named J. P. Feldmayer, who held multiple titles including acting Political-Military Affairs Unit Chief for what remained of the U.S. embassy in Kabul. Forty-seven years old, a father of six, on a college campus Feldmayer might be mistaken for an assistant professor of political science. But his path to the Foreign Service was even more unusual than Sam's.

The son of a Philadelphia police detective father and a Catholic school teacher mother, Feldmayer dropped out of college and spent thirteen years in the army, including six years as a Green Beret. Deployed in Afghanistan from October 2004 through July 2005, he received a Bronze Star and a combat infantryman's badge for his Special Forces work fighting Taliban insurgents. After leaving the military, Feldmayer became a Diplomatic Security special agent, then made the jump to junior diplomat. In 2017, he returned to Afghanistan as an embassy political officer.

By coincidence, in 2018 Feldmayer was the ex-Diplomatic Security Agent-turned-Foreign Service Officer whose experience encouraged Sam to make his career switch. Feldmayer's line about being sick of standing outside the door still rattled around Sam's brain. Feldmayer returned to Kabul in July 2021 to help with the evacuation and, he thought, to remain at the U.S. embassy afterward. The Taliban takeover changed that plan.

When Sam first heard that Feldmayer was at the airport, they reconnected via email and then by text. Feldmayer forwarded to Sam and several others an urgent message that a qualified Afghan interpreter had made it into the airport only to be separated from his fifteen family members, who also were approved for evacuation. Two Marines were driving all fifteen to North Gate to be ejected. The situation was top priority: the message came from the staff of Zalmay Khalilzad, a former U.S. ambassador to the United Nations who was in Doha negotiating with the Taliban on behalf of the Biden administration. Sam joined a team that rushed to resolve the crisis before the Marines could expel the interpreter's family.

AT A JOC briefing on Wednesday morning, August 25, Sam learned
how Feldmayer planned to do what seemed impossible to help Afghan
employees of the U.S. embassy.

He intended to somehow slip the fifty-plus coach buses he hired
into an airport where every known entrance was barricaded, besieged
by crowds, or like Freedom Gate at Camp Alvarado, already being
used as an access point under the watchful eye of the Taliban.

Feldmayer's solution: a secret gate to the airport.

Only a select few members of the State Department team knew the
gate existed, first among them Feldmayer in his role coordinating with
the U.S. intelligence community in Kabul. Little more than a week
old, the unofficial entrance had multiple names. Some called it Liberty Gate. Some covert operators tried to name it after an American
intelligence operative who helped to establish it. Its most common
name was Glory Gate.

Glory Gate's creators were CIA paramilitary operatives and members of the army's elite Delta Force. Its armed guards were members of
the CIA-trained Afghan paramilitary force known as the Zero Units.
Unlike the more formal airport gates, Glory Gate didn't have nearby
Taliban checkpoints where Talib fighters might block access to Afghans whom the Americans were desperate to save.

Glory Gate's initial purpose was to serve as a clandestine way to
evacuate high-value intelligence sources and local agents. Some people
brought through Glory Gate were chosen by officials at the highest
levels of the U.S. government, from the White House down. The
gate's controllers also used it on an ad hoc basis to provide stealthy exit
from the streets of Kabul for Afghan interpreters, soldiers, and others
at risk of death for having helped the United States.

The plan Feldmayer negotiated with American intelligence operators called for the hired buses to pass through Glory Gate up to eight
at a time. Once inside the airport, the buses would drive to Camp
Alvarado or directly to the passenger terminal, where Marines would
search the Afghan employees from the U.S. embassy and their families

for weapons, explosives, or contraband. Document screening would follow.

On Wednesday, August 25, Sam was assigned to oversee that screening process. After the morning briefing, he hurried the short distance from the JOC to the passenger terminal to await the buses.

First, Sam needed to commandeer enough space on the tarmac outside the terminal for a holding area large enough to contain several hundred people as they waited to be searched and screened. Each bus would carry about fifty-five men, women, and children, so if three buses passed through Glory Gate at once Sam needed room on the tarmac for 165 people. Even more if the process backed up and additional buses arrived.

As Sam worked on the logistics outside the passenger terminal, a gruff bearded American approached him. The man had the look and demeanor of a Special Operations commando. With him were thirty or so Afghans. The man made it clear that he had no time or patience for screenings or anything else from a young State Department diplomat.

"This group needs to go in," the operator said. "They're special interest cases."

"Who are you with?" Sam asked.

A quick back-and-forth confirmed Sam's first impression: the man was part of a classified unit that prefers asking questions to answering them. The conversation also persuaded Sam that the Afghans with the man were legitimate evacuees who'd been flown by helicopter to Camp Alvarado as part of an ongoing U.S. intelligence airlift. Sam stepped aside.

As the temperature soared past ninety degrees, Sam returned his focus to organizing and overseeing the search and screening area for local embassy staff. One break came when the leader of a Hungarian special forces team that controlled space behind the terminal told Sam his group was leaving. Sam noticed that the Hungarians left a pickup truck blocking the area. The truck was still running, so Sam climbed in, only to spot the stick shift. "I'm such a millennial," Sam thought. "I can't drive a manual transmission."

He grabbed a State Department doctor in his fifties who knew how to drive a stick, but the engine stalled when the doctor put the truck in gear. The doctor reached for the ignition key, only to discover the truck had been hot-wired. Sam leaned in, eager to apply his lesson from a day earlier. One by one, Sam touched the battery wires to other loose wires under the dashboard. The windshield wipers swished. The horn blared.

The Hungarian returned with the attitude of a commando finding a thief inside his truck.

"Can I help you?" he asked.

"Oh," Sam sputtered. "We're sorry, we're just trying to move it. We weren't going to steal it."

"Whatever," the Hungarian said, as Sam and the doctor cleared out.

Before the Hungarian drove away, Sam asked, "Do you think we could have it, once you guys leave?"

The Hungarian smiled. "I already promised it to the Belgians."

MEANWHILE, SAM HAD continued texting with Asad, aka Ryan, the interpreter trying to help his sister's family. Their exchanges throughout the week gained steam as the final hours of the withdrawal approached. The last civilian evacuation flight from Kabul was only days away: 6 A.M. on Saturday, August 28, to give the last American troops and diplomats enough time to clear out before the August 31 deadline.

Wednesday morning, August 25, shortly after Sam attended the briefing at the JOC about the embassy employee buses, he texted Asad with encouraging news: the policy of allowing at-risk Afghans had been restored, at least temporarily.

"Abbey Gate might be good for your family this morning," Sam told Asad. "Our consuls are finally letting in families with a credible fear of the Taliban."

Asad didn't respond.

WHEN THE FIRST bus of embassy employees arrived at the passenger terminal, Sam climbed aboard.

His voice raspy, Sam yelled to the bus captain over the roar of C-17s taxiing nearby: "I need you to translate what I'm about to say. 'Okay, I'm going to take you off the bus, single-file line. Please collect your luggage from underneath the bus. Then you'll follow me into a holding area where I will explain the next step.'"

Sam stepped off the bus and walked backward like a tour guide to a station where male and female Marines conducted body and luggage searches. The previous day, a search turned up a loaded revolver, and this day's searches produced contraband including kitchen knives and powdered opium.

By the end of the day, having cleared nine busloads of embassy employees despite some backups and hiccups, Sam turned over the operation to the night shift.

His voice gone, wrung out from twelve hours on his feet in the heat with no lunch and little water, Sam returned to his quarters to rest.

MEANWHILE, DANGER SIGNS of terrorist plots kept rising.

While Sam spent the day working to clear embassy staff buses, the shadow U.S. embassy staff issued its first public warning in four days: "Because of security threats outside the gates of Kabul airport, we are advising U.S. citizens to avoid traveling to the airport and to avoid airport gates at this time unless you receive individual instructions from a U.S. government representative to do so." Then, in bold: **"U.S. citizens who are at the Abbey Gate, East Gate, or North Gate now should leave immediately."**

Around the same time, the White House press secretary announced that about 19,000 people had been evacuated the previous day, bringing the total to 82,300 since the fall of Kabul.

Almost simultaneously, other top officials in Washington told reporters the United States and its allies were tracking a "specific" threat to the airport from ISIS-K. The Australian government warned of "an ongoing and very high threat of terrorist attack."

ON THURSDAY, AUGUST 26, after his predawn ritual of a shower and a quadruple espresso, Sam arrived at the JOC shortly before his shift began at 6 A.M. With forty-eight hours left until the last civilian evacuation flight, Sam learned about another change of plan.

The coach buses hired by J.P. Feldmayer for the State Department still cruised the streets of Kabul picking up local embassy staff and their families. Sam's job remained focused on screening documents and vetting stories. But a supervisor told him he'd be working from a new, more dangerous location many of his colleagues didn't know existed.

Sam was bound for Glory Gate.

He arrived there a half hour later, accompanied by a security team and another State Department consular official. Instantly Sam understood why Glory Gate remained a secret: it was hidden in plain sight. In fact, Glory Gate was less a formal airport gate than an improvised back door.

Glory Gate's entranceway was located two kilometers west of North Gate, where an unused, unnamed service road to the airport intersected with Tajikan Road. The service road was roughly paved, dusty and pitted, ten meters wide. The closest landmark was a twenty-four-hour gas station and mini-mart on the opposite side of Tajikan Road called the Panjshir Pumping Station, better known as the Panjshir Pump. CIA operatives, U.S. Special Operations Forces, and other covert operatives used the gas station as a meeting place and transit point for numerous evacuees.

Coils of concertina wire stretched across the opening of the service road where it met Tajikan Road. Afghan Zero Unit paramilitary soldiers, working as guards for the gate's CIA and Delta Force operators, moved aside the razor-sharp wire whenever vehicles needed to enter. A small gap in the concertina coils allowed approved pedestrians to pass.

Beyond the concertina wire, on the east side of the service road's entrance at Tajikan Road, stood dirt-filled barriers called Hesco bastions that looked like huge hay bales. Stacked two to three meters high, the barriers were arranged in a square fifteen meters on each side. The result looked like a primitive hut missing its roof. A door-sized opening in one wall of the barriers allowed Glory Gate's operators and evacuees to use the Hesco square as a rocket bunker or as cover from gunfire. It also served as a safe space to search incoming evacuees for weapons and explosives.

Moving south along the service road toward the airport, the Glory Gate operators had used heavy equipment to position several concrete barriers, to slow or stop entry. Some of the barriers stood upright while others lay toppled on the ground.

Beyond the barriers, seventy meters south of Tajikan Road in the direction of the airport, American operatives had used forklifts to arrange more concrete blast walls roughly in a U shape, to create an improvised holding area where they could control entry. The protected area served as another location for searches or for cover. The operators widened the opening between the blast walls to give the State Department's hired coach buses enough room to enter.

Past the U-shaped holding area, continuing south toward the airport, the service road ran straight and narrow for 125 meters. Operators positioned blast walls on either side of the road the entire length of that stretch, creating a protected chute that looked like a roofless tunnel.

At the end of the straightaway was a single-lane bridge over a dry culvert that resembled an empty moat. From there, the service road snaked another three hundred meters through a desolate no-man's-land to its true destination: a gap in the airport wall at the remote western end of the airport, not far from Camp Alvarado. The opening in the wall was the actual Glory Gate. The long, winding service road that led there from Tajikan Road was its driveway.

Sam and the others from the State Department team drove northwest from the JOC and exited the airport through the gap in the wall. They parked along the service road well back from Tajikan Road. As Sam walked north toward the intersection with Tajikan Road, he saw trucks and cars driving past the service road entrance in both directions. The Panjshir Pump did steady business selling fuel and groceries even in the early morning hours. Market stalls shaded by tattered rugs or swaths of faded canvas lined the sidewalk. The fall of Kabul and the mad rush to the airport couldn't stop vendors from hawking fruits, vegetables, cotton candy, car parts, on-the-spot tailoring, shoe repairs, and kitchenware.

Sam felt the temperature rising along with his apprehension. Hundreds of people walked along Tajikan Road, including more than a dozen Zero Unit guards who patrolled the area for the American covert gatekeepers. The Afghan guards kept the crowd on edge and away from Glory Gate's concertina wire-blocked entranceway by firing semiautomatic guns and large-caliber truck-mounted weapons above the heads of pedestrians. Any unauthorized person who detected Glory Gate's potential as an airport entry and moved toward it could expect a gun-barrel beating or worse.

Around 8 A.M., as Sam awaited the day's first embassy buses, he saw a green pickup truck with a white Taliban flag stop near the Panjshir Pump. Out jumped six Taliban fighters in desert camouflage. Sam took cover, knowing that the Zero Unit paramilitary Afghans and the Taliban were sworn enemies. But the Taliban fighters seemed to be observing the negotiated cease-fire around the airport, eager as they were to see the United States leave Afghanistan.

The Talibs steered clear of the Zero Unit paramilitary soldiers, and vice versa. With black beards and hardened expressions, the Taliban fighters flogged Afghans along the street seemingly at random. They drove off within minutes, which made Sam conclude they were simply cruising around the airport looking for people to beat. They showed no sign they understood how the service road was being used as an airport entranceway. When the Taliban truck left, Zero Unit guards reclaimed full, aggressive control of the noisy street.

The Afghan paramilitary fighters proved useful in a different way when Sam asked around for an energy drink. A U.S. Special Operations member motioned to a Zero Unit guard, who ran like a cabana waiter to the Panjshir Pump and returned with cold Red Bulls for each.

As Sam absorbed his surroundings, he knew he'd assumed his highest level of risk since arriving six days earlier in Kabul. He couldn't rationalize his presence at Glory Gate the way he did when he ventured outside Abbey Gate. There, he assured himself he was still somewhat safe because he traveled only a few meters beyond the airport wall. Now, in military lingo, he was well "outside the wire," nearly half a kilometer from the comparatively secure zone inside Kabul International. He'd broken his "Don't leave the airport" promise to Liana. The loud, close pop-pop-pop of semiautomatic rifle rounds made it hard to argue he hadn't also broken promise number two: "Don't do anything unnecessarily dangerous."

All that remained was promise number three: "Don't be a hero."

But the day was still young.

FOR THE PREVIOUS week, the email, text, and voicemail inboxes of every member of the State Department team, from Ambassador Bass and his top deputy Jim DeHart to lower-level diplomats including Sam, overflowed with official, semiofficial, unofficial, and personal requests to help Afghans escape the carnage overtaking their country.

With each passing day the flood intensified.

Pleas came from the White House and from the offices of senators, members of Congress, and current and former U.S. government officials. The Vatican sent a list of names. Foreign governments, major corporations, religious groups, media companies, military members, veterans' associations, and non-governmental organizations did the same. More requests arrived through informal networks and daisy chains of contacts that bloomed out of desperation. J.P. Feldmayer, operating on three hours of sleep a night, was afraid to close his eyes. He feared he'd miss a message about someone he might save through Glory Gate. He'd battled the Taliban as a decorated Green Beret, yet he considered these to be the most intense days of his life.

Sam's parents and in-laws still didn't know he was in Afghanistan, but it seemed as though the rest of the world did. Word spread among former colleagues at the embassy in Nigeria about Sam's temporary assignment, and soon he was barraged with evacuation requests sent by friends in Abuja who'd served in Afghanistan with the military or nonprofit organizations. Friends of friends reached out, too. A colleague of Liana's in Mali texted Sam on behalf of an Afghan American Marine whose family members were trapped in Kabul.

A college friend of Sam's who'd served in Afghanistan as an Army Ranger sought help for his onetime interpreter. A beseeching text pinged his phone from a member of Sam's State Department diplomatic training class. Another came from someone with a Washington, D.C., area telephone number: "Hi, Sam. I hope this reaches you well. I'm in the US helping at-risk Afghans to evacuate Afghanistan. Received your contact info as someone on the ground. . . . Can you verify?" Sam shook his head at the thought of confirming his identity and location to an anonymous stranger.

Sam couldn't focus on every request, but he kept them all and responded to as many as he could. He offered no false hope but vaguely pledged to help if the opportunity arose and if he could determine whether the person or family qualified for evacuation. That's not what people wanted to hear, and he knew it. They wanted Sam's sacred vow that he would personally rescue their loved ones or friends, no matter the risk or cost.

Only days earlier, when Sam first volunteered to help with the withdrawal, he was driven in large part by a hunger for adventure and the potential for career advancement. Now he understood the real reason to be there. It had nothing to do with his needs or desires. Sam felt a crushing weight of responsibility for the thousands of people outside the airport gates who feared for their lives and clamored for deliverance. He also suffered from heavy guilt about those he'd turned away or couldn't help.

As requests poured in, Sam was too busy, too tired, and too focused on self-preservation and professional detachment to dwell on every text or email plea. But he recognized that at the far end of each one was a scared human being or family, potentially facing a death sentence. Men, women, and children, mothers and fathers, grandparents, aunts and uncles, boys and girls. Teachers, journalists, and soldiers. Shopkeepers and homemakers. Cooks and custodians. Artists, activists, and government officials. Sam could imagine that even some of the youngest Afghans seeking seats aboard the C-17s understood that the Taliban executed and imprisoned dissidents, severed limbs of accused thieves, stoned women for disobedience, and lashed anyone in its way.

Sam also recognized that the people seeking a way out of Kabul were no different from him, Liana, and their families and friends. People like his great-uncle who stayed too long in Poland and was killed by the Nazis. Or the old men and women who showed school-children their tattooed forearms. Or the Jewish refugees in Marseille who Hiram Bingham refused to turn away. Sam knew that some people seeking his help were within a few kilometers of where he stood, outside a locked gate, crushed by their fellow freedom seekers, buffeted by the roar of planes departing without them. Or maybe they hid inside their homes, too afraid to face the Taliban fighters who roamed the city like they owned it. Which they did.

Standing in the hot sun on the service road that led to Glory Gate, Sam knew he couldn't help even a fraction of the people who needed saving. He couldn't save all the people in his texts or emails. But maybe he could save a few, even if it meant breaking his last promise to Liana and endangering himself and his career.

AS HE STOOD near Tajikan Road, Sam spotted his colleague J.P. Feldmayer, who'd organized the embassy buses. Feldmayer held a spreadsheet listing license plate numbers and expected arrival times of several dozen buses heading their way. To stay updated, he spoke repeatedly by phone with Afghan bus captains as the rented coaches crawled through the city's snarled traffic. At Feldmayer's side was a local embassy staffer named Sadiq, who fought his way into the airport days earlier then declined immediate evacuation to help the American officers plan his colleagues' evacuation and to serve as an interpreter.

One reason for Sam's reassignment to the front lines of Glory Gate was the new plan called for the Afghan embassy staffers and their families to have their documents screened immediately inside the service road entrance. Then they and their luggage would be searched at Camp Alvarado, to speed the process and prevent backups that occurred the day before when the buses went directly to the passenger terminal.

Close to 9 A.M., three big, dusty coach buses appeared about two hundred meters down Tajikan Road. It took the drivers about ten minutes to creep the rest of the way through the pedestrians and traffic. Zero Unit guards, under the direction of their CIA bosses, fired enough rounds to scare the curious, after which they pulled back the concertina wire, opening the service road to allow the buses to turn in.

As the buses entered the service road, Feldmayer directed them past the Hesco bastion square toward the concrete blast walls, and then farther south toward the airport. Feldmayer, Sam, and a third State Department official had already agreed the safest place for an initial document screening would be just past the small bridge, where the buses could be steered onto a shoulder where the road curved and widened. The area had the added advantage of being well back from Tajikan Road, where the buses' arrival made some pedestrians suspect their destination and try to rush in alongside them. Zero Unit guards used flash-bangs, smoke, tear gas, and rounds fired into the air to drive them back.

By parking the buses off the service road, the State Department team also avoided conflict with U.S. intelligence operatives who continued to drive cars through Glory Gate to bring in small groups of at-risk Afghans and speed them to the passenger terminal.

When the first three embassy staff buses parked at the screening spot, Sam, Feldmayer, and the third State Department official each climbed aboard one with a security contractor or Diplomatic Security Agent. Some local embassy staff worked as gardeners, mechanics, or in other roles that didn't require English, so Sam asked the bus captain to translate.

One family at a time, he ran through his screening protocol: "Who's the embassy employee? Okay, let me see your embassy ID. What section did you work in?" Then he'd ask the employee to identify each family member. "Great, perfect. Okay, please get off the bus. Don't worry about your luggage for now. Go stand over by the side."

In less than a half hour, Sam confirmed that all fifty-five passengers were legitimate embassy employees or family members. As the Afghans awaiting evacuation stood in the dirt beside the bus, Sam climbed back aboard to search for stowaways. Finding none, he stepped off and invited everyone to retake their seats. One man hung back.

He told Sam his name was Ebad, and in broken English he begged Sam to allow his younger brother to join him and his family at the airport. Ebad explained that his brother had accompanied him to the rendezvous location, but the bus captain had refused to allow him on board. Sam thought, "Of course. He's not part of your nuclear family. No brothers, no sisters, no cousins, no aunts, no uncles."

"I'm sorry, these are the rules," Sam told Ebad. "We really have to move now. Please get back on the bus."

Ebad didn't budge. "My brother, I take care of him. He doesn't have anyone else. He's all alone."

Ebad explained that his brother was seventeen, with no parents in the picture. That made him effectively part of Ebad's nuclear family, a circumstance the State Department hadn't anticipated. Siblings of adult embassy staff members were assumed to be adults, too.

"Please, is there anything you can do?" Ebad implored Sam. "He's nearby." His brother was near the Panjshir Pump, having followed the bus to its supposedly secret destination.

"There's really nothing I can do," Sam said. He vacillated, briefly— "If he's able to make it across the street . . ."—then reconsidered. "Actually, no, I'm sorry. You have to get back on the bus. I can't do this. I'm really sorry about the situation, but there's nothing I can do."

Ebad climbed onto the bus but continued to plead with Sam. He hung over the bus driver, halfway out the driver-side window. Sam found Ebad credible, and his status as an embassy employee meant he'd been well vetted as trustworthy. It pained Sam to imagine the fate of a seventeen-year-old on the cusp of manhood in a city under Taliban control.

Sam asked for a phone number for Ebad's brother and began typing it into his cellphone. Halfway through, Ebad interrupted: "Just take my phone."

"I don't want your phone," Sam said. "I don't want to be responsible for that. Just give me his phone number."

"No, take my phone. It has his number," Ebad said, reaching out of the bus window with a Samsung smartphone.

"Then how am I going to get in touch with you?" Sam yelled.

"I have another phone," Ebad answered, still hanging out the window.

In a flash of inspiration fueled by dread, Ebad had improvised an evacuation plot for his teenage brother, with Sam as its central player. Ebad's plan would require Sam to ignore the State Department's evacuation rules about nuclear families, rescue Ebad's brother, get him inside the airport, evade questions from other American officials, then contact Ebad to reconnect the two. The wildest part was that Sam thought it actually might work.

Standing below the driver-side window, looking up at the bus like a kindergarten student on his first day of school, Sam calculated his next move. The other two buses pulled away. Pops of gunfire crackled nearby. A security contractor insisted to Sam it was past time for the bus to leave for Camp Alvarado.

By chance, the State Department's plan called for Feldmayer and the other consular screener to ride aboard two of the buses to Camp Alvarado for body and luggage searches by members of the 82nd Airborne. In a stroke of potentially good fortune for Ebad and his brother, Sam had been assigned to remain at Glory Gate with a security contractor to greet and guide the next convoy of embassy staff buses.

Torn between wanting to help and wanting Ebad to leave him alone, Sam reached up and accepted Ebad's spare smartphone. Ebad shouted out the password numbers that would unlock it.

"Fuck," Sam thought as he typed them into his own phone, so he wouldn't forget.

"I'm going to call my brother!" Ebad yelled as the bus pulled away. "He's going to call the phone. Pick up!"

The spare phone rang almost immediately but again it was Ebad providing Sam with more information. Sam could barely hear him.

Sam rasped: "I don't know anything about you. I don't know how I'm going to link you guys up. Can you send me a picture of your embassy badge?" Sam provided his contact information, and Ebad sent an image of his yellow embassy badge via WhatsApp.

When the buses drove off, Sam walked back toward Tajikan Road.

His security contractor bodyguard told him to go no farther than the doorway of the protective Hesco barriers. Despite Sam's body armor and helmet, stepping beyond that point would exponentially increase his exposure to additional dangers, from kidnapping to stray gunfire. The thought of a U.S. diplomat being killed, hurt, or abducted outside a secret CIA entrance to the Kabul airport was too troubling for either of them to contemplate.

Sam accepted the limits even as he angled for a better view of Tajikan Road. Amid bursts of gunfire and flash-bang explosions from the Zero Unit guards, Sam watched as U.S. intelligence operators and their Afghan allies rushed Afghan evacuees from the Panjshir Pump to the pedestrian path that led to the Glory Gate service road.

The longer he watched, the more fully Sam understood how Glory Gate functioned. Not only was it an off-the-books airport entrance for embassy staff buses and cars driven by American operators, it was an escape route for anyone the United States government wanted to evacuate on foot.

Sam took a beat. He considered his position and his options. As a Foreign Service Officer and a vice consul of the U.S. State Department, Sam concluded that he theoretically had the authority to decide who to allow inside the airport, as long as he stayed within the evacuation guidelines established by his superiors. He ignored the fact that his assignment at Glory Gate didn't include freelance pedestrian rescues of at-risk Afghans.

The logical progression from Sam's conclusion about his authority was an idea that seemed certain to break his third promise to Liana. It revolved around the friendly Afghan interpreter with the California surfer vibe, the young man Sam met on his first day in Kabul and saw again at East Gate: Asad.

To bring in evacuees on foot, someone would need to cross Tajikan Road, walk more than a hundred meters through a busy street market, collect at-risk Afghans at the Panjshir Pump, then guide them back. Sam understood the State Department security team wouldn't allow him to step beyond the end of the Glory Gate service road. No such restrictions existed for Asad. Then again, by enlisting Asad, Sam would be putting the young man's life at risk.

Sam felt certain that Asad would accept the danger to help his own family to escape Afghanistan. After that, maybe Asad would stick around and serve as a translator and retriever to bring in other people whose painful stories filled Sam's inbox. Plus Ebad's younger brother.

One more factor played into Sam's reasoning: with Feldmayer and the other State Department consular official busy with the buses at Camp Alvarado, Sam had a window of opportunity and complete autonomy.

In another stroke of good timing, Asad had reestablished contact after a twenty-four-hour gap between texts.

THAT MORNING, THURSDAY, August 26, Asad answered Sam's suggestion from the previous day that his family might be able to enter the airport through Abbey Gate. In his reply, Asad reminded Sam that his mother and brother had already made it into the airport, but his sister, her husband, and their two children still needed help. They remained holed up in their Kabul apartment, traumatized by their previous attempts and too afraid to return to the streets.

By the time Asad replied, the U.S. State Department had already issued its warning about dangers at Abbey Gate, East Gate, and North Gate. Sam could no longer urge Asad to send his sister's family to one of those entrances. But now, with his new understanding of Glory Gate, Sam formed the stirrings of a plan for how it might be put to even greater good, while also assuaging some of his guilt about all the people he'd turned away from Abbey Gate.

Sam's priority remained American citizens and Afghan staff from the U.S. embassy. But in the lull between those arrivals, maybe he could do more. Maybe he could help more.

"Hey man, what's your plan today?" Sam texted Asad. "Can I get you to be our terp [interpreter] for a few hours near [Camp] Alvarado?" By mentioning only the general location—the airport's northwestern corner—Sam was trying to preserve Glory Gate's secret status.

Sam added: "It may"—he put the word may in bold—"also help with the rest of your family if we can get them there."

Asad answered within minutes: "How bro."

Sam texted that he'd explain by phone or when they were together, then added: "We would have to move pretty quick this morning though—like in the next few hours."

Without naming Glory Gate, Sam instructed Asad how and where to find him.

"I'm here now," Sam wrote. "Outside the gate. It's very secretive right now so please do not spread this beyond only who absolutely needs to know. It will burn the op." For emphasis, Sam added: "Lots of shooting."

Sam and Asad texted back and forth about how Asad could reach Sam. The rapid-fire texts resembled an exchange between two high schoolers trying to get rides to the mall.

"Can you come and pick me up?" Asad asked.

Sam: "I don't have a car."

"I don't have a car too. Do you need me?"

After several more exchanges, Sam texted: "If possible please" with a praying hands emoji.

Asad got a lift from an army intelligence team member he'd been helping. When Asad arrived, he told Sam he'd already been to this location the previous night with the intelligence unit, although they called Glory Gate by one of its other names. Asad told Sam the army team had sought permission from the gate's clandestine operators to bring in his sister and her family, but they refused.

Asad pointed out the main gatekeeper, a combat-hardened, olive-skinned, thick-bearded man in his forties who oversaw the Afghan Zero Unit guards. Asad told Sam he'd badgered the man the previous night with no luck.

"I can't go with you," Asad said. "He hates me."

Sam assumed the bearded man was an Afghan paramilitary commander. "I hope he speaks English," Sam thought. On the positive side, Sam knew that J.P. Feldmayer had won approval from Glory Gate's controllers to bring in embassy staff buses. On the other hand, Sam's plan was an unsanctioned operation trying to help Afghans who fit no neatly defined category for evacuation. Asad's sister and her family might qualify under the shifting rules as at-risk Afghans, but Sam didn't know for certain and didn't intend to ask.

"Good morning," Sam said as he approached the gatekeeper. Asad hung back, trying to stay inconspicuous.

"How are you?" Sam inquired. "I'm with the U.S. State Department. I'm wondering if your unit might be able to allow my interpreter to go collect a family outside."

To Sam's surprise, the man answered in perfect English. He pointed to Asad: "I remember you from last night. You're a pain in the ass."

Sam regrouped, if awkwardly, not fully comprehending the situation and still thinking the man was Afghan.

"Oh, well. I understand, but this is me, from the State Department, asking would you be able to help out the U.S. State Department." Sam might have repeated "State Department" one or two additional times in the same sentence.

The man mocked Sam with a patented brand of American hard-ass sarcasm.

"Could you remind me who you're with again? I don't think I remember."

Sam finally got it. The man, known by the call sign "Omar," was an American special operator whose low opinion of junior State Department diplomats had been confirmed. Sam apologized and tried again.

"Forget what I said. I was being an idiot. Anyway, do you think we can do this?"

"I don't care," Omar said. "Do whatever you want. Just don't get in our way and don't blow our gate. This is the last functioning method that we have to get people in. Don't fuck it up."

With Omar's crude blessing, Sam got a spare set of keys to Glory Gate. Keeping his promise to Asad, Sam decided his first improvised rescue mission would involve Asad's sister, her husband, and their two children.

Asad phoned his sister with the good news, but the call went badly. Sam couldn't understand the language but he knew the sound of siblings arguing. Dejected, Asad hung up.

"She's not coming," Asad said.

"What do you mean she's not coming?"

"She's too scared. They tried the other day and they got beaten. She got hit in the face. She's got two young kids. At this point, she's given up. She just wants to stay here, stay out of the craziness."

"That's crazy," Sam said. "Come on, this is our only chance, but we have to move quickly. Call her again."

Asad hesitated.

"Call her again. If you want I'll talk to her."

Asad called and again the siblings bickered. Without putting Sam on the phone, Asad hung up.

"I'm sorry, she's not coming."

Their first rescue plan had gone sideways. But Sam still needed Asad if he wanted to bring in people who otherwise had no way to reach the airport through the teeming crowds. Asad shared Sam's desire to help others, even if he and his family received no benefit.

Despite his disappointment about his sister, Asad agreed to stay with Sam at Glory Gate. He also hoped somehow he might change his sister's mind.

WHEN EBAD TOSSED Sam his spare cellphone, he said his younger brother was waiting nearby. Sam decided Ebad's brother would be their new test case.

Sam texted Ebad from his personal phone, with a deadline: "Call me directly. If he's here in the next ten minutes, I can snatch him, or send me your brother's phone number immediately. I have a ten-minute window to make this happen."

With Asad translating, Sam spoke with Ebad's teenage brother and pinpointed his location near the Panjshir Pump. Sam asked him to text a photo of himself as confirmation and to help Asad identify him. When the photo arrived, Sam thought the young man with a trimmed mustache and beard looked older than seventeen. Sam hesitated, then decided to trust Ebad as an embassy employee. The security contractor protecting Sam didn't care one way or another, as long as Sam didn't personally go into Tajikan Road to snatch anyone.

Sam gave Ebad's brother a code word Asad suggested: "devils." Asad chose the password because he thought it sounded like something from a movie. Sam told Ebad's brother to say it without calling attention to himself when approached at the gas station by a young Afghan man in body armor.

Before Asad left his side, Sam explained the plan to Omar, the surly American overseer of Glory Gate. Either Omar was bored of standing around, or Sam's initiative impressed him enough to set aside his macho indifference.

On Omar's signal, the Afghan paramilitary guards who roamed Tajikan Road created a distraction by firing their weapons over the heads of pedestrians. At a break in traffic, Asad sprinted from the service road entrance into Tajikan Road. He cut through an opening in a median strip, crossed to the far side, and wove through the anxious crowd east toward the gas station.

A lone, unarmed man in American body armor on Tajikan Road could become an easy target for thugs or opportunists, or for Taliban or ISIS-K fighters. That would be doubly true for an American, but even a native Afghan like Asad needed to stay alert. Asad moved fast enough to be efficient but not so fast as to draw unwanted attention. He also had an emergency plan in mind.

Days earlier, Asad saw Zero Unit guards being fired on by an un-known sniper at North Gate, an incident that left one Afghan soldier dead. Based on that attack and his two years of battlefield experience among the U.S. Special Forces, Asad assumed the Afghan paramilitary guards would be the primary targets if the Taliban or ISIS-K showed up near Glory Gate and started shooting. Asad resolved to run toward any Zero Unit guard who was killed or wounded, take his weapon, find hard cover, and shoot back until he could retreat.

Asad's motivation was straightforward. Risking his life for Ebad's brother might eventually enable him to do the same for his sister's family. "I'm going to do whatever it takes to help them," Asad told himself. "If there is a chance I'm going to take it."

Sam waited anxiously at the Hesco barriers. He knew Asad could find himself with a bull's-eye on his back, if for no other reason than his style of body armor. "In Afghanistan," Sam told himself, "they know the difference between U.S. camo and Afghan camo." Sam recognized that Asad would willingly jeopardize his safety for his sister's family, but now he'd gone into the street at Sam's request for a stranger. If anything happened to Asad, it would be Sam's fault.

Sam also worried about consequences for his career. No one in the State Department knew that he'd recruited a young Afghan inter-preter who seemed to have connections with army intelligence. For all practical purposes, Asad was "this random Afghan guy I met in the passenger terminal." Now Sam had sent him outside the wire to grab some other random Afghan guy who didn't qualify as a nuclear family member of an embassy staffer.

"What if he gets taken by the Taliban?" Sam thought. "I am re-sponsible."

The longer Asad was gone, the more Sam spiraled.

"Ultimately, the State Department, the White House, is responsi-ble, but I would have caused that disaster. If anything goes wrong, Asad is fucked. I'm fucked. My career is over."

9

WOLVES

Aᶠᵗᵉʳ ʙᵉⁱⁿᵍ ᵗᵘʳⁿᵉᵈ away from Abbey Gate, Homeira enjoyed her best sleep in weeks.

She awoke with so much energy on Saturday, August 21, she cooked
breakfast for Siawash, Jaber, and everyone else in their two apartments: her parents; her brother Mushtaq, his wife Jahedah and son
Shahzad; her brother Khalid; her sister Zahra; and her cousins Qasem
and Basir.

Afterward, Homeira still felt restless. For two years she'd admired
the bright blue domes of the Sakhi Shrine from her window, but she'd
never visited. "I was about to lose the whole country yesterday," she
thought, "and now every inch of Kabul is valuable to me."

She invited her mother on a walk to the mosque.

Her father scoffed. "You didn't go anywhere in Kabul these past
two years. Now that the Taliban is here, you want to go to different

places?"

"My daughter feels like going there," Ansari shot back. "We'll go there together."

Zahra joined them, and the three women rounded up Siawash and Mushtaq's son Shahzad, an impish four-year-old who looked like Siawash's younger brother. As they left the apartment, Homeira noticed Jaber and Khalid bent over a laptop, furiously filling out evacuation requests.

HOMEIRA DRESSED MORE modestly than she had at the airport, wearing muted colors and a shawl that hid her chest, to avoid endangering her mother. Normally reserved, Zahra wore a bright red cloak and a matching scarf. Her makeup surprised Homeira the most.

"I've never seen you wear red lipstick. Why now?"

Zahra shrugged. "I don't know. I just wanted to."

They walked through side alleys as a shortcut to the thirty-acre cemetery that surrounded the shrine. Thousands of dusty green flags hung on poles to mark the graves of war casualties.

"Do people turn into flags when they die?" Shahzad asked.

Homeira, Ansari, and Zahra gazed up at the mosque's six domes, covered in glazed tiles that shimmered in the midday sun. Quranic excerpts, poetry, and prayers snaked up the exterior walls in elaborate script. Sacred to all Muslims, the mosque is especially revered by Hazara Shiites, an ethnic minority frequently targeted by both the Taliban and ISIS-K. On a holy day in October 2016, an attacker at the mosque dressed as a police officer sprayed gunfire and threw hand grenades at worshippers, killing eighteen and wounding dozens. ISIS-K claimed responsibility. The marble floors were washed of blood and the mosque reopened, only to be struck again seventeen months later by a suicide bomber who killed thirty-four people nearby.

Outside the mosque's terraced entrance, Taliban fighters stood at ease beside police cars, ignoring the women and boys as they passed.

Siawash steered Homeira toward a popcorn vendor. She stood in line behind two Talib fighters. One stepped farther away, to avoid being close to a woman, eventually leaving the line altogether. Homeira felt something like pity. In other circumstances, he might have been a handsome green-eyed boy from Kandahar, visiting the mosque on a day off from school. She despised the viciousness and beliefs of Taliban leaders, but she suspected that individual Talibs, brainwashed and brutalized, indoctrinated into violence, had been robbed of their childhoods.

"There is a child in every Taliban soldier who never got to eat popcorn, lick an ice cream, or be on a swing in the park," she thought. "When they're in a different situation, these men forget they're supposed to be willing to blow themselves up. This is the tragedy of Afghanistan."

Back home after the outing, Homeira's translator Zaman Stanizai called to pressure her to try again to reach the airport despite the bedlam at Abbey Gate.

"I did my best," she shouted. "I want no one to tell me to leave again. If anyone feels that I ignore myself and Siawash, this is the proof that I don't. I went to the airport and couldn't leave, so I don't feel indebted to myself or my child. Let me live my life in peace."

But the stay-or-go whipsaw couldn't be resolved so quickly. After the call, Homeira had a conversation with her cousin Qasem that tested her resolve to remain in Kabul.

Quiet and thoughtful, with short dark hair and a neatly trimmed beard, Qasem was the family's most devout member. A week earlier, before the fall, he was a promising lawyer who'd worked as a prosecutor, on track to become a judge. Now he feared reprisals by Taliban members he prosecuted or whose prison sentences he'd announced as a court clerk. He wanted to flee Kabul as badly as Homeira's brothers Jaber and Khalid.

"I'm sure you'll survive this," Homeira reassured him. Afghanistan's laws have always followed sharia to some degree, she said, so he would adapt and continue to practice law.

The Taliban respects no laws but its own, Qasem replied. He echoed what Homeira's new lawyer in her financial support case said nearly two weeks earlier, when the idea of the Taliban reaching Kabul was distant speculation.

"The Taliban doesn't even officially recognize divorces that happened during the republic era. They're calling for all divorced women to go back to their families," Qasem said. "How is that same Taliban going to accept my studies from the republic era?"

Homeira didn't worry about her divorce; her husband initiated it, so that wouldn't offend the extremists. But she had a chilling thought: "If the Taliban doesn't recognize the sharia laws of the republic, how will they recognize the civil laws of the republic?"

Specifically, she worried about court decisions involving child custody.

Homeira slipped back toward despair.

LONG WALKS HELPED her mood, so the next morning, Sunday, August 22, she brushed off Siawash's pleas that she stay home. She followed her usual route through Kabul University wearing clothes that made her stylish in Iowa, but shameful under Taliban rule.

The campus was quiet, disturbed only by the constant hum of engine noise from planes overhead evacuating more of her countrymen. A week after the Taliban's arrival, Homeira noticed that women had largely disappeared from the streets. She saw no one like herself, walking alone in public in what Siawash and his friends now called "infidel clothes."

Heading toward home on a narrow footpath, Homeira saw two men walking toward her at a distance. A few more steps and she noticed their long, loose clothes.

A few more and she saw their guns.

Her mind raced. "Should I just keep walking like in the republic era and make them step aside, or will they step aside before reaching me? Should I jump to the other side of the street?"

She weighed the pros and cons. Staying on the path might result in a beating, but it might strike a symbolic blow for women's rights. Scurrying away might save her from harm, but it might trigger the shame of having surrendered to Taliban oppression without a fight.

Homeira continued straight ahead. With each step, she imagined how they might interrogate her.

"Why did you keep walking?" one Talib might ask. "Why are you even outside?"

Maybe he would declare: "You made a big mistake to walk through us." And then the other might smash her head with his gunstock.

Still she walked on. She held her breath as the distance between them closed.

When they were a few meters apart, the Talibs stepped aside.

Homeira marched past them, shoulders back, chest out.

HOMEIRA RETURNED TO a quiet apartment. Before she could share her small victory, Qasem came home looking traumatized. Her devout lawyer cousin trembled as he told his story.

He'd also walked that morning near Kabul University. He, too, crossed paths with two Taliban fighters. But they didn't step aside. They stopped him and asked where he was going. Taking a walk, he said. One demanded his phone. Qasem refused, but the Talib insisted.

"I swear they didn't even know how to read," Qasem told Homeira.

His social media and texting apps were unlocked, and the Talibs saw photos of fully dressed foreign women who revealed enough skin to offend fundamentalists. They whipped him.

"You have no honor," one sneered. "We need to teach you how to be Muslim."

Shielding himself from the blows, Qasem replied: "Yes, sir. I'm sorry. Forgive me, please?"

Homeira's father overheard the story. He felt sad and angry, but he thought Qasem was wise not to fight back. He worried how his impulsive sons Jaber or Khalid might have responded. He'd already told them repeatedly, "Don't clash with the Taliban!"

That afternoon, Zahra invited Homeira on a walk to a nearby ice cream shop. Homeira declined. She was busy replying to messages from her translator and others asking for updates. She'd learned that her name had been placed on a list for evacuation to Belgium, but details were scarce and she hadn't changed her mind about remaining in Kabul. Homeira also kept busy by posting articles about herself on Facebook from publications in Finland, France, and England.

An hour later, Zahra rushed through the door out of breath, her face bright red. She'd sat in the women's section of the ice cream shop near two young girls. Two Talibs came in and sat in the men's section. After the men ate they hovered outside, staring through the window.

"I thought they were waiting so they would beat us when we got out," Zahra said.

When the Talibs left, she sprinted home.

Homeira comforted her sister, then asked if Zahra thought she could ever stand up to the Taliban. She'd need to, Homeira said, if she wanted to continue to work as a doctor.

"The Taliban I saw today wouldn't let me eat an ice cream," Zahra replied. "It was terrifying. I don't think I'll be able to challenge them or negotiate with them."

In Zahra's response, Homeira recognized the quandary facing all modern women in Afghanistan: "The Taliban won't give us our rights unless we demand them, but we are placed in a situation where we're forced not to want our rights and to be scared."

That night, the family fell into a familiar conversation, bashing the United States for what they called the betrayal of leaving. Homeira's mother rarely talked politics, but with her hands still raised as she finished her evening prayers, she chimed in with a rebuttal.

"The U.S. made enemies for us, but why couldn't we settle things with the Taliban in all these twenty years?" Ansari asked. "Now we blame the U.S. for everything. This country has always been at war. This isn't the first time."

As Ansari spoke, her youngest son Khalid returned home covered in dirt, with red bruises on his face, neck, and back. He'd gone to the airport with a friend from Herat, the friend's wife, her sister, and the couple's infant daughter, all of whom arrived in Kabul by bus that day. Both women had Green Cards, and Khalid secretly hoped to impersonate the sister's husband, who'd already left the country. The plan went awry when the crowd became agitated. Taliban fighters drove them back and whipped Khalid.

Khalid's friend and his family followed Khalid into Homeira's apartment, hungry and tired. They intended to try again in the middle of the night, when they hoped the mobs might be quieter.

Fifteen years separated the oldest and youngest of the six siblings, and Homeira occupied an almost maternal place in Khalid's life. Worried that he would be killed or seriously hurt, Homeira insisted he stay behind. She told him returning to the airport without documents would guarantee another beating. Reluctantly he agreed.

Homeira took stock of the day's toll on her family. Her mild defiance on the university footpath had risked a beating. Qasem and Khalid were beaten, one on the street and the other at the airport. Zahra ran home in terror. That didn't include Jaber's multiple lashings on other days when he tried to enter the airport. This was their new life if they remained in Afghanistan.

A generation of Homeira's family—including an author, a lawyer, a journalist, a doctor, and a presidential aide—were transformed overnight from Afghanistan's highly educated future leaders to Kabul's latest victims. And it would get worse. For the moment, the Taliban remained in disarray, surprised by its sudden takeover of the capital. When the extremists consolidated control, Homeira felt certain they would systematically impose their oppressive will.

As they discussed the day's events, Homeira glanced at her father.

After nearly every suicide bombing, Wakil Ahmad called each of his children and nephews to be sure they were alive. Yet Homeira hadn't seen her father look so anguished since she was a child, on the night the family became refugees and he shouted for her to "Run!" at the Iran border.

EVERYONE ELSE WAS asleep when Homeira exited her bedroom early the next morning, Monday, August 23. On the living room rug she found a pile of clothes left behind by Khalid's friends from Herat. As planned, the family had taken a taxi to the airport at 2 A.M. with only their documents and a small bag.

Homeira picked up the baby girl's abandoned shoes. She'd seen reports on television and the internet about children being trampled or squeezed to death outside the airport, and her own experience approaching Abbey Gate showed how easily that might happen. Homeira held the tiny shoes and prayed for the baby's safety.

At 5:30 A.M., she left for her morning walk, still carrying the shoes.

With the streets empty and Kabul University quiet, Homeira was reminded of the beauty of her Kabul-jan. She knew she was in denial, but she wanted to enjoy the cool air and the feeling of freedom until the heat rose, the Talibs awoke, and the city became theirs again.

The apartment was quiet when she returned home. Homeira heard water running in the bathroom and the muffled sounds of a man crying under the shower. The calm she felt from her walk dissolved into sorrow.

Jaber exited the bathroom. Surprised to see Homeira in the kitchen, he looked away. She poured him a glass of milk tea. Neither spoke of what Homeira heard.

Later that morning, Homeira recalled a dream from the night before about a childhood friend in Herat named Zarghuna. Forced by the Taliban to spend much of their time inside their homes, Homeira and Zarghuna used Homeira's brothers as delivery boys to exchange notes. Twenty-five years had passed since Zarghuna's brother forced her to marry a Taliban fighter.

"All these Taliban soldiers have come back," Homeira told her mother. "What if Zarghuna has come back with them as a soldier?"

"God knows how many children Zarghuna is a mother to, or if she is still alive," Ansari said.

Before the fall of Kabul, Siawash and his cousins often pretended to spot enemies approaching their building. Peering from a window with binoculars, one would yell, "They're at the end of the alley!"

"Open fire!" another would order. "Shoot the rockets!"

Now when Siawash woke he immediately pulled closed the curtains.

"The Talibs are here," Homeira told him. "You can easily see them without your binoculars. Why don't you shoot at them from the windows anymore?"

"Those Taliban wouldn't see me," he replied. "These Taliban in the alley can see me. They will shoot and kill me before I shoot them."

When Siawash and other children gathered in the stairwells, they no longer ventured below the fourth floor. By avoiding the lower floors, they thought, they wouldn't be among the first ones the Taliban encountered if they entered the building.

Homeira spent part of the day replying to emails from dozens of people who hoped she could use her international contacts to help them evacuate. Pleas came from Khost and Kandahar, Helmand and Herat. A female cousin, a widow with two children, wrote: "I'm afraid. All the neighbors know that I used to be a police officer here for years. . . . Get us out of Afghanistan if you can." The cousin had heard rumors that Taliban fighters were taking widows as second or third wives. With no plane seats to provide, Homeira offered prayers.

The incident at the ice cream shop frightened Zahra, but she agreed to join Homeira and their mother on a shopping trip. Homeira's father warned her to leave her cellphone and carry a simple flip phone, so if she was stopped by Talibs they couldn't use her photos, social media, and foreign contacts against her.

The three women took a taxi to a large bazaar, but they found most shops closed and Talibs walking the streets. Mushtaq's wife Jahedah asked why they returned so quickly.

"Wolves have eaten the city," Ansari said.

That evening, Khalid's friend from Herat texted him triumphantly: "We got past the gates."

Khalid felt joy for his friend but crestfallen for himself. Homeira had only wanted to spare him from another beating, but now she felt terrible for telling him not to go. He could have been on a plane by now. Her one consolation: the baby girl was safe.

Next Homeira learned a group of her female friends had also left the country. Their work and writings, which covered similar ground as Homeira's, had qualified them as at-risk Afghans. Homeira tweeted: "I feel lonely these days. Now, this country is so big for me and my pain."

The departures of those women and Khalid's friends counted among the 16,000 people evacuated from Kabul that day. Within a day, the escalating number of daily departures would exceed 21,000

THAT NIGHT AT dinner, no one in the family felt like eating.

As the moon rose, Homeira sat by a window feeling torn. Her heart wanted to remain in Kabul, but her head tilted toward leaving. She considered the entreaties of her translator and her literary agent, especially if she could save the rest of her family.

Homeira reviewed recent events as she weighed her options.

Her conversation with her cousin Qasem about sharia and custody heightened her fear of losing Siawash. She believed if she and her ex-husband both remained in Kabul, he might ask the Taliban to take Siawash by force. Or if he left Kabul with his new family, he would insist upon taking Siawash with them. He had said as much in a text: "Siawash's life and prosperity is on the line. Whoever leaves first has to take the child." Days earlier, she'd decided to allow Siawash to go with his father, but now she wasn't sure she could handle losing him again.

Roiling Homeira further were the beatings of Qasem and Khalid, the desperation of Jaber, and the intimidation of Zahra. Homeira feared the "wolves" would destroy them all. The empty bazaar and her friends' evacuation made her dread feeling isolated in a vacant city. Compounding it all was her parents' fear for her life, which Homeira tried to ignore but couldn't.

As Homeira weighed her future, other family members found their own places by open windows to catch the night breeze and listen to the planes overhead. They scrolled their screens for news updates and the latest awful images from the airport. Several applied for as many evacuation lists as they could find, hopeful the next day would be their last in Kabul.

MEANWHILE, HOMEIRA'S AGENT Marly Rusoff and translator Zaman Stanizai intensified their struggles to find her and Siawash a path to safety, throwing darts at every imaginable wall.

They explored arranging for a helicopter filled with mercenaries to land in Homeira's neighborhood and fly her, Siawash, and possibly other family members over the crowds and into the airport. They discussed an overland trek to Iran, and from there to India and beyond. Neither of those ideas proved viable.

Days earlier, Marly enlisted the help of a client, Deborah Rodriguez, author of *Kabul Beauty School,* a memoir about teaching hairdressing and empowerment to Afghan women in the early 2000s. Rodriguez added Homeira's name to an already swollen evacuation list she'd assembled from her extensive Kabul contacts. They held conference calls and traded dozens of texts and emails, the urgency of the messages' tone rising as the evacuation deadline loomed.

Zaman remained in regular contact with Homeira, pressing her to keep trying to reach the airport and offering suggestions that weren't always well received. When Homeira mentioned her family was nearly out of food, he encouraged her to put on a burqa to shop safely. She replied: "If you think I would wear a burqa then you don't know me!"

One evacuation plan after another stalled or fell apart, in some cases over the inability to add Homeira's family to oversubscribed lists. Refusing to give up, individual members of the ad hoc rescue group reached out to everyone they could think of, no matter how far-fetched.

Marly reached the farthest when she wrote to an old boyfriend from her college days in the 1960s at the University of Minnesota. In 2016, decades after he and Marly dated, Sam Heins became the U.S. ambassador to Norway during the Obama administration. He served two years then settled into a comfortable retirement as a lawyer and human rights activist. With nothing to lose and time running out, Marly asked Heins if he knew anyone in the U.S. State Department who could help a prominent Afghan writer and women's advocate trapped in Kabul.

Some of the ideas floundered because of implausibility, while others ran aground because of Homeira's insistence that seats for herself and Siawash weren't enough. She wanted help for her entire extended family.

Another one of Marly's clients, who had connections inside the State Department, pulled strings and called in favors to secure Homeira and Siawash precious seats on a coach bus cruising the streets of Kabul to transport at-risk Afghans to the airport. Once on the bus, they wouldn't have to endure the violence in the crowds outside the gates, and their places on evacuation flights would be assured. But Homeira didn't want two seats. She asked for fourteen, only to be told that wouldn't be possible. She declined, frustrating Marly, Zaman, and the others.

The extraction planning group expanded to a Finnish journalist named Maria Manner, who published a long interview with Homeira after seeing her on Tolo TV. Christopher Merrill of the University of

Iowa worked to secure Homeira a fellowship at Harvard University, which would provide her with a destination and a justification for leaving. Officials at Homeira's London publisher, Harper UK, worked around the clock. Publisher David Roth-Ey investigated adding Homeira and Siawash to a list of employees from Harper's parent company, News Corp., who were being spirited from Kabul to Qatar.

The effort to save persecuted people by placing their names on special lists made Roth-Ey feel like history was repeating itself in the worst way. As he tried to help Homeira, the publisher couldn't help but think of Oskar Schindler and his list of Jewish workers rescued from the Nazis.

WHILE MARLY, ZAMAN, and the others strategized and spread their net, Homeira received a message out of the blue on Twitter from a man named Gaël Perdriau. His offer sounded too good to be true.

"Hi, I am the mayor of Saint-Étienne, France," Perdriau wrote. "You are welcome in my town with your family . . . if you want with your words and your heart."

Perdriau was, in fact, mayor of an industrial city south of Lyon with a population of 175,000, a famed soccer club, and a miniature Statue of Liberty. Four days before he messaged Homeira, he publicly invited Afghan political refugees to settle in Saint-Étienne. He learned of Homeira and her plight from her Twitter feed.

Feeling guilty about holding Khalid back from the airport, Homeira told her youngest brother first about Perdriau's offer. He ran through the apartment spreading the news. Family members pressed for details, believing their deliverance had arrived courtesy of a minor French politician.

That is, all except Wakil Ahmad and Ansari. For once, Homeira's parents agreed.

"I haven't come here to leave to another place," Homeira's father said. "I've only come to visit you."

"I won't go anywhere," her mother said.

Homeira decided to argue with them later, after details were worked out and her parents faced the prospect of witnessing the departures of nearly their entire family. She devoted her attention to texting with Perdriau in English, with varying degrees of fluency.

"Hi," she replied. "Thank you so much. We are trap of Taliban. Can not go to airport."

"And if the French embassy helps you?" he asked.

"If they can help me go to airport I will appreciate it. My book put us on danger. . . . My family is under high risk. I am so concern. I wrote the book and my brothers should [not] pay."

"If there is something I can do, are you ready to go?"

"Yes. But we are 14 person. I can not leave them alone."

Homeira wished she could save forty people or four hundred. For now she'd seek Perdriau's help for herself and Siawash; her parents; her four siblings in Kabul, and also her brother Tariq; Mushtaq's wife Jahedah, their son Shahzad, and Jahedah's eleven-year-old brother; and her cousins Qasem and Basir.

"Well understood," Perdriau replied. "I do my best with the embassy and keep you informed."

"It means a lot for us. Never forget. Thank you in advance."

Perdriau told Homeira he'd made the same offer to another high-profile Afghan woman in danger: Zarifa Ghafari, who'd survived multiple assassination attempts as the country's youngest female mayor. Homeira knew Ghafari and discovered she'd already left Kabul for Germany. When she told Perdriau, he replied: "If she wants I am OK to protect you both with your family in my town."

Hours after his first message, Perdriau told Homeira he'd already brought her family's case to the French Ministry of Foreign Affairs. He signed off, "I'll keep you informed. Courage."

As she thanked him, Homeira stressed, "The big problem is time. I do not have time."

DURING HER MORNING walk on Tuesday, August 24, Homeira saw Taliban fighters breaking into homes and seizing the property of former government officials who'd left the country. She rushed home.

On her way inside, the building manager cornered her: "Ms. Qaderi, some of the people in the building are worried that you're here. I mean, they're worried that Taliban might come for you." He suggested she move elsewhere for her own safety.

"If other people are worried," she told him, "please tell them that this apartment is the only thing I have. If Talibs come for me, tell them not to come upstairs. Just ring the door and I'll come down myself. There's no need for any violence."

Inside her apartment, Homeira told her father about the manager's warning. Wakil Ahmad explained the neighbors weren't concerned about her safety, but about their own. He reminded her of the Taliban's behavior during its previous regime.

"They came and took things with them," Wakil Ahmad said. "Some people lost their heads. They took sisters instead of brothers, and they took brothers instead of sisters. People have experienced these wars. They're worried the Taliban might take one of them instead of you."

Meanwhile, Homeira's ex-husband called Siawash: "I'm heading towards the airport. If you want, you can come with me."

Believing that he'd soon leave for France, Siawash replied: "No, Dad, I'll go with mom."

He told Homeira the happy news: "If Dad leaves Afghanistan, he can't use the Taliban to take me away from you." Siawash soon learned that his father and his new family were turned away at the gates, but they intended to try again.

That morning, Homeira resumed her text exchanges with Perdriau.

"Hi," she wrote. "Please help us. I scare to stay with the Taliban alone."

The French mayor replied within minutes: "I do my best. Believe me."

Perdriau asked if Homeira and her family could travel secretly to

Tajikistan. From there, he said, he thought he could get them to Abu Dhabi and then to Paris. Homeira said that would be impossible. He asked for Homeira's address, "for the military to come and get you," to take her family to the airport under armed guard for an evacuation flight. She gave it to him immediately.

"Then I welcome you to my city in Saint-Étienne with pleasure," he wrote.

With each new promise, each suggestion from Perdriau that he could send soldiers and secure visas, the family's spirits soared.

Homeira told Zaman about Perdriau's offer. He and Marly embraced the plan they dubbed the French Connection. Publisher David Roth-Ey used Perdriau's promise of sanctuary for the family in negotiations with Qatari officials, who wanted guarantees that anyone evacuated to Doha would treat it as a way station en route to a final destination.

All the while, Perdriau radiated confidence. When Homeira tried to connect Perdriau with the Finnish journalist Maria Manner, the mayor replied, "I prefer to let the French army act. Trust me."

With other avenues rapidly closing, Zaman, Marly, and Deborah Rodriguez pressured Homeira to promise to leave with Siawash if that were her only way out. Homeira knew how hard they were working and she didn't want to seem ungrateful. She also didn't want them to grow frustrated and stop trying to help her. She told them she wouldn't turn down any evacuation plan that included passage to the airport, even if it covered only herself and Siawash.

Privately, though, Homeira felt more certain than ever she wouldn't leave her family. She loved having them within arm's reach, three generations crowded together as they'd been in her childhood home in Herat. She focused on Perdriau's promise of salvation for them all.

As she waited, Homeira sought financial details from the French mayor. She didn't have access to banks, the apartment was her main asset, and language barriers would make finding work difficult. She told Perdriau she was embarrassed to ask, but she worried how her family would support itself in Saint-Étienne.

He replied: "Do not worry. We will welcome you as it should."

By all indications, Perdriau's promises were sincere and his efforts were intense. But as mayor of a midsize city in France, he was trying to practice international diplomacy without a portfolio. With each passing day, it became more evident he couldn't send French soldiers to Homeira's building to transport her family past the airport crowds. He couldn't direct French diplomats in Kabul to act expeditiously on her behalf. He couldn't get the French government to immediately issue visas for fourteen members of her family.

Homeira did receive an email from French officials saying it might be possible for her to leave with Siawash and her "husband."

"I don't have a husband," she fumed. She disregarded it, holding tight to Perdriau's assurances he'd do everything possible to save her entire family.

In the meantime, Perdriau continued to console and support Homeira. He urged her to accept any valid evacuation plan, even if it meant arriving in France with only Siawash. If something else came through, he would continue working to resettle her other loved ones. But Homeira found it difficult to abandon the dream of her entire family leaving Kabul for life in the French countryside under the mayor's protection.

Eventually, though, Perdriau's inability to deliver visas or safe passage to the airport became apparent. The mayor grew desperate. Without Homeira's knowledge, he beseeched her British publisher, David Roth-Ey, to pay for an elaborate escape plan that sounded like a movie plot. Perdriau wrote: "The diplomatic solutions seeming very slow and random, the threat . . . being increasingly strong, I propose another solution to you. A team can exfiltrate Homeira and her family, but this requires resources: 140,000 Euros. Do you think the publishing group can mobilize them please? This action can be within 48 hours."

ON WEDNESDAY, AUGUST 25, Homeira experienced more hopes raised and then dashed. She wrote more posts on social media and did more interviews with international reporters. Her appetite hadn't returned, so she continued to lose weight. Most upsetting of all were her brothers and cousins arriving home abused and dispirited.

Khalid returned to the apartment twitching with anger after a walk near Kabul University. He showed Homeira and their father his broken glasses. Khalid said he and a friend saw several Talibs order a group of boys to stop playing in the street. One boy protested that they'd done nothing wrong. A Talib struck him with his gunstock. Khalid and his friend ran to help.

"What business is this of yours?" the Talib asked. He threw Khalid's glasses on the ground and crushed them under his shoe.

Wakil Ahmad scowled.

"There are no stores open to get your glasses fixed," he said. "You'll get headaches."

"He was beating the poor boy," Khalid replied. "Should I have stood and watched?"

"You shouldn't have gotten involved."

Wakil Ahmad had worried most about Jaber, fearing that his temper would get him killed. Now Wakil Ahmad added Khalid to the top of his worry list.

While her mother and sister paid another visit to the shrine, Homeira tweeted bitterly. After Vice President Kamala Harris defended the decision to leave Afghanistan, Homeira wrote: "You ruined our dreams. You put us in a big jail. Congratulations." And later, " 'Kabul Airport' was the greatest human tragedy ever created. That geography will be erased, but we will never forget the history of sorrow and humiliation that befell us."

Again defying warnings from her translator and international friends, Homeira returned to the Tolo TV studios to criticize the Taliban and advocate for women. Each time she spoke out, Homeira thought, "This might be the last time. I might never get back home."

Her father worried for her safety and the welfare of the entire family, but he never asked her to stop. Homeira loved him all the more for it.

That afternoon, Homeira saw her cousin Qasem looking upset as he worked on his prayer beads, a tasbih, or rosary, given to him by their grandfather. Qasem prayed without fail five times a day. He often said he'd called the name Allah a million times on each bead.

"Qasem-jan, would you like a glass of tea?" Homeira asked.

He didn't seem to hear her. She assumed he was upset because several potential evacuation lists would only accept a few names, and she included her unmarried siblings Jaber, Khalid, and Zahra. As she handed Qasem a glass of tea, Homeira promised she would never stop trying to help him leave. He stared forlorn at the beads. To distract him, she tried to make him laugh.

"Either you and I need to leave this country," she said with mock seriousness, "or these Talibs need to leave. There's no other way."

"I can't find some of my prayer beads," Qasem said.

She looked more closely and saw he was restringing the tasbih. She noticed a fresh cut on his palm. Homeira questioned him to piece together the story.

Despite his beating three days earlier, Qasem refused to step aside that morning when a group of Talibs crossed his path. One pushed him against a wall.

"I didn't even get in your way," Qasem protested.

As the Talib ripped away his prayer beads, Qasem held tight. The string sliced Qasem's palm as it broke.

"You infidels got along with the Americans for twenty years," the Talib said. "You never stood up to them. You have no right to pray to God with a tasbih."

They left him in the street, trying to recover all one hundred brown wooden beads. Qasem gathered all he could find, but some beads were lost forever.

"We're all Muslims," Qasem whispered to Homeira as he resumed his work.

HOMEIRA SPENT THE early hours of Thursday, August 26, exchanging more texts with Perdriau. The mayor warned her about news reports predicting a suicide bombing at the airport. She promised she would stay away. Then her translator Zaman called with the opposite message.

"Get yourself to the airport," he said. He explained that she was under the mistaken impression that evacuation flights would continue until August 31, when in fact they would end within forty-eight hours. "Get there and get past the gates however you can!"

Weeks of simmering stress came to a boil. Homeira felt her cheeks flush with emotions: guilt over endangering her family with her book and her activism; love of her home; frustration at being asked to sacrifice so much for doing nothing wrong; and anger, so much anger, at the Taliban, at the Americans for leaving, and at everyone telling her what to do.

She exploded at Zaman.

"You live your best life in one of the best areas in California, and you're deciding for me from there? You think going to the airport is like getting in a taxi, showing your passport, being welcomed, and sent off to the plane? Men are being trampled there under people's feet. Children are crushed and asphyxiated. Every day, more bodies come out of that airport."

The more furious she became, the more committed Homeira became to staying in Kabul, consequences be damned.

"I've survived wars for almost forty years," she yelled through tears, "and I've not been hit by a rocket. You have to be really lucky to survive all wars for forty years. The rocket killed others and now it's my turn. I'll stay here and die."

Homeira hung up.

Awakened by his mother's shouts, Siawash began to cry. They weren't leaving for France or anywhere else. The game of trying to spot Talibs stalking his home was now reality. Siawash stared out a window, watching military planes in the sky.

"If you had decided to leave we could be on one of those airplanes now," he said.

Homeira dressed in a long blouse, grabbed her purse, and left the apartment.

Kabul University had been transformed. The campus where she loved to walk looked like a military installation, with Taliban guards outside every building. She wept as she walked, refusing to wipe away her tears. At her favorite spot, where students used to congregate around the *bolani* vendors, she fell to her knees and sobbed. Men stepped around her. No women were around, so no one helped her. Finally she dragged herself home.

The sight of Homeira terrified her mother, who thought she must have been beaten. Homeira showered until she ran out of tears. She composed herself and resolved to face the rest of her life, no matter how brief it might be.

WHEN HOMEIRA SHUT down talk of leaving, her brothers Khalid and Jaber and their cousins Qasem and Basir understood they could no longer hope she would bring them to France or anywhere else. They clustered in the guest room and plotted their next moves as young, single men determined to start their lives anew. They left the apartment one by one.

It had become a running joke to call out when leaving, "I'm going to the U.S.!" This time no one said it. Homeira noticed all four wore shoes or sneakers, instead of their usual loose Kandhari sandals. She hoped she would see them again.

Wakil Ahmad wondered if the foursome was headed to the airport or to confront the Taliban directly.

"I hope these children don't do anything stupid," he told Homeira. "I hope they don't destroy themselves. It's not the time to start a resistance."

Homeira reassured her former mujahideen father with gentle

humor.

"No, Dad. They're not like your type who would go on the streets and get killed. They're all still trying for their lives."

"I hope that's the case," Wakil Ahmad said, "because we made a mistake. We took a wrong route and the result was that we failed."

Both tried to hide their worries from Ansari. She thought her sons and nephews were going to meet friends. "Don't stay hungry outside," she called as they left. "Come back quickly."

Homeira's sister Zahra accepted whatever fate awaited her. "This is destiny," she said.

The situation was more complicated for their brother Mushtaq, who had to consider his wife Jahedah, their son Shahzad, and his wife's young brother.

To demonstrate her new resolve, Homeira posted on social media a photo taken several days earlier in Jaber's apartment. With Siawash at her side, Homeira held court as she sat on a rug with her father, three brothers, and two male cousins. She captioned it "Our little republic." She knew it would be a provocation to fundamentalists. Her head was uncovered, and as she spoke the men around her listened intently.

By the afternoon, Homeira had regained her equilibrium. Yelling at Zaman on the phone and crying on her knees at Kabul University felt like a long time ago. She texted Khalid, subtly urging him to abandon his airport plans: "Poor Mom has made some food. Don't eat out. There is a lot of food left for tonight."

He replied: "If our destiny is in the house, we'll come back. If not, we're off to the U.S. Goodbye."

HOMEIRA INVITED HER sister Zahra and sister-in-law Jahedah on a twenty-minute walk to the Pole Sorkh neighborhood. They left behind their smartphones, so their photos or social media sites couldn't be used against them if they were stopped. They carried simple flip phones.

Zahra and Jahedah had spent less time outside the house than Homeira, so as they walked they alternated between excitement and fear at the sight of Talibs.

"We're looking for trouble," Homeira's sister joked. "We want Talibs to look at us, so we say something to them and start a fight."

"It wouldn't be a fight," her sister-in-law said. "They would just kill us off. Who even dares start a fight with the Taliban?"

They walked on, but Zahra's comment weighed on Jahedah. "Zahra, if Talibs said something and you wanted to say something back, we'd leave you and go. Don't think we'd stay here and defend you. I have a child and don't want my child to be motherless."

Pole Sorkh normally hummed with activity on Thursdays, so Homeira hoped it would be more lively than on her last visit. But it was worse. Shops were closed or empty, and the girl who sold flowers on the street was long gone. The only cars were driven by Talibs speeding around a traffic circle. Homeira sat on the ground outside The Cup Cake and cried.

Homeira's tears weren't only for herself. She wept for the young men and women who'd experienced freedom in Pole Sorkh but now were shuttered inside their homes or had become refugees scattered around the globe. She told Zahra and Jahedah, "Let's go home."

Jahedah's phone rang. She answered and heard her son's voice: "Mom, where are you?"

"We're outside," she said. "We'll come back later."

Wakil Ahmad took the phone and asked for Homeira.

"What's wrong?" she asked her father.

"There's been a suicide attack at the airport."

Homeira fought panic as she thought of the goodbye text from Khalid. She understood it meant he'd gone to the airport with Jaber and their cousins Qasem and Basir.

"People have died," Wakil Ahmad said. "Come back home."

10

ABBEY GATE

Outside Glory Gate on the morning of Thursday, August 26, Sam stood anxiously beside the Hesco barriers at the edge of Tajikan Road. He struggled to hold it together as he waited for Asad to return from the Panjshir Pump with Ebad's brother.

Long minutes later, Asad rushed back with the young man in the photo Ebad sent, who'd whispered "Devils" as instructed. With the Zero Unit guards still firing over the crowd to create a distraction, Sam and the security contractor pulled Asad and Ebad's brother into the opening of the Hesco barrier square.

Relief washed over Sam. Asad had lived up to a name that translates as "lion."

Just as in the photo, in person Ebad's brother looked older than seventeen to Sam, but both his passport and his *tazkira* confirmed his age. He had the same last name as the one listed on Ebad's yellow badge, but Sam didn't take note of his first name. The security contractor searched the young man for weapons and explosives. Finding none, the next challenge was getting Ebad's brother to the airport and through security there, then reconnecting him with Ebad.

Sam and the contractor left Asad near Tajikan Road and walked south down the service road. As they approached the blast walls, Sam realized he needed to do one more thing.

"Hold up, let's take a picture," Sam said. Shortly after 9:30 A.M., Sam texted it to Ebad with a two-word caption: "Got him."

Ebad replied: "I will remember your kindness for ever. I can not express my feelings."

Goosebumps rose on Sam's sunburned forearms. He forced back tears and choked down a knot in his throat. Rereading Ebad's text, Sam recognized he'd crossed an invisible line. After tiptoeing around the evacuation rules for days, Sam had committed a Hiram Bingham–like act outside the official State Department regulations. It felt as good as he imagined it might.

Sam, Ebad's brother, and the security officer ran down the service road past the blast walls to a white armored Mercedes Benz Sprinter van the size of an ambulance. They drove to the rear of the passenger terminal, where Sam faked his confidence about the situation. He adopted an air of arrogance, copying the don't-bother-me demeanor of the intelligence operator he encountered a day earlier. He didn't want to explain what he'd done or where he'd been, and he didn't want anyone to learn the young man wasn't part of an embassy staffer's nuclear family. If that happened, Ebad's brother faced eviction from the airport, and everything Sam and Asad did at Glory Gate would have been for nothing. Sam also might be reprimanded or worse.

Without stopping, Sam rushed Ebad's brother past the State Department screening officials stationed outside the terminal. He muttered "special interest case," which suggested that he was acting under a higher government authority. Sam's colleagues stood by as he led Ebad's brother through the terminal's back door.

Sam brought the young man upstairs to the Marines overseeing the wristband identification process and the C-17 manifests for evacuations.

"He's not an unaccompanied minor," Sam told them. "He's seventeen, but his brother who's his guardian is on his way. He's a local embassy staff member, so keep an eye on him until his brother arrives in probably no more than thirty minutes."

The Marines accepted Sam's explanation.

The test had worked. Sam sprinted back down the stairs. He began plotting to bring others through Glory Gate. Only later would he realize he never learned Ebad's brother's first name.

BY THE TIME Sam exited the passenger terminal, the Diplomatic Security officer assigned to him that morning had already turned around the armored Sprinter van, pointing it back toward Glory Gate. Sam felt a good vibe about his bodyguard, a hardworking introvert in his forties who'd previously been a soldier deployed in Afghanistan.

On the ten-minute drive back to the airport's northwest corner, the security officer turned to Sam with a question: "Hey, man. Can you help me with my old interpreter? He worked with me up in Mazar-i-Sharif"—the scene of fierce battles—"and I've been trying to figure out a way to get his family in this whole time. Can you do that?"

Sam thought, "Why are you asking me for permission?"

Sam felt as though he was the one who needed approval from the State Department security team to stand near Tajikan Road and to send Asad to the Panjshir Pump. If an armed security officer with a military background wanted to pull in his onetime interpreter, Sam thought he could simply do it himself. Then it dawned on Sam: the security officer understood the rules. Only a State Department consular officer like Sam had the authority to designate a former interpreter without an SIV as an at-risk Afghan eligible to enter Glory Gate.

Sam nodded. He told the security officer to give his old interpreter directions to the Panjshir Pump.

When Sam returned to the edge of Tajikan Road, he learned that Asad had continued trying to persuade his sister to make a run for the airport. Again she refused. Through tears, Taiba Noori had told her brother: "I'm sorry, I can't do it again. My children might get hurt and I can't risk my children's life for this."

Asad also told Sam he'd reached his mother in Doha, where she'd arrived a day earlier with Asad's older brother. Asad had connected his mother and sister on a call, and Horya Mohammadi told her only daughter: "Don't leave me here alone. I can't live without you."

Still Asad's sister hesitated.

Asad told Sam his sister was considering one last attempt, but she and her husband remained too fearful of the Taliban and the Zero Unit guards to brave the streets.

"Call her again," Sam insisted. "Let me talk to her. You saw this last one worked. Tell me why this won't work for your sister?"

"I know, I know," Asad said.

Sam's voice rose. "Tell her we just made this work. We did the proof of concept. She's not going to be the first one. This will work!"

Asad called again. Worn down by pleas from Asad and their mother, Taiba Noori and her husband Noorahmad Noori finally agreed to go to the Panjshir Pump with their son Sohail and daughter Nisa. Asad hung up and smiled.

"She'll be here in thirty minutes," Asad said.

While they waited, Sam thought about the UN program officer named Mohammed, whom Sam's former boss in Nigeria asked him to help. Sam had tried to evacuate him four days earlier, when he urged Mohammed to bring his family to Abbey Gate. At the time, Mohammed told Sam he returned home "because Taliban are everywhere and they may follow." Sam kept hoping for another opportunity. Now Sam texted him: "Are you in Kabul still?"

Mohammed answered quickly: "Yes I am still in Kabul."

Sam: "Be available for a WhatsApp phone call at 2:15 P.M. and be ready to move to an area I tell you to go to."

ASAD'S SISTER TAIBA Noori and her family reached the Panjshir Pump close in time to the arrival of the security officer's former interpreter, his wife, and their two young children. Sam decided that on this second Glory Gate run they should attempt to bring in both families at once, a total of eight people, an exponential leap from the single target of Ebad's brother.

Sam explained the plan to Omar, the American intelligence operator who controlled Glory Gate, who again signaled the Zero Unit guards to scatter and distract the crowd with gunfire. Asad and the security officer ran into Tajikan Road.

With no one to tell him to stay back near the Hesco barriers, Sam edged within a stride of the road to anxiously await their return.

As minutes passed, Sam noticed several male crowd members who seemed to understand why a group of Americans had gathered there. Sam saw a few young men trying to climb over a cement wall 150 meters to their west, to attempt a sprint toward the airport, even if it meant risking gunfire. Two Zero Unit guards standing beside Sam opened fire low above the men's heads, with bursts of four to eight rounds each. The would-be wall jumpers retreated.

Sam flinched in pain, having never heard the sound or felt the percussive pressure of assault rifles so close without earplugs. After that, it happened so often he got used to it.

Two other Zero Unit guards appointed themselves as Asad's bodyguards as he moved toward the gas station. Asad connected quickly with his sister's family and shepherded them through the crowd back toward Glory Gate. As they neared the concertina wire at the pedestrian entrance, Asad noticed two young Afghan men crowding close to his sister's family.

Alarmed, Asad yelled to them in Dari, "Who are you guys?"

"We're getting in," one replied.

Asad alerted the Zero Unit guards and pointed out the interlopers. The paramilitary soldiers beat the men away with their rifle butts and tossed flash-bangs to scare away anyone else who thought about sneaking in through the concertina wire.

Still at the edge of Tajikan Road, Sam spotted Asad, breathing heavily, carrying his five-year-old nephew Sohail. Asad's sister Taiba ran toward Sam, screaming as she pulled and dragged her three-year-old daughter Nisa by the hand. Her husband carried all their luggage. As bullets from the Afghan guards flew low over their heads, Sam reverted to Diplomatic Security mode, determined to put himself between danger and the people he needed to protect.

Asad flew past with his nephew.

Sam rushed toward Taiba, whose eyes blazed with fear. Closing the gap, Sam yelled, "Can you pick her up?" She lifted Nisa to her chest. Sam grabbed Asad's sister and niece as protectively as he would have Samantha Power for an emergency evacuation. Sam's right hand crossed over his left, grasping Taiba by the shoulder as she carried Nisa in her arms. He felt both shaking uncontrollably. With a move drawn from muscle memory Sam spun the mother and daughter and placed himself squarely behind them. He hoped the steel plates in his body armor would shield them if anyone shot in their direction from the street.

"Okay," Sam shouted, his right hand still on Taiba's shoulder, "let's move!"

Sam's left hand gripped the cloth of her abaya at the back of her waist. He push-carried her forward, his feet spread wide so he could move Taiba and Nisa ahead of him double time without running them over.

Gunfire and flash-bangs mixed with the cries of Asad's sister. She gasped for air as Sam rushed them farther from Tajikan Road, up the service road toward the blast walls. They reached a low concrete barrier where Sam felt safe enough to stop. Still terrified, Taiba wailed as she fought to catch her breath. Asad and his niece, nephew, and brother-in-law crouched alongside. Taking cover nearby were the security officer and the four members of his interpreter's family.

Sam led them into a protective alcove within the blast walls, a spot where American intelligence teams searched evacuees. Sam directed Asad's family members to a small ledge.

"Sit down, sit down," he told them. He grabbed water bottles that felt as warm as toast and gave them to Asad and his family. He gave fist bumps to Sohail and Nisa, which made the children smile. Asad radiated relief. Still Taiba wept.

"You're safe now," Sam said.

His eyes burned with tears behind his dust-covered sunglasses. He swallowed hard. His voice cracked as he told her, "You're going to be okay." Her crying ebbed.

After quick body and luggage searches, Sam, Asad, and the security officer led the eight new refugees to the Sprinter van. Still wrung out, Sam climbed into the front passenger seat, while Asad crowded in back with his family and the interpreter's family.

As they drove to the passenger terminal, Sam thought about how different, how intimate this felt compared to the hundreds of brief interactions he had with people outside Abbey Gate, Afghans whose faces had already blended together in his mind. By the time the van stopped, Sam had formed a vivid memory of what he'd seen, done, and thought minutes earlier at Tajikan Road: "Get her behind the cement barrier," he'd told himself. "This is mine to own. I made this decision. Good or bad, I made this decision. I just put my ass on the line, literally my life on the line, not to mention my career on the line. I'm going to see this through. Get them safe inside."

When they reached the passenger terminal, Sam led the eight evacuees past his consular colleagues using his new brusque approach: "Special interest case, can't talk about it."

Glancing over at Asad, Sam felt overwhelmed with admiration. Sam had learned that the army intelligence team Asad helped had found him a room to shower and sleep, but he hadn't done either because he didn't want to miss an opportunity to help his sister's family. Now Sam watched with satisfaction as they all exited the van and headed into the terminal.

They climbed upstairs to the Marines processing evacuees and assigning them to planes.

Along with his relief, Sam felt a physical toll from the previous week. Infected blisters on his right foot oozed blood into his sock. Sunburn peeled his neck and arms. His lips cracked and his nose bled. His sandpaper throat made him sound like a two-pack-a-day smoker. In fact, Sam had been bumming Camels and Marlboro Reds from Special Ops members who always had ready packs. The cigarettes calmed his nerves and gave him a nicotine boost, but they trashed his gullet.

After guiding the new evacuees to the Marines, Sam told Asad: "We're going back to the JOC for a little bit. Let me touch base with you in an hour or so. Stay with your family. I'm going to ask for your help for a few more this afternoon."

Sam still had Mohammed the UN program officer on his mind, but he silently vowed he wouldn't prevent Asad from leaving Kabul any longer than necessary.

"We'll get you on a plane tonight," Sam told him. "I will personally make sure I will get you and your family on a plane tonight, as long as the planes are taking off."

Asad thanked him, calling Sam "brother." The term of endearment was common among military men, but now it landed differently.

"I don't know how to thank you for what you've been doing today," Sam said. He opened his wallet and pulled out his emergency cash. Sam reached toward Asad with two hundred dollars.

Asad refused.

"Please, take it," Sam said. "You need it more than I do right now. You're going to need money when you get to Doha."

Again Asad refused.

"Take the money!" Sam insisted.

"I'm not taking your money," Asad said.

Sam knew that was his final answer.

Asad left to shower, change, and eat. For the first time in weeks, he could do so without fearing for his family's lives.

SAM AND THE security officer drove the Sprinter van the short distance from the passenger terminal to the JOC. As Sam walked inside, his supervisor spotted him.

"Good, there you are," she said. "I need you for a special project. I've got to run out for ten minutes. Sit tight. I'll be right back."

She disappeared and Sam tried not to lose what remained of his cool.

"I'm just getting this thing going," he thought. "Now she's going to pull me for something else? If I'm not out there doing this, nobody will be."

He thought about disobeying her order to wait, but that didn't seem like a great plan. He considered handing off the Glory Gate access he'd negotiated with Omar to another State Department official, but that didn't seem likely. Sam knew the system that he and Asad created worked, and their teamwork could make the difference for other last-minute evacuees. Sam weighed telling his supervisor what he'd been doing and asking permission to continue, but that risked bureaucratic machinery grinding his operation, and his career, to a halt. Sam knew several State Department staffers had already been sent home for being unable to handle the situation.

"Shit," Sam thought. "How am I going to get out of this?"

Fresh out of good ideas, he texted a friend he'd made on the small State Department team, a logistics manager who earlier in the week provided the $60,000 in cash for Feldmayer to rent the embassy staff buses. He and Sam had bonded in part because they shared the same mentor, the senior State Department official who Sam asked for help when he volunteered nine days earlier. Sam also admired his new friend for the way he conducted himself, as a mature ex-army soldier-turned-diplomat who had his act together.

"You around the JOC?" Sam texted. "Need your help with something."

When they connected, Sam took his friend into his confidence about what he'd been doing at Glory Gate. His friend already knew about the gate, but he didn't know it might be used for individual evacuations. As Sam explained his conundrum, he grew close to exploding.

"She's trying to pull me for some bullshit project, but I'm getting people off the road right now. If she pulls me, we're not getting anybody else in."

Sam's friend, far more experienced in the art of bureaucratic avoidance, calmed him down. He also recognized a way he could capitalize on Sam's Glory Gate enterprise.

"Dude, you're getting people in?" the older man said. "I've got a family I've been trying to get in this whole time." Sam's friend wanted to help a former interpreter from his army days, to repay the man for saving his life more than a decade earlier.

Sam leapt at the deal: "If you can do damage control to distract her or something so she doesn't realize I'm gone, I'll go get your interpreter's family in, plus others."

"Absolutely."

"I don't want to get in trouble. I don't want to go AWOL," Sam said. "What do I do?"

"Just go," his friend said. "Get the security guys and go. I'll handle her."

As Sam rushed back toward the Sprinter van, he called the security officer he worked with earlier in the day to explain the plan. The officer told Sam he'd round up more security contractors for their return to Glory Gate. Still, Sam's supervisor weighed on his mind.

"Hide by the van," the security officer replied.

Sam crouched like a hubcap thief and called Asad to summon him to the JOC. Asad raced back, ready for more clandestine pickups.

As Sam, Asad, and the security team drove to Glory Gate, the friend who promised to provide cover for Sam texted him the name of his former interpreter, along with information for the man's wife. He also sent a recent photo and a plea: "Get them in dude."

Sam told him to direct the couple to the Panjshir Pump and await his call. A few minutes later, Sam's friend texted with another at-risk Afghan couple to add to Sam's "please get" list.

To keep track of the people he was trying to help, Sam used a Sharpie to write descriptions and coded names of his target evacuees on his left forearm and the back of his left hand. He also scribbled "23," the number of embassy staff buses yet to arrive. The code Sam used was simple by design. For instance, the security officer's former interpreter and his three family members from Mazar-i-Sharif became "4 Mazar." Each time Sam and Asad brought a group through the gate, Sam drew a line through the code. The skin on his arm soon looked like the canvas of an amateur tattoo artist with crossed-out names of ex-lovers.

As Sam rode in the van, he realized he hadn't eaten anything all day except two Nutri-Grain bars. He found a brown plastic MRE on the van floor marked "Menu 4: Spaghetti with Beef and Sauce." It bore a U.S. Defense Department seal and a guarantee it was "Warfighter Approved." Sam tore it open and shoveled the cold gruel into his mouth with a plastic fork.

Sam's frenetic pace put him in conflict with an email an embassy staffer sent that day to the entire State Department team in Kabul. With the tone of a wellness letter, it told them to stay "hydrated, fed, and rested," and noted they were already short-staffed because of illness and fatigue. The email sounded an ominous note, as well, instructing them to keep their bags packed and to be ready to leave within thirty minutes in case of emergency.

BACK AT TAJIKAN Road, Sam learned the gate's intelligence operators had received a warning of a terrorist car bomb heading their way.
If it wasn't intercepted, they expected it to arrive sometime in the next
two hours.

Ignoring an impulse to run as far and as fast as he could, Sam sent
a voice message to his friend at the JOC, cautioning him that a vehicle-
borne improvised explosive device, or VBIED, might complicate their
plans.

"There's an active vbied threat right now at this gate," Sam said on
the voice message, shouting over low-flying planes. Sam explained
that he and Asad needed to prioritize six Green Card holders they had
newly learned about, and then the seven members of UN program
officer Mohammed's family.

"Then I'm going to try to get your guys, but things are really fucking fluid and we've got to move fast because they're probably going to
shut this gate and boot us pretty soon. So I'm gonna do everything I
can. I'll keep you updated."

At times, Sam seemed more worried about his supervisor than
about a car bomber. He followed the voice message with a text to his
friend: "Have u spoken to [the supervisor] so I can be at ease on that
front?" His friend replied: "Working on it. She's venting her spleen.
About someone else. You are probably in the clear. And I'll work to
settle her down."

On high alert for the possible car bomb, Sam and Asad resumed
their operation. Sam learned from the gatekeeper Omar that two
evacuation-eligible families, a total of nine people, had shown up un-
expectedly at Glory Gate with American passports. It wasn't clear who
told them about the entrance, but there they were, already searched.
Omar asked Sam to make the official U.S. consular determination to
approve their evacuation, an easy task considering they were documented U.S. citizens. Sam herded the two families into the Sprinter
van and brought them to the passenger terminal, again using his "special interest case" swagger to cut the line.

By the time Sam returned to Tajikan Road, a new U.S. intelligence operator had taken Omar's place at Glory Gate. Sam needed to renew his informal use permit. The new gatekeeper was another combat cowboy, also bearded and battle-tested, with a Glock on his hip, a black T-shirt, and no body armor. But he was friendlier than Omar. As they got to know each other, the operator began coughing. Sam offered a medicated lozenge supplied by the State Department doctor who'd helped hot-wire the Hungarians' pickup truck. A mentholated friendship formed.

Sam noticed that between crowd control distractions, the Zero Unit paramilitary soldiers kept busy by disassembling AK-47s that once belonged to the Afghan Army so they wouldn't be claimed by the Taliban, ISIS-K, or civilians. Sam asked his new acquaintance if he could grab a bayonet from the pile. The operator shrugged, so Sam chose a razor-sharp knife nestled in a steel scabbard. He found green parachute cord and attached the bayonet to the left side of his body armor, keeping it out of his way yet easy to unsheathe by cross-drawing with his right hand.

WITH HOURS PASSING and no sign of Mohammed the UN program officer, Sam sent him a voice message: "Give me an update. I'm working on a really tight window right now. I have only about twenty minutes before we have to go."

Soon Mohammed and his family reached the Panjshir Pump, where he texted Sam a map with a pin showing his location, along with a photo and a video of himself, his wife, his parents, and his three children. Asad was busy, so Sam sent an Afghan Army interpreter known as Jessie to reel them in.

Earlier in the day, Jessie had asked Sam for help bringing in four family members he attested were at-risk Afghans. The U.S. operator at the gate had warned Jessie they'd be allowed to enter only if he gained State Department approval. When Jessie first approached Sam, they cut a deal: Sam would screen Jessie's evacuees if Jessie brought them from the Panjshir Pump at the same time he collected Mohammed and his family.

Jessie took the same approach as Asad, and the system worked again. Sam cleared the four Afghans for Jessie, while also fulfilling the promise he'd made to his old boss, the deputy chief of mission in Nigeria, to do everything he could to help Mohammed. Sam's last text exchange with her had been four days earlier, when she wrote plaintively: "I hope he can find some miraculous way to make it through."

When Mohammed and his family reached the Sprinter van, Sam arranged a group photo. Sam and Mohammed's elder son displayed thumbs-up signs, while Mohammed's daughter held up her pointer and middle finger, indicating "V for Victory" or peace.

After rushing them through the passenger terminal, Sam sent his old boss the photo with the caption: "Got your UN guy! More details to come but it was an amazing recovery op outside the wire. He's being put on a plane as we speak."

She replied: "OMG thanks. I am actually crying. Sam you are awesome." Later she added: "So crazy but you are a true hero today Sam!"

So much for Sam's third promise to Liana.

SAM RESUMED WORKING with Asad. His next mission was a return to the Panjshir Pump to collect eight Afghan women who were American citizens or Green Card holders.

The women came to Sam's attention from a colleague at the JOC who knew about Glory Gate but didn't know the extent of Sam's operation there. She was the same colleague Sam befriended at Dulles Airport when he helped her prove she had a negative Covid test before they flew to Doha.

The eight women who needed help were members of Afghanistan's Hazara population, a persecuted ethnic and religious minority who feared genocide under the Taliban. Their anxious husbands in the

United States had banded together to bring out their wives as a group.

Passwords for the women were "Friends of Khalil" and "Devils." They were easy to find, and Asad returned safely with the women to the edge of Tajikan Road, under the protection of Zero Unit guards.

Around the same time, Sam and his friend at the JOC exchanged a torrent of text messages trying to coordinate the snatch of the two couples his friend wanted to evacuate, including his former interpreter. Sam soon learned that the woman in the second couple was pregnant. After repeated missed connections, they finally worked out timing and details, including exchanging photos and phone numbers of Asad and the two couples.

Despite all the planning, the couples proved nearly impossible for Asad to find. He knew one man wore a red Nike hat, the other had a red scarf, and one of the women wore a white headscarf with bright flowers. None of it helped. Communicating with them via text, sometimes with Sam's friend as an intermediary, Sam grew agitated. He told the couples to position themselves near a tanker truck at the back of the Panjshir Pump. Still Asad couldn't find them.

Multiple texts and photos flew back and forth between Sam and his friend, as Sam kept Asad in the loop with repeated phone calls. The couples sent more photos of themselves at the gas station. Still nothing.

Asad returned to Tajikan Road then resumed his search. Asad spent more than twenty minutes around the Panjshir Pump. More fruitless searching followed, as did frustrated calls and text exchanges. Asad's missions normally took four or five minutes. He'd never been outside the wire nearly this long. Out of desperation, Sam suggested the couples wave their passports in the air, despite knowing that might attract unwanted attention. The half-hour mark approached. With no sign of the couples, tempers flared.

Sam texted his friend to warn that he was on the verge of reeling in Asad and abandoning the couples: "He has another 2 minutes before he has to roll back to the gate because he's exposed as fuck right now."

"Dude," his friend replied, "he's gotta find them. They're there."

Sam repeatedly tried to call the couples, but their phones were busy.

"Tell the wife to get off her fucking phone too," Sam texted his friend, then apologized. "Sorry I'm feisty and stressed."

"Me too," his friend replied. "Fuck."

Finally, Asad spotted them. After the "Devils" password confirmation, he called Sam.

"Got em," Sam texted his friend. "They're running back to the gate now."

"FUCK YES!!! Double that dude's pay. Right fucking now."

Sam seconded his friend's appraisal: "Amazing. This terp is incredible. Fucking hero."

With no female security officers nearby, Sam and the security officer were as culturally sensitive as possible while searching the Hazara wives and the two women from the other group. After uneventful searches, Sam climbed into the Sprinter van with the Hazara wives so a contractor could drive them directly to the terminal. Another security officer drove Asad and the two couples in a small SUV to Camp Alvarado. Asad didn't know why they took the detour.

At Camp Alvarado, Sam's friend from the JOC greeted Asad, his former interpreter, the man's wife, and the other couple. He thanked Asad profusely then handed him a surprise: $1,200 in U.S. government cash for "emergency translation" work. The money didn't come from Sam's wallet, so Asad tucked the dozen Ben Franklins in his pocket.

AMID THEIR EXCHANGE of texts, Sam mentioned to his friend that U.S. intelligence operatives at Glory Gate had alerted him about a car bomb possibly headed their way. During the hours since the threat first emerged, the likelihood increased. Now it seemed imminent.

At 4:38 P.M., Sam texted his friend: "Active vbied threat on our gate." Then he returned to their texts extolling Asad's bravery.

Although Sam didn't dwell on the threat in his texts, it preyed on his mind.

During the time when Asad searched in vain for the couples, Sam watched American covert operatives take defensive action to prevent any threatening or unauthorized vehicles from entering Glory Gate. They moved blast walls with a forklift and positioned an armored personnel carrier sideways across the service road. Sam's stress rose further when the gatekeeper told him this would be the last operation of the day. The heightened atmosphere during Asad's search helped to explain Sam's profanity- and frustration-filled texts to his friend, as well as his less-than-clandestine suggestion about waving passports in the air.

When Sam asked the gatekeeper for details, he said: "They're tracking it very closely right now. It's going to happen in the next two hours, so be ready to pull back. If we say run, run." If a terrorist car bomb was being tracked, Sam didn't know why it couldn't be stopped.

While Asad had continued his search and the commotion intensified, Sam learned that other, more public gates also were bracing for an attack. His handheld Motorola radio crackled to life with a State Department alert: "Attention all officers at Abbey Gate. Return to the JOC immediately!"

The situation spiked Sam's anxiety about the moral and legal implications of repeatedly placing Asad's life in jeopardy. Sam could only hope that if the Glory Gate keeper told him to run, he would have enough time to call Asad and bring him in. They could speed to the terminal with the eight Hazara wives, with or without the two couples. Sam told himself this would be Asad's last run, no matter what. Asad would be on a plane with his sister's family by nightfall if Sam had to drag him on personally.

Only later did Sam register that, as he stood at the edge of Tajikan Road, he'd been in nearly as much danger as Asad.

Meanwhile, during Asad's search for the eight Hazara wives and the two couples, Sam received a text from Mohammed the UN program officer: "Hi Sam thank you very much. My sister and family 4 people are also waiting if possible can you plz help them. She has two kids."

Mohammed explained that his sister worked at the Afghan presidential palace and her husband was a contractor for the Americans and the British. The Taliban wouldn't allow them to reach the airport.

"Sorry," Sam replied. "I'm on the last group I'm allowed to grab. They're shutting down this gate."

His reluctant refusal of Mohammed's request reflected a reality that would haunt Sam: he and Asad were lifeguards in a tsunami. For every at-risk Afghan they helped, countless others remained hopelessly in peril.

At the passenger terminal, Sam handed off the Hazara wives to a State Department colleague. From there, Sam and the security officer parked the Sprinter van near the JOC. Sam noted the time: 5:08 P.M. As he looked at his watch, Sam could see that he'd crossed out every Glory Gate target name on his left forearm.

Not including several hundred embassy staffers on buses, Sam, Asad, and the State Department security team—with help from American intelligence operatives, Special Operations Forces operators, and Afghan paramilitary troops—personally brought fifty-two people, from thirteen families, through Glory Gate.

OUTSIDE THE JOC, Sam stopped in a courtyard to smoke a cigarette. He crushed the butt under his heel, showed his ID to a Marine guard, and entered the State Department command center. Dehydrated, limping from his infected foot blisters, nursing a fiery throat and shredded lips, caked in sweat and dust, Sam peeled off his helmet and body armor.

He sank deep into a fake leather couch.

At that moment, less than a mile from the JOC, a former engineering student named Abdul Rahman Al-Logari walked among several hundred fellow Afghans waiting to be searched by Marines outside Abbey Gate.

Logari had neither hope nor interest in clearing the Americans' search and screening process. He had emerged eleven days earlier from a high-security prison at Bagram Air Base, where he spent four years for plotting a suicide bombing in New Delhi. When the Taliban took over Kabul on August 15, they threw open the prison's gates indiscriminately, releasing not only thousands of their own fighters but also supporters of their domestic enemy, ISIS-K. Logari was among the newly freed ISIS-K militants.

As Logari moved through the Abbey Gate crowd, having somehow evaded or cleared Taliban checkpoints en route to the airport, he wore a twenty-five-pound explosive vest under his clothing. While U.S. officials searched on the ground and from the air for a car bomb, Logari arrived on foot. He drew close to American service men and women frisking other Afghans. At 5:36 P.M., he detonated his suicide bomb.

Ball bearings the size of peas tore through the crowd at high velocity, killing thirteen U.S. troops and at least 170 Afghans. The bomb seriously wounded hundreds more Afghans seeking evacuation, along with forty-five American service men and women. Bodies filled the open sewage canal that divided the roadway leading to Abbey Gate. Victims covered in blood and burned flesh writhed in agony. Screams of pain and grief filled the air. Survivors pleaded for help, raced to rescue others, and sought cover, running from the scene or trying to climb the airport walls.

Believing they were under secondary attack by ISIS-K gunmen, Marines opened fire. Later they learned there was no second wave. They had most likely heard warning shots by British troops and other American units.

ISIS-K claimed responsibility and identified Logari as the bomber.

Eighteen months had passed since the last American service member died in Afghanistan. At Abbey Gate, the American dead included eleven Marines, a navy corpsman, and an Army Special Operations soldier, most of them new to Kabul. Days earlier, one of the Marines, a twenty-three-year-old sergeant named Nicole Gee, posted a photo of herself on Instagram cradling an Afghan baby. She captioned it: "I love my job."

Criticism of the Biden administration, for failing to anticipate the speed of the Taliban takeover, increased to a roar. Biden vowed to hunt down the perpetrators and make them pay. He called the U.S. military victims "heroes who've been engaged in a dangerous, selfless mission to save the lives of others."

WORD OF THE terrorist attack spread instantly through the JOC.

A voice boomed: "Attention. . . . Unconfirmed report of blast at Abbey Gate. Stand by for more information."

Sam jolted from the couch to full alert.

Confirmation came in real time, in grainy live footage from a drone flying overhead, projected on the wall of televisions. Details on the image were hazy, but Sam realized that the blast occurred within a few meters of where he'd stood among the Marines screening evacuees outside Abbey Gate four days earlier. When the names of the dead were released, Sam recalled the navy corpsman, 22-year-old Maxton Soviak of Ohio, whom Sam had befriended when Soviak cared for a teenage boy who'd passed out in front of him.

Sam absorbed the scene in the JOC as his diplomatic colleagues on one side of the building and the military officers on the other whirled into action. He admired how quickly yet quietly they worked, issuing steady commands and typing furiously, answering phones and disseminating information. The loudest noises came from outside, as cars screeched past with horns blaring. Marines rushed from a barracks attached to the JOC and shouted obscenities at pedestrians to clear the way as they bolted full speed toward the danger.

Warnings sounded in the JOC about multiple follow-up attacks.

One report, which turned out to be mistaken, claimed that a second bomb exploded at the Baron Hotel across from Abbey Gate. Sam heard a report of a grenade tossed over the airport wall in the same area. Another alert said terrorists breached the airport, but soon that report was withdrawn. Yet another alert said an enemy drone above Camp Alvarado was preparing to drop explosives. Soon a correction explained it was a benign U.S. drone.

"Oh my God," Sam thought. "This just keeps going on and on."

The alert system resumed, with a blaring siren warning of an imminent rocket attack. A robotic female voice repeated: "Incoming, incoming, incoming. Take cover."

A security officer yelled: "Everybody, helmets on, helmets on!"

As they huddled in a corner, Sam remembered to sing to save his lungs if he heard the whirring engine of a rocket about to strike.

While they waited for either an explosion or an all-clear signal, a supervisor reminded everyone to text their families. Sam realized he had tunnel vision. He focused on the bombing and the impending danger, without thinking Liana would soon see media reports about Abbey Gate, if she hadn't already learned through an alert from the State Department Operations Center.

"I'm okay," Sam texted her. "You're about to see something on the news."

He followed with an email. When Liana didn't immediately reply, he texted a mutual friend at the Bamako, Mali, embassy. "Can you find Liana and let her know I'm okay?" He also texted a State Department friend in Beirut, asking him to use a secure communications channel to reach Liana.

In Mali, Liana first saw a message on a work computer from a friend: "Have you heard from Sam?" She ran to her phone to find multiple messages that Sam was unhurt. In her relief, the first question Liana texted to him was, "Are you going to leave?"

"It's ongoing right now," he replied.

Even as he shared some details, Sam downplayed the danger, just as he'd done in his email three days earlier. He didn't describe all the alarms about the incoming rocket alert or his belief that he might die.

Liana remained worried regardless. She knew Sam, and that meant she knew he was trying to protect her. Adjusting to the new circumstances, Liana rephrased the third promise she'd elicited from Sam before he left: "If they offer you a plane out, do not be the hero who stays."

Despite having already broken all three promises, Sam agreed.

Soon after, Liana texted: "Love you."

"I love you too," Sam replied. "It's gonna be a long night."

"Just get home."

"I will soon."

Liana replied with a red heart emoji.

Sam also texted Asad, who was awaiting a C-17 flight to Doha with his sister's family.

"Hey brother," Sam texted, "there was a suicide vest at Abbey Gate just now. Just wanted to let you know. It's pretty bad, we're assessing now." What seemed like a straightforward update in fact reflected gnawing guilt. A suicide bomber might as easily have targeted Glory Gate and killed Asad when he was working off-the-books for Sam.

"Oh, shit bro," Asad replied. "Are you fine?"

Sam assured Asad he was unhurt. It felt good to hear from Asad. Sam felt even better knowing that after all Asad did for Americans in Afghanistan, as well as for his fellow Afghans, the United States would soon welcome Asad and his family in return.

Finally the all-clear came, with no rocket attack on the JOC or anywhere else.

No one expected the quiet to last long. Marine Corps General Frank McKenzie, head of the U.S. military's Central Command, told reporters he anticipated more attacks by ISIS-K: "We believe it is their desire to continue these attacks and we expect those attacks to continue—and we're doing everything we can to be prepared."

When the alarms ended, Sam continued to watch and learn from the JOC's response to the bombing. He kept one eye on media reports about the blast on the big televisions. He exchanged more texts with Liana, with his brother Jacob, and with several friends and State Department colleagues who knew he was there. His parents remained in the dark.

Sam also provided on-the-ground reports to a staff member of Ambassador Zalmay Khalilzad, who headed U.S. negotiations with the Taliban in Doha. Sam and the Khalilzad aide had remained in touch after Sam helped to stop the airport eviction of fifteen members of an interpreter's family, at the ambassador's request.

Unlike Sam, many of the thirty to forty members of the State Department team still in Kabul had never been close to an airport gate. Focused on the logistics of coordinating vehicle convoys with thousands of evacuees who entered through the main gate, aka South Gate, they'd spent the week shuttling between their quarters, the JOC, and in some cases the passenger terminal. Some were better equipped than others to handle the stress. During the rocket alarm, Sam noticed two newly arrived consular officers frozen in place, not responding to orders to put on helmets and body armor. One pacified herself by playing Candy Crush on her phone. Sam offered them support and made sure supervisors at the JOC knew they were struggling.

By midnight, all warnings of imminent additional attacks were lifted.

Sam returned to his room with about thirty hours left until the last civilian evacuation flight. Despite bone-deep fatigue he couldn't sleep. He replayed the day's events, from the highs of rescuing people at Glory Gate to the tragedy at Abbey Gate.

Sam felt certain the suicide bombing meant that Glory Gate wouldn't reopen, even as emergency evacuation requests continued to pour in via email and text.

Sam didn't know what job he'd be assigned the next morning, but with gate security tightened and the possibility of more bombings, Sam assumed he'd seen the last of Tajikan Road. Plus, Asad was gone, so Sam had no one to send out to find people at the Panjshir Pump.

As he lay in bed and closed his eyes, Sam had no clue that his most dangerous moments in Kabul were still ahead of him.

11

LAST CHANCE

MINUTES AFTER THE explosion at Abbey Gate, the city
seemed empty as Homeira, her sister Zahra, and sister-in-law
Jahedah sped home from Pole Sorkh in a hired car. As Homeira stared
out the window, her father's summons echoed in her ears: "People
have died. Come back home."

She burst through the apartment door, raced to her phone, and
logged on to Facebook. Horrific images of the massacre filled screen
after screen. She recognized landmarks she'd seen with Siawash and
Jaber outside Abbey Gate six days earlier. She looked out her tenth-
floor window and spotted black smoke rising from the blast site.

Feeling weak, Homeira called to her father: "Khalid messaged me!"

Everyone crowded around as she shared the goodbye text Khalid
sent hours earlier, after he left the apartment with Jaber and their
cousins Qasem and Basir. The message confirmed what her father sus-

pected, but her mother was caught by surprise.

"Good God, my children have gone to the airport!" Ansari shrieked.

Wakil Ahmad's hands shook as he tried to call one after another. Each call went unanswered. Never before had he been unable to reach "the boys" after a suicide bombing.

Siawash and Shahzad cowered, unsure what to do as the anguished adults screamed and argued. Siawash began to cry. He remembered that his father planned to try again to enter the airport that day. Siawash called his father's phone but couldn't get through.

Mushtaq arrived home during the frenzy, unaware what happened.

"Go to the airport," Wakil Ahmad told his eldest son. "Bring the boys back, dead or alive."

Ansari nearly fainted.

Mushtaq rushed out while the others joined Wakil Ahmad dialing and redialing the four cellphone numbers. None of the calls connected.

Wakil Ahmad gathered himself. He realized he'd been so nervous he'd misdialed the numbers multiple times. But even when he and others dialed correctly they received no answer.

The fact that none of the four young men had called home more than a half hour after the blast heightened their dread.

Several plausible explanations existed for the communications blackout. The men's phones might have been off, or the system was overloaded, or commercial cell service was disrupted intentionally to prevent attackers from remotely detonating another device. But none of those reasons occurred to Homeira's family. The silence from Jaber, Khalid, Qasem, and Basir convinced them all four were lying dead in the blood-soaked dirt outside Abbey Gate.

A neighbor heard the family's cries. She came inside to help, comforting Ansari and offering her a glass of sugar water.

Homeira begged her father: "I'll go to the airport. If there's anyone alive and we make it to the hospital, I'll donate blood. We have the same blood type. We'll help each other."

"No," Wakil Ahmad said. "Stay home. It's not a time for you to become a brave woman outside."

He weighed whether to follow Mushtaq or manage the situation at home.

Long minutes passed.

Screams gave way to sobs.

Decades of experience with suicide bombings, some within blocks of where they stood, created unwelcome mental images of their loved ones' ravaged bodies. Ansari prayed feverishly, promising God that if her boys came home alive she would return to Herat and give thanks every week at the fifteenth-century Shrine of Khwaja Abd Allah.

More time passed. The anguish intensified.

Homeira's phone rang.

Over loud noises and voices in the background, she heard: "We're alive."

Homeira screamed: "They're alive!"

It was Khalid. He continued in an aggrieved tone: "No one even called me. You are very indifferent people. I said that I would be at the airport!"

Homeira could barely hear him over her family's celebration. She was too delighted to explain the misdialed numbers and the countless failed calls.

"Where are you now?" she asked.

"Jaber and Qasem are somewhere else. Basir and I are coming home. They're all fine."

Homeira called Mushtaq and told him to come home, too.

Siawash remained subdued, clinging to Homeira in fear for his father. Shortly after the call with Khalid, Homeira's ex-husband called to say he, his wife, and Siawash's half brother weren't near the gate when the bomb went off. With all airport gates closed and rumors of more attacks, they went home with no plans to try again.

"It's not worth going to the U.S.," Siawash's father told him. "Please stay home and don't go to the airport. It's dangerous there."

HOMEIRA'S BROTHERS AND cousins arrived home tired, dirty, and traumatized. She didn't know whether to curse or hug them, so she did both.

The joy was brief. Homeira's sorrow turned to the families whose loved ones would never come home. Death counts during the war were notoriously unreliable, so Homeira suspected the true number of Afghans killed and wounded at Abbey Gate was double the announced figure. She heard that one family lost four young men.

Grief for other families hardened into anger as word spread on social media that Taliban fighters outside the airport didn't help the wounded. This was an unforgivable offense in Homeira's eyes. After countless previous suicide bombings, police and public safety officials risked their lives to save the wounded and transport them to hospitals, despite knowing that secondary explosions were often timed to the arrival of first responders.

"The Taliban isn't for the people," Homeira said bitterly. "They came only to enforce their power onto others."

Zahra pressed her head against a window and wept. Homeira's brothers and cousins felt no need to hide in the shower to shed tears. Her father stopped trying to lift the family's spirits.

They clustered before the television to watch reports about the bombing. They scrolled their social media accounts, but logged off when families began posting photos and tributes to the dead. The images were too painful to contemplate.

Rage turned again toward the United States for abandoning them to the Taliban, ISIS-K, and whatever other terrorists would fill the void after a twenty-year war.

"There is no difference between Taliban and ISIS. They are all murderers," Homeira said.

Her family directed some of their fury toward the Americans' chief negotiator, Afghan-born Zalmay Khalilzad, whom they considered a countryman who'd betrayed them. By negotiating with the Taliban during talks that excluded the Afghan government, Homeira said,

"He left us to the wolves."

Hours passed. Slowly the four young men began to share what they experienced at Abbey Gate.

When the suicide bomber detonated his vest, they'd already been separated by the crowd into two pairs, brothers Khalid and Jaber, and cousins Basir and Qasem.

Khalid felt the explosion in his ears. "All of a sudden, I couldn't hear anything," he said.

Jaber felt it with his feet. The earth shifted beneath him and he collapsed on the ground.

Basir and Qasem, farther from the gate, experienced it with their eyes. They saw the fiery flash and billowing smoke.

All but Jaber immediately ran, fearing more explosions. In the seconds it took Jaber to stand, Khalid was gone, swallowed among hundreds of panicked, screaming people. Jaber heard volleys of gunshots, but he couldn't tell the source. He expected to see waves of terrorist attackers streaming toward the gate to force their way inside, to kill every American they could find and any Afghan seeking evacuation who crossed their path. He sprinted away.

Somehow Jaber found Khalid and they reconnected by phone with Basir and Qasem. Then Khalid called home.

THAT NIGHT, HOMEIRA couldn't sleep.

She stopped trying around 5 A.M. and went to make coffee. Khalid followed her to the kitchen, his eyes red. He nodded good morning. Homeira had never seen him so sad. The sounds of them walking around attracted other sleepless souls.

Homeira suddenly felt claustrophobic. She thought she'd have a heart attack if she didn't get outside. She poured her coffee into a travel mug and put on sneakers. Khalid followed her out of the apartment.

As they walked in the first light of Friday, August 27, Homeira was surprised to see the skies filled with planes. The airport had resumed operations after the attack, for the final full day of the evacuation. The streets were quiet except for Taliban soldiers driving past at high speeds.

Homeira told Khalid she'd been speaking with the author Deborah Rodriguez, who'd enlisted the son of one of her former beauty school students as a translator. The hairdresser-turned-writer-turned-activist had spent days coordinating with a private group of U.S. military veterans working largely in secret to transport at-risk Afghans to the airport.

At one point Rodriguez messaged Homeira with instructions and a code: "To establish trust, they will text you the word Orange, and you need to respond with the word Apple. . . . This is not an evac for your entire family. This is only for you and your son." During phone calls and texts the previous day, Rodriguez seemed certain a clandestine team would come to the apartment building to fetch Homeira and Siawash, but the mission was scrubbed by the explosion at Abbey Gate.

On their walk, Homeira told Khalid she felt relieved that no one had come for her. They'd weather future tragedies as a family. Homeira expected him to agree. More than anyone, Khalid had insisted on solidarity, especially when it seemed as though Homeira might leave without them. "If we go," he'd said repeatedly, "we need to go together. If we don't, we stay together." To Homeira, in recent days his expression read: "Sister, don't go without me."

But now, after his trauma at Abbey Gate, Khalid's new perspective stunned Homeira: "It doesn't matter whether we all live or not. Take your child and leave this country."

Homeira saw no point in arguing. She had no desire to leave, and the last evacuation flights were less than twenty-four hours away. Even if she agreed with Khalid, she had neither the means nor a plan to reach the airport and gain admission through a gate.

She simply nodded and said: "Okay, we'll see what happens."

Back home, Homeira went to her office for an interview over Skype with Afghanistan International TV. While waiting to speak, Homeira listened to another interview subject describe his experience at Abbey Gate with his mother and child. After the explosion, the man picked up his child and ran. His mother survived, but he was crippled with shame. "I'll never be able to look my mother in the face because I took the child and I left her," he said.

The man's story lit a fuse in Homeira's psyche. It triggered all the pressure she'd felt for weeks and all the crises and impossible choices she faced. It sparked her fears for herself and Siawash. It revived the agony of believing that four of her brothers and cousins were dead. A sleepless night after days of uneaten meals magnified her emotional turmoil.

On Skype, sitting before her laptop at her elaborately carved desk, Homeira cried throughout the interview. She struggled to articulate her thoughts. When the interviewer asked about resistance to the Taliban, she made a comment open to misinterpretation. She detested the Taliban more than ever, but instead of rallying opposition the way she usually did, Homeira said confronting the Taliban made sense only if the motives were clear, and if leaders of the resistance weren't the same men who ran from the fight when Kabul fell. Her goal was to avoid pointless bloodshed and to encourage the rise of new leaders, but that's not what people heard.

Homeira came under heavy fire from online commenters. Even some allies construed her remarks as suggesting accommodation with the Taliban. One frustrated supporter wrote: "It's better she stays quiet, and she needs to leave if she has the chance." Death threats flooded her social media sites from anti-Taliban groups and her other erstwhile allies.

Homeira felt angry about the misunderstanding and overwhelmed by the absurdity. The Taliban and its opponents had finally found something to agree on: she should leave or be killed.

The threats also reached her father and brothers via social media.

Wakil Ahmad entered her office. He embraced her and rubbed her back, just as he'd done when she was a child. Upset by the close call at Abbey Gate and the violent reaction to her latest interview, Homeira's father launched into their most profound conversation in years.

"Some of these people are ungrateful," Wakil Ahmad said. "They will analyze your words however they want. They're not aware of your good deeds. I understand completely what you said, why you cried, and why you emphasized it matters who leads the resistance."

But the damage was done.

"From this moment, your presence in Afghanistan is a danger not only to yourself, but also to your brothers," he said. She knew he also meant her cousins. "They will get in trouble because of you. You've talked on media many times since the Taliban showed up. Don't put these boys in even more danger than they are already in. . . . It's time you thought about the rest of the family, too.

"You need to leave so your brothers are safe. That'll be enough."

Homeira felt unmoored. She didn't want to leave, but she didn't want to die. She didn't want to endanger her family, but she couldn't remain silent. If she stayed and protested, her family might pay the price. If she left with Siawash, she might never again see her parents, her siblings, her other family members, or her Kabul-jan.

Wakil Ahmad cut through the confusion.

"Nothing will be solved with your death," he said. "This country has sucked the blood of other young people like you, and it's as if nothing happened. I'm your father and I can't do anything to stop it. If they kill you, the only thing I can do is bury your dead body—if they give it to me. What use is there in death?"

Homeira's mother joined them.

Ansari often described her younger self as a mother cat who scooped up her kittens, to protect them from danger and hunger during the Soviet and Taliban wars. Now, she said, it was time for Homeira to do the same, to protect Siawash and herself.

"This is the only place on earth where death has never brought changes," Ansari said. "You'd be wise to save your life and your son."

Homeira reminded her mother how, many years earlier, she explained what it meant to be a refugee: "It means becoming a stranger in a foreign country. It means dying alone."

Ansari waved her off.

"It's not the time to think about all this. Life will go on once you leave."

HOMEIRA WENT TO the guest room for a quiet place to think. She found her sister-in-law Jahedah crying as she used Homeira's curling iron on her long, straight hair.

"I was supposed to start working after all these years of studying," Jahedah said. Homeira knew Jahedah's father was ill, and Jahedah and her sisters had hoped to find jobs to support their parents. She felt certain the Taliban wouldn't let women work outside the home, which spelled doom for Jahedah's parents.

Homeira sat beside her. She took the curling iron and went to work on the silken hair that flowed down Jahedah's back.

"Homeira-jan," Jahedah said softly, "you need to go. Don't wait for us. We'll be relieved if you leave."

As Homeira continued curling Jahedah's hair, she took stock. In the past few hours, her brother Khalid, her parents, and her sister-in-law had all delivered similar messages. Homeira thought: "I'm being selfish and endangering everyone's life."

Homeira hugged Jahedah from behind, tears dripping onto her freshly styled hair. Siawash watched the two women from the doorway then walked away.

When Homeira finished, Jahedah gathered the beauty supplies, to clean and put them away. Homeira said she'd take care of it, so Jahedah left her there alone.

Homeira looked at herself in a hand mirror. Her face was drawn from the weight she'd lost. Her mouth turned down at the corners.

Her eyes were puffy, her skin pale. Her waist-length hair was a mess. She couldn't recall how many days had passed since her last shampoo. The shower had become a place only to think and cry.

Her hair felt heavy on her shoulders. A burden on top of her other burdens.

She picked up a brush and a pair of scissors.

With the first cut, a foot-long clump fell to the floor. Homeira cut again. More hair tumbled around her. She felt lighter with every snip. Soon a thick brown carpet surrounded her feet. More cutting. Tempted to shave it all off, she hesitated. She lacked the audacity to go bald.

When Homeira finished, her remaining hair reached her shoulders.

She returned to the living room to shocked expressions from her father and Siawash. But she had a bigger subject to discuss than her new hair length. If the opportunity arose, she announced, no longer would she hesitate or demand evacuation for everyone.

"With Siawash," she declared, "I will leave the country."

WITH PRECIOUS FEW hours until the last evacuation flight, a huge gap existed between deciding and doing.

Homeira had already missed or rejected several opportunities to leave, and the Abbey Gate explosion scuttled Deborah Rodriguez's clandestine evacuation plan. Still, Homeira's team of international supporters had continued their frenetic efforts to find a way out via the French Connection, the Qatari option, the London publisher's contacts, the White Scarves' list, or any other possibility. Despite their endless strategizing and pleas, none looked promising.

In a call with her translator Zaman, Homeira insisted she couldn't go to the airport without a travel plan, recalling the events at Abbey Gate and fearing that she and Siawash would be beaten or worse. A friend of Jaber's reported that Taliban whippings had increased for evacuation seekers who arrived without documents. Social media bristled with rumors of another suicide attack.

"Now that I have one hundred percent agreed to leave," Homeira told him, "it's better I have someone to help me go through with it."

Zaman wrote urgent messages to her agent Marly and the others: "This is one last time to share her message with the outside world that unless and until they can send a vehicle to pick her up, any and all promises would have no use. SOS, SOS, SOS. . . . If she is not evacuated, we might lose to the Taliban the greatest women's rights defender Afghanistan has ever produced."

AS THE DAY wore on, Homeira's parents became anxious every time their sons and nephews left the house, fearing they'd try again to reach the airport.

Ansari's only peace of mind came from Homeira's new promise to leave with Siawash if an evacuation plan emerged. But every time the doorbell rang from the building lobby, she'd shake with fright that the Taliban had come to seize her eldest child.

"Mom," Homeira reassured her, "the Taliban won't ring the door if they get here. They'll break in like insects. If anyone calls, just be glad."

Eventually Ansari became so restless she decided to return to the Sakhi Shrine. She and her husband resumed their bickering.

"On Fridays," Wakil Ahmad warned, "usually men are in the shrine because of the Friday prayers."

Ansari yelled back as she put on her scarf. "It's not a public bath," she said. "Why do you separate men and women? It's a shrine. There are dead people buried there. Everyone's naked."

She invited Zahra to join her, but she declined.

"Homeira might leave, so I want to be with her."

"God willing," Ansari said. "If she goes, may she be safe and sound. I'll go to the shrine to pray and come back."

She left but quickly returned, her scarf stained with tears. Homeira feared that Ansari had somehow angered Taliban fighters. Wakil

Ahmad thought men in the shrine had chased her away. Ansari sat and corrected them both.

"What Zahra said about not going because Homeira might leave today got me thinking. I was on the way when I got afraid and said to myself, 'What if someone calls my daughter and I never get to see her again?'"

Jahedah brought her a cup of tea.

"Have patience," Jahedah said. "If dear Homeira leaves, only God knows when we'll get to see her again."

Siawash, who'd been spending most of his time in the stairwell, was in the apartment and overheard the conversation. Thinking they had a plan to leave, he hugged Homeira then rushed to find Sangi.

"Wherever in the world we go, I'll take my turtle with me. I'll put it in my bag!"

Homeira's nephew Shahzad, who'd been shadowing Siawash everywhere, approached her shyly.

"Auntie, are you going to America?"

"Yes Shahzad," she said quietly. "We're going."

The little boy wrapped his arms around her neck: "Take us with you. The Taliban will kill us, too."

Homeira couldn't find words to answer him. She knew if she and Siawash did leave, her nephew's pleas and the warmth of his hands on her skin would haunt her.

HOURS PASSED. ONE cup of tea, then another. Homeira exchanged calls and texts with Zaman, Marly, and other supporters. Mayor Perdriau's ongoing stream of encouraging texts remained a source of comfort. But no evacuation strategy emerged.

They talked of cooking meat stew for dinner but no one was hungry. Wakil Ahmad mused about making soup, a traditional meal to share with family and neighbors to wish a person well before a trip. But with no travel plan, they'd make no soup. Homeira told her father she'd make him soup with his favorite fried garlic, after the last evacuation flight left.

A strange sense of relief settled over Homeira. Her friends had left the country, but until the Taliban came for her, at least she'd have her family, her apartment, her city. Homeira confided her feelings to Jahedah, but her sister-in-law urged her to keep trying to leave.

"Homeira-jan, if there's a head, there are hats to wear. You'll get another house. Your life is more important. Who will this apartment be for if they kill you?"

THE SUN HUNG low above Kabul's western mountains. The evacuation's last full day, Friday, August 27, neared an end.

For several days, anytime Homeira's phone rang with an unfamiliar number, her father answered it. He worried the Taliban or its supporters might call to discover if Homeira remained in Afghanistan, and he wanted them to think she'd already gone.

Homeira's phone rang with an Afghanistan number she didn't know, so Wakil Ahmad answered, "Hello?" The caller said nothing then hung up.

Minutes later, around 6:30 P.M., her phone rang again. Wakil Ahmad put the call on speaker.

"Are you Homeira?" a man asked in American-accented English.

She spoke up: "Yes, yes, this is Homeira."

"We want to help you get out. This is your last chance."

12

FINAL SPRINT

B ARELY FIVE HOURS after leaving the JOC, Sam dragged himself out of bed on the morning of Friday, August 27, to begin his eighth day in Afghanistan.

Blaring sirens and gruesome images from Abbey Gate flashed in his mind. Even inside the windowless vault of his barracks room, Sam knew sunrise in Kabul wouldn't arrive for another half hour. In the bathroom, he turned on a light, pressed his head against the cool white tile, and burst into tears. He pounded his fist against the wall as he sobbed.

Sam pictured Asad's sister Taiba Noori, her face a mask of terror as she ran to him. He thought of the risks he took and the ones he'd asked of Asad. Still crying, Sam shuddered at how he kept pushing the boundaries, stopping only when Glory Gate's operators fell back and shut the portal to the airport. Time and again he could have decided

"I've done enough," and retreated to safety, only to go further. That's what Liana meant by "unnecessary" danger, wasn't it? What if a suicide bomber had come to Tajikan Road, or if he'd gone back to Abbey Gate, where the oldest of the dead U.S. service members was his same age? Sam wept for them, too, and for the Afghans murdered or crushed to death as they sought new lives in America, and for breaking his promises to Liana, and for misleading her about how much danger he'd been in.

Two minutes passed. Sam caught his breath and turned on the shower. Hot water washed away his tears. He took deep breaths.

"I can do this," Sam told himself. "Final sprint. I need to keep it together for one more day." It helped to remember that with nearly all airport gates closed or severely limited, he'd likely be spending the entire day inside the JOC.

He pulled on his armor, grabbed his helmet, and looked in the mirror to see a scraggly week's growth of beard. His cheeks were hollow. His deep brown eyes looked tired, but they were clear and dry. More deep breaths squared him away.

As he left the room, Sam repeated to himself, "One more day."

WHEN SAM ARRIVED at the JOC his supervisor pulled him aside.

"Hey, I have a special assignment for you. Ambassador Bass needs someone to staff him today, they're really busy."

This was the job Sam wanted from the moment he arrived in Kabul, when he went upstairs to the second-floor conference room and tried to wheedle his way out of consular work and into a role as a staff aide. Despite that initial bid for office-based work, and despite his breakdown that morning, Sam had no regrets about the days he spent roaming the airport and the work he did at Glory Gate. He'd altered the course of hundreds of lives.

Now, though, the bombing changed everything. He doubted Glory Gate would reopen. Even if it did, he thought it might be used exclu-

sively for a few top-priority cases such as American citizens, Green
Card holders, and embassy employees with established qualifications
for evacuation. Maybe there would be room for a few SIV holders and
special interest cases connected to powerful people in Washington.
Unsanctioned snatches of Afghans without SIVs seemed too far-
fetched and hazardous to contemplate.

With twenty-four hours left in the civilian airlift, Sam relished the
idea of staying safe and making himself useful to the most important
American diplomats still in Kabul: the men and women overseeing
the last phase of a historic, if chaotic, effort that many critics thought
would fail to rescue even a fraction of the number of people who'd
already left.

Shortly after 6 A.M., Sam climbed the spiral staircase.

He spotted Bass in the twelve-by-twenty-foot nerve center, amid
maps, a conference table covered with laptops, a whiteboard, televisions, secure communications equipment, and a small green cot in the
corner for sleeping. Nearby were Bass's chief deputy Jim DeHart, who
personally chose Sam for this assignment, another staff aide, and a
veteran State Department Foreign Service Officer named Mustafa
Popal.

No one on the State Department team had more of an affinity with
the people trying to flee Kabul than Mustafa. A native of Afghanistan,
he escaped with his family from the same airport in 1981, when he was
five years old, during the Soviet-Afghan War. After arriving in Vir-
ginia as a refugee, Mustafa graduated from Georgetown University
and the Fletcher School of Law and Diplomacy at Tufts. Before joining the diplomatic corps, he worked in the Office of the Secretary of
Defense, where he was honored for his contributions to Afghanistan
policy after 9/11. Bald and bearded, with gentle eyes and a generous
smile, Mustafa now served as chief of staff to the deputy secretary of
state. Among his multiple languages were Farsi and Dari.

Sam felt nervous as he approached Bass, a calm presence whose
wire-rim glasses and Vandyke beard gave him the look of a high school

guidance counselor. After enduring days of gunfire, flash-bangs, sudden arrivals by Taliban fighters, a suicide explosion at a gate where he'd worked, car bomb warnings, and rocket alerts, now Sam's hands trembled. If he hadn't been so focused on calming his jitters he might have found it funny.

"Ambassador, sir, I'll be your staffer today," he told Bass.

Bass welcomed him and sent him to DeHart, who asked Sam to help figure out how to help roughly two hundred remaining local embassy staffers who'd burned their yellow identification cards out of fear of the Taliban. Now they had no way to prove their employment to get past Taliban checkpoints aboard the last embassy staff buses still trying to reach the airport. Sam worked on the problem, and eventually high-level negotiations between U.S. officials and Taliban leaders resulted in a deal under which the Taliban accepted a list of embassy employees and ordered its fighters at checkpoints around Kabul to grant them safe passage to the airport.

Sam simultaneously managed multiple other assignments from DeHart. He fielded special interest evacuation requests from top officials in the State Department, including one involving the rescue of fifty-three at-risk White Scarves and a group of Afghan journalists who'd gathered at the Serena Hotel, a fortified luxury hotel popular with foreigners.

Sam also coordinated with U.S. Special Operations Forces and kept tabs on efforts to gain airport entry for remaining American citizens who wanted to leave. Some of those U.S. citizens had intended to stay in Kabul, only to change their minds after the Abbey Gate bombing. Most would be directed to the former Ministry of the Interior building, then brought on foot through Freedom Gate, which quietly remained open as a passageway to Camp Alvarado.

But soon even that entrance closed. Based on additional intelligence about more suicide bombings, the U.S. embassy issued another updated security alert: "Because of security threats at the Kabul airport, we continue to advise U.S. citizens to avoid traveling to the airport and to avoid airport gates." Then, in bold, **"U.S. citizens who are at the Abbey gate, East gate, North gate or the New Ministry of Interior gate now should leave immediately."** Almost no entrances to the airport remained active.

Sam filled page after page of a small green notebook with scrawled briefing summaries, acronyms, and updates, juggling a dozen high-priority projects as the clock wound down toward the last flight. The notebook replaced his forearm as his scorecard for evacuation success.

During a morning briefing, Sam learned evacuation priorities had tightened even more than he expected. He wrote in his notebook: "Main efforts—Amcits, LPR, LES," meaning American citizens, Green Card holders or legal permanent residents, and local embassy staff. Next came U.S. non-governmental organizations and "federal affiliates" such as Voice of America, the U.S.-funded broadcast network. Sam's eclectic list also included workers from Roots of Peace, a California nonprofit that helped Afghan farmers and small businesses; the Rockefeller Foundation; Johns Hopkins University; and Lincoln Learning Centers, which provided Afghan youths with educational and cultural opportunities.

Afghans of "high interest" remained technically on the list, and initially so did holders of approved Special Immigrant Visas. But the SIV system, beset for years by bureaucratic delays and political interference, had grown even more muddied after the State Department issued electronic versions of the visas without individual names or document numbers. Afghans copied them as screenshots for relatives and friends. Unauthorized copies flooded the city.

Sam amended his priority list with a firm note about Afghans who held SIVs: "Won't happen. TB [Taliban] not allowing."

The Taliban had begun stopping Afghans with U.S. visas at checkpoints. Negotiations to allow legitimate SIV holders to exit proved unsuccessful, and the Americans could do nothing about it. DeHart explained that two Taliban fighters had been shot by unknown assailants, and Taliban leaders blamed the Americans and their remaining

Afghan Army allies. They retaliated by dragging Afghans off buses headed to South Gate and largely ending their cooperation.

In DeHart's words, "The wheels are coming off."

As Sam worked to help arrange last-minute evacuations, he scribbled a stern note to himself: "Don't over promise. Most will not get in."

In addition to the groups whose entry Sam sought to arrange, DeHart forwarded him several extreme long-shot pleas for at-risk individuals. DeHart had become something of a clearinghouse for such appeals, scores of which begged for his attention every time he checked his email. He considered the requests to be the inevitable result of twenty years of relationships built between Americans and Afghans in the aftermath of 9/11.

AT 7:43 A.M., DeHart forwarded Sam a long, plaintive email from someone Sam had never heard of, on behalf of someone else Sam had never heard of, mentioning a friend of DeHart's who Sam also had never heard of.

The writer of the email identified herself as a New York literary agent: Marly Rusoff. The subject line read: "[A] friend of Samuel Heins who seeks help for Homeira Qaderi."

At his post on the second floor of the JOC, Sam was the last link of a communication chain that started with Marly's far-fetched plea to her old college boyfriend, the former ambassador Sam Heins, seeking contacts in the State Department.

Unknown to Marly, when Heins was U.S. ambassador to Norway five years earlier, none other than Jim DeHart was his top deputy. The two men struck up a friendship that endured after Heins retired and returned to the United States, while DeHart left Oslo for a diplomatic post in Afghanistan, then became U.S. Coordinator for the Arctic Region, only to return to Kabul amid the crisis.

In an extraordinary coincidence, Heins knew that DeHart had

landed in Kabul a week earlier on an emergency basis for the evacuation. So he gave Marly a State Department email address for DeHart and wished her well. When Marly thanked Heins, he replied: "Obviously they are bound by the official line but who knows, maybe some serendipity will intervene."

With dozens more pressing matters demanding DeHart's time and attention, and with his primary focus on busloads of endangered Afghans, DeHart glanced at Marly's email but didn't dig in. That's what junior staff aides were for, to handle impossible requests, even if they mentioned a friend who was a former ambassador.

"I don't think there's anything we can do about this," DeHart told Sam. As a courtesy, he added, "Maybe you can email her back and get the contact points if an opportunity comes up."

DeHart thought that would be the last he heard of it.

Sam barely knew where to begin. In his haste, he misread one of the names in the subject line and wondered if Samuel Heins was part of the Heinz ketchup dynasty. Sam wasn't even certain how to pronounce the name of the person who needed evacuation. He decided if Homeira Qaderi held a U.S. passport or a Green Card, he might be able to help her, although he wasn't certain how. Otherwise, like countless other endangered Afghans, she was out of his reach and out of luck.

As Sam skimmed Marly's email, he noted that Homeira was described as a brave, celebrated author and activist facing death threats from the Taliban. He read quickly about the apparent involvement of a mayor in France, officials in Qatar, and a State Department contractor whose name he couldn't find in a department directory. Sam's eyes raced past a description of an aborted bus evacuation for the author and her son, and a failed plan for a helicopter pickup.

Most of it didn't register. But he absorbed the email's ominous concluding paragraph, which read: "Homeira may be killed if she does not get out of Afghanistan soon."

Mostly, Sam focused on everything the email didn't include. It said Homeira Qaderi had an Afghan passport, but made no mention of a

U.S. passport. It didn't say if she had a Green Card, a valid SIV or even a blank one, or whether she had done work directly on behalf of the United States. He found no indication that she had a French visa or political asylum there, in Qatar, or anywhere else. The email didn't include contact information for Homeira, although it said "her phone number is available."

Sam sent DeHart a tactful reply familiar to any midlevel bureaucrat trying to prove he didn't ignore a superior's request: "Sir—working on this." Sam also told DeHart he'd discuss it with one of their colleagues who was due at the JOC later that morning. The colleague was a covert operative whom Sam expected to return to Glory Gate sometime that day.

If DeHart had forwarded Marly's email one day earlier, when operations at Glory Gate were in full swing, Sam might have written "2 Author" on his forearm, provided directions to the Panjshir Pump, and added Homeira and her son to one of Asad's pickup runs. Not anymore. The woman and child described in the email might be at high risk, but so were innumerable other Afghans for whom the window of opportunity had slammed shut.

If he found time, Sam thought, he might make a brief call to Marly Rusoff. He'd politely deliver a message she didn't want to hear and he hated to give: "Sorry, but nothing can be done." Then he'd cross the email off his to-do list, tell DeHart, and move on to the next assignment.

AS SAM PLOWED through one task after another, he learned that a ceremony would be held that afternoon on the tarmac to start the journey home for the remains of the thirteen U.S. service members killed at Abbey Gate. An hour before the service, Sam's supervisor announced that only a few senior State Department leaders would attend.

Sam followed her to her office and closed the door.

"This is bullshit," Sam said. "What do you mean we can't go?"

She explained they had too much work to do, with too little time to get it done. Also, it wasn't clear anyone except a few top diplomats had received invitations from the military.

"That's ridiculous," Sam said. "We've been busting our asses, as you know, as you've been doing. We need to go to this. This is very personal to a lot of us."

His supervisor let down the steely veneer that sustained her and kept the JOC's day shift humming.

"I know," she said. "I cried last night when I got home. I cried this morning. We're on the same page, Sam. But this is out of my hands." She wanted to attend the ceremony, too, and she took Sam into her confidence about traumatic events she'd witnessed at a previous posting.

Sam dropped his outrage. He said he understood and described his experience in Niger, when the deaths of four Special Forces soldiers in an ambush sent him to his knees to recite the Mourner's Kaddish. After sharing their emotional scars, Sam and his supervisor agreed on the importance of processing their trauma when they got home.

Before Sam left, his supervisor casually asked where Sam had been the previous day, in the hours before the Abbey Gate bombing. She'd either forgotten or chose not to mention that he'd gone AWOL.

Sam considered the question, weighing in an instant how best to respond. He decided to lean in to the new trust between them. Sam came clean and confessed the details of how he spent the day orchestrating snatches at Glory Gate using a young Afghan interpreter as his deputy, which technically made Sam an operator and Asad a casual State Department contractor, with both of them acting without authority as agents of the United States government.

"I'm telling you this now because I'm doing staff work today and because I'm not going back to Glory Gate," Sam said. "I'm probably not leaving the JOC until we leave on our flight tomorrow."

Sam's supervisor knew he'd been assigned to screen incoming Afghans at Glory Gate, but she assumed that meant routine document checks for families arriving on embassy staff buses, in a safe area far from the dangers of Tajikan Road.

"I'm not going to get mad at you for this," she said. "I think you've got your own emotions to deal with. But it's a good thing you didn't fucking tell me that yesterday, because I would have stopped that."

She added, "I'm glad you're safe."

Pleasantly surprised by his supervisor's reaction, Sam returned to work.

Twenty minutes later, she made an announcement to the JOC reversing her earlier message about the memorial service: "Okay everybody, be ready at 1:30 to go to the flight line."

DURING THE PAST few days, Sam had grown troubled by how many people he'd given his cellphone number, the same one he'd had since high school. He spotted a box in the JOC filled with burner phones and grabbed a knockoff iPhone and a spare SIM card. After a colleague got it to work, Sam carried it outside the JOC into a maze of concrete blast walls and razor wire where he got better cell service.

"Hi, I'm looking for Marly Rusoff."

"Yes, speaking."

From the gargle of Marly's voice, Sam realized he'd momentarily forgotten Kabul was eight and a half hours ahead of East Coast time. He'd woken her up before 5 A.M. at her second home in Beaufort, South Carolina, where Marly was nursing her husband back to health after his bout with Covid-19.

"I'm calling from the U.S. State Department," Sam said. "I'm currently in Kabul, at the airport, and I was passed your information by my boss."

The words Kabul and State Department roused Marly from sleep.

"Yes, yes, okay! What can you tell me?"

"I'm just trying to get more information about what exactly is the situation and who I'm trying to get out."

Not realizing what Sam needed or that he'd already seen her email to Jim DeHart, Marly launched into an impassioned description of Homeira, her bravery, her writing, her celebrity, and her peril. She mentioned death threats and unsuccessful evacuation efforts. Marly added sidebars about a French mayor, a British publisher, and a Qatari sheikh.

Sam's head spun. He jotted down a few basic details.

Worried about missing the memorial ceremony, Sam stewed as Marly kept pitching him on the urgent need to save Homeira. Not wanting to be rude, he hesitated to interrupt her. But the more Marly explained, the more certain Sam became: Homeira sounded like an incredible person, at dire risk, but she didn't qualify under the strict last-day State Department evacuation rules in Sam's notebook. She wasn't an American citizen, so even if Freedom Gate reopened, the Taliban wouldn't let her travel to the Ministry of Interior building.

Even if Glory Gate were an option, Sam had no way to use it. He wouldn't dream of going AWOL again, especially not from his new role as an aide to an ambassador. Also, he would have no one to guide Homeira and her son from the Panjshir Pump to the service road. Asad was in Doha, and the Afghan Army interpreter Jessie had also caught a flight out.

Homeira fell squarely under the rule Sam created in his notebook: "Don't over promise. Most will not get in."

Finally, he interrupted Marly.

"I understand, and we're keeping it on our list to hopefully try and rescue her today, but I want to explain the context here. There was a massive attack last night. All the gates are currently closed. I don't want to say it won't happen, that it's impossible, but I think the chance of this happening is one percent."

Marly ran to her computer, hoping to find some magical extra information that would reverse Sam's decision. Silently, Sam told himself: "Don't bother, it's not going to change."

He tried again, this time leaving no room for misunderstanding: "I'm really sorry to have to tell you this news, but I can't tell you with any confidence this will happen."

Despairing, fully awake, Marly tried repeating Homeira's accomplishments and the failed evacuation efforts, emphasizing that her life was in Sam's hands.

The longer Marly continued, the more excruciating it became. Sam cut her off.

"I'm sorry I couldn't be more helpful," he said. "I really hope this is able to work out somehow for her."

He thought about his breakdown hours earlier in the bathroom and the soon-to-begin sendoff for thirteen dead Americans. Sam recalled a group email he received that morning from Secretary Blinken offering condolences and praising the State Department team for their heroic efforts: "Children, women, and men whose opportunities and even lives may have been stamped out will now get to have futures, in no small part because of what you've done."

Sam knew that by rejecting Homeira and her son, he'd placed them among those who Blinken described as "stamped out." It felt like he was shouting "Red" at Abbey Gate.

Marly understood that she'd run out of appeals. She felt certain Homeira would be killed and Siawash's father would regain custody. Marly wanted to scream about the injustice. Instead she focused on the sadness and fatigue she heard in Sam's voice. Marly could tell he was young, and she suspected this wasn't the only life-and-death decision he'd carry with him forever.

"I appreciate your candor," she told Sam softly. "It's nice of you to tell me honestly how it is."

Marly's reply washed over Sam. He expected her to express rage or sorrow, not kindness toward him in return for denying salvation for her friend. Marly's words sounded like a benediction meant to ease his heartache about all the people whose lives he couldn't save.

Unintentionally, Marly's compassion made Sam feel miserable. He said goodbye.

After the call, Marly sent a follow-up email to DeHart that expressed more sympathy for him, Sam, and their colleagues at the airport.

"I so appreciate the phone call from your office this morning and understand that your hands are tied, and that you must prioritize those with U.S. passports. . . . Even a fast 'no help is forthcoming' is appreciated at this time as we struggle to find a path forward. I wish you and your team strength."

After sending the email, Marly pulled on a bathrobe and went outside to walk in her garden, the one place she felt a sense of peace. Still quarantined from her ill husband, Marly watched the sky turn pink as the sun rose over the South Carolina low country. She felt certain that when the sun rose the next day in Kabul, Homeira would be at the mercy of the merciless.

DeHart glanced at Marly's second email then forwarded it to Sam.

SHORTLY AFTER THE call with Marly, Sam stood in the shade of a military plane to pay his respects to the fallen Americans. He found a place under the plane's wing behind Ambassador Bass, Jim DeHart, and Mustafa Popal. Nearby stood Ambassador Ross Wilson, who oversaw what remained of the United States' diplomatic presence, while Bass oversaw the evacuation.

Several thousand U.S. troops in desert camo lined the tarmac in the relentless heat. Bearded special operators with long hair and ball caps stood silently alongside.

Eight pallbearers carried each flag-draped steel transfer case up the cargo ramp of a C-17 from McGuire Air Force Base, in Sam's home state of New Jersey. One by one, the dead disappeared into the open belly of the big gray plane.

Sam's memory returned to the nighttime ceremony four years earlier for the four U.S. Special Operations soldiers killed in Niger. His emotions now were every bit as strong, with one glaring difference. Despite the endless danger in Niger, he felt safe at that ceremony. In Kabul, anyone who hated the United States knew exactly how and where to find thousands of Americans, Afghan friends of the United States, and their allies. With each passing minute of the ceremony, Sam's anxiety grew about another terrorist attack.

Afterward he texted a photo of the lined-up soldiers and the lowered cargo ramp to "The Squad," his far-flung friends from Foreign Service Officer training: "Just watched 13 heroes who died protecting us get loaded onto a plane. It was horrible and tragic. We need to get the fuck out of here. I think we may get hit again tonight."

Back inside the JOC, Sam joined Bass, DeHart, and other State Department officials for a sensitive mission briefing by Rear Admiral Peter Vasely, a Navy SEAL who was the highest-ranking U.S. military officer still in Afghanistan. Sam had never attended such a senior-level briefing, and initially he expected to be asked to leave. Only later would Sam be excluded from a meeting, when Bass held a secure video call with President Biden.

After being sworn to secrecy, Sam heard Vasely describe plans for a retaliatory drone airstrike to be carried out within hours against an ISIS-K leader believed to have plotted the Abbey Gate bombing. That strike would be declared a success by the U.S. military, with no civilian casualties, but it would be overshadowed by the mistakes of a later drone strike in Kabul that killed ten innocent civilians, including seven children.

IN THE COURSE of his day's work, Sam learned that Glory Gate's covert operators had, in fact, resumed operations, primarily for the narrow categories of evacuees he'd been told to prioritize. Sam also learned that at least some Taliban checkpoint commanders were preventing anyone who wasn't an American citizen from approaching the airport.

One item still pending on Sam's to-do list was to help secure passage through Glory Gate for a bus and a van carrying the fifty-three at-risk Afghan journalists and women involved in human rights who'd gathered at the Serena Hotel. The request to help the White Scarves carried extra weight, having arrived in an email with support from Suzy George, the State Department's chief of staff.

As Sam worked on that case, his thoughts returned to his call with Marly. When he met with an intelligence operator about the White Scarves and several other priority groups, Sam spotted an opening.

"There's some other people I'm trying to get in today," Sam said.

The covert operator, who served as the liaison between the State Department and the operatives who ran Glory Gate, gave Sam a sour look. It translated as "Yeah, join the club."

Sam persisted. "Well, if I give you the information, could you add it to your list?"

The operator told Sam he'd see what he could do. But the existing list was long and time was short, so no promises. Sam tore Homeira's contact information from his notebook and handed the operator the scrap of paper.

Sam returned to work. He solved as many problems as possible, although some proved intractable and others were resolved by colleagues. His twelve-hour shift ended at 6 P.M., but he had no intention of returning to his quarters. Sam's earlier requests to work double shifts were denied, to avoid burnout, but with only hours until the 6 A.M. Saturday end of the evacuation, Bass and DeHart allowed him to keep working. Even if Sam couldn't accomplish much before they began destroying sensitive materials prior to departure, he wanted to see it through.

"Final sprint," as he told himself that morning.

Shortly after the overnight crew arrived, Sam was downstairs in the JOC when Mustafa Popal approached him. The two met six days earlier, when Mustafa arrived in Kabul from Doha with Sam's lost luggage in tow. In the days that followed they crossed paths in the JOC, and Sam felt growing admiration for the polished, soft-spoken diplomat who casually said he worked for Deputy Secretary Wendy Sherman without mentioning that he was her chief of staff. Sam became more impressed when he learned Mustafa participated in negotiations with Taliban officials. Further connecting the two, they discovered they had a mutual friend in Beirut, the same official Sam asked to send a secure message to Liana after the bombing.

Mustafa had gained an appreciation for Sam, too. He judged Sam to be a young man with a sense of adventure and energy to match. He especially liked that Sam always seemed eager to help in any way he could.

"I heard you were able to get people in through a secret gate yesterday," Mustafa said. He made the statement calmly, his poker face a tribute to his long diplomatic career.

Sam made a hundred instant calculations. He feared someone had flagged his transformation from consular officer to unsanctioned operator, and he worried that Mustafa had been deputized to determine what level of punishment he deserved.

"Yes," Sam said, trying to see where this was headed before admitting to details.

"Well," Mustafa said, "there's one family I've been trying to get in, but I know we're not getting many people in at this point."

Mustafa didn't want to sanction Sam, he wanted to enlist him.

Mustafa had been trying without success to help seven Afghan family members of Uzbek descent. The family came to his attention through his sister-in-law, who ran a non-governmental organization that advocated for Afghan women. The group on Mustafa's radar included the family matriarch, her brother, four of her daughters, ages five to twenty-two, and a son-in-law. The matriarch had been a provincial official and so had her husband, who was killed by the Taliban. Complicating their attempts to reach the airport, the one married daughter was pregnant and had difficulty walking as a result of childhood polio.

Mustafa texted regularly with the pregnant woman as the family tried repeatedly to enter the airport. On one attempt, two days earlier, they approached Abbey Gate, but withdrew when fights broke out and Taliban soldiers began beating would-be refugees. A Talib smashed the pregnant woman's husband in the face with a rifle butt.

Like so many others, they were at high risk but didn't qualify under the current rules.

Sam knew the covert operators had their own priorities and wouldn't take responsibility for the Uzbek family. If he wanted to help Mustafa's special interest family, Sam knew that he would have to return to Glory Gate himself.

Sam was operating on little sleep, bad food, and harsh cigarettes. Daylight was fading. Asad was gone. Sam limped from blistered feet. The rising threat of more suicide bombings preyed on his nerves. Tens of thousands of Afghans in the streets were increasingly desperate to catch a flight out. He'd already done his part. He'd decided to ride out the last hours of this temporary assignment in the safety of the JOC. Another trip to Glory Gate promised to be the most perilous act of Sam's life. It far exceeded the definition of "unnecessarily dangerous," in Liana's phrase.

"Just get home," she'd texted him the night before.

"I will soon," Sam promised.

And yet, as much as he valued the office work he'd done alongside Bass and DeHart, Sam felt best about having helped Asad's sister and her family, Ebad's brother, the interpreters and their families, and everyone else he shepherded through the secret gate.

A thought occurred to Sam. If he helped Mustafa's group, maybe he could also tackle a piece of unfinished business he feared would plague him long after he left Afghanistan.

"Okay, yes," Sam told Mustafa. "And I'm going to add two to that list."

13

"RUN, HOMEIRA!"

THE MOMENT SAM decided to help Homeira and Siawash, new worries arose.

First, he had to be certain that the JOC's covert Glory Gate liaison, the man to whom he gave Homeira's information on a scrap of paper, hadn't already taken steps to bring her in. A much bigger question was whether he'd made the right call.

After the Abbey Gate bombing, the consequences were limitless if anything went sideways or if the wrong people gained access to the airport. Even if the mission went smoothly, Sam could pay a high price for his serial rule twisting. He didn't have nearly as much leeway as Mustafa Popal, chief of staff to the deputy secretary.

To settle his fears, Sam googled Homeira and read about her achievements. It impressed him that she'd accomplished so much as an internationally celebrated author and a single mother who advocated for other Afghan women.

Next, Sam reread the first email Marly sent to Jim DeHart. This time, instead of skimming for details about passports and visas, Sam focused on Marly's description of Homeira's bravery for promoting women's rights and writing a memoir that offended the Taliban. Sam also read Marly's sympathetic follow-up email, forwarded to him by DeHart, which she'd sent after Sam told her the rules gave Homeira no way out. Along with that email, Marly included a pleading letter Homeira's British publisher sent to a sheikh who was Qatar's foreign minister.

"The safety of Homeira Qaderi is of paramount importance," that letter read. "[T]he worldwide community of authors, readers and publishers would be indebted to you for your brave action in helping this family. . . . You alone have the ability to save this woman's life and the lives of her close family by allowing them to join the Qatari convoy out of Kabul."

Sam understood that with so little time before the last flight and so few options for airport entry, the letter's core message—"You alone have the ability to save this woman's life"—more accurately applied to him.

Sam stepped outside the JOC for better reception and privacy. He called Marly a second time.

"Hello, this is Sam Aronson from the State Department. We spoke this morning. Do you remember me?"

"Of course," Marly said.

She told him Homeira still hadn't found a way to reach the airport, which confirmed Sam's suspicion that the Glory Gate operators had other priorities.

"Listen," Sam said. "I have an idea. But it's dangerous. Do you want me to try to help your person?"

"Yes, please!" Marly said. "She's already in grave danger."

Marly sent him Homeira's phone number and other contact information.

Afterward she texted her long-ago college boyfriend, former ambassador Sam Heins: "OMG I just got a second call from Afghanistan. . . . The caller said he may have found something they can do to help, but no promises. It is dangerous."

After speaking with Marly, Sam thought about all the people he and Asad helped the previous day at Glory Gate. This would be no harder, Sam told himself, knowing it wasn't true.

AS THE SUN set, Sam called Homeira from the burner phone he plucked from the box in the JOC. A man answered, so Sam hung up. Wakil Ahmad was still screening Homeira's calls to protect her from the Taliban. Sam called back. When a man answered again, he asked, "Are you Homeira?"

That's when Homeira, on speaker, called out in English: "Yes, yes, this is Homeira."

After Sam explained he was offering her a last chance to leave Kabul as part of the evacuation, he backtracked and introduced himself: "My name is Sam. I've been in touch with Marly. I think that's your agent."

"Yes, Marly!" Homeira said.

Homeira began describing the horrors she'd experienced since the fall of Kabul, including her trip a week earlier to Abbey Gate. When she asked about evacuating her extended family, Sam interrupted.

"The only thing we can do is get you and your son out. Two people," he said.

With the call still on speaker, Siawash translated for his grandparents. In Farsi, Wakil Ahmad repeated Sam's central message to Homeira: "This is your last chance!"

Homeira thought about the promises she'd made to her parents and to Zaman, Marly, and everyone else trying to help her. She reluctantly accepted Sam's terms: only herself and Siawash.

"Okay," Sam said, "where are you exactly?"

"I'm in Kabul."

"I know. Whereabouts in Kabul?"

Sam realized it was a foolish question. His knowledge of the city ended at the airport walls. Homeira told him she lived in the Fourth District, which Sam had never heard of.

"How far is your apartment from the airport?"

"If there's no traffic, half an hour. But there will be traffic, so maybe an hour."

"Okay, do you know the Panjshir Pump on Tajikan Road?"

"I don't know it," Homeira said, "but I'm sure I can find it."

Sam insisted, "Write it down or say it out loud, Panjshir Pump on Tajikan Road. I need you to be there by no later than 7:30 P.M. on the dot. I'll be calling you at 7:30 with instructions of how to get across the street to where we are."

That was less than an hour away.

"I don't think I can make it there by 7:30," Homeira said.

"I need you to try your hardest. I might have a few minutes of flexibility, but we really need to move by 7:30." Privately, Sam expected it might take Homeira longer, but he wanted her there as quickly as possible.

With Siawash still translating, Wakil Ahmad chimed in: "Tell him okay! We'll get you there."

"I'll do my best," Homeira said.

Sam told her: "Homeira, don't bring anything except your son. You can't bring any bags. Bring your passports, *tazkira*, cellphone, money, and anything else that can fit in your pockets."

"What about a backpack?"

"No. I'm sorry, this is not my rule. You have to understand that we think everything's a bomb right now. We're on high alert. They will not let you in with a bag. If you show up with a bag, a handbag, a backpack, anything, we're tossing it out onto the street."

Sam wasn't bluffing. Fear of hidden explosives was so great that Afghans weren't the only ones being denied bags on the last flights. A military force protection order required U.S. service members leaving Kabul to ditch their rucksacks before boarding planes.

"Okay," Homeira said.

Sam said he'd call again with more instructions.

In the meantime, Mustafa made similar arrangements with the Uzbek family he wanted to help. The plan was in motion.

WAKIL AHMAD TORE through the apartment gathering Homeira and Siawash's passports, money, and a few small essentials.

Homeira locked eyes with her mother as Ansari rose from her prayer rug. Ansari looked pale. She tried to reassure Homeira, and also herself.

"You will be back in no time," she said. "In the blink of an eye."

Homeira disregarded Sam's warning and grabbed her MacBook, which contained financial and personal documents as well as eleven short stories she'd been working on for more than a year. No backups existed. She slid the laptop into a black foam sleeve and placed it with her charger in a pink shoulder bag, along with Siawash's watch.

Zahra plucked a pair of Homeira's favorite pearl earrings from atop a dresser and handed them to her. Homeira felt her sister's cool skin and thought back to when she left Herat for Iran as a new bride. Now she felt a rush of guilt and grief at abandoning Zahra to the Taliban for a second time. Homeira wordlessly placed the earrings inside the pink bag.

Siawash picked out a bold red T-shirt with the outline of a body-builder and the words "Generation Iron Fitness Network." With his grandfather's help, he selected a blazer with a crest on the breast pocket, so he'd look like a proper young man. Siawash held a small iPad he used for games, but couldn't find a larger one he used for school. Amid the excitement, Siawash forgot about Sangi.

Suddenly Siawash threw his arms around his grandfather.

"Don't forget me," Wakil Ahmad said.

Ansari kissed Siawash on the head.

"Get her a taxi!" Wakil Ahmad commanded. Mushtaq sprinted to the elevator.

The four unmarried brothers and cousins were out, so Wakil Ahmad called them to say Homeira and Siawash were leaving. He only reached his son Jaber and nephew Basir, both of whom rushed home.

Homeira hugged Zahra and her sister-in-law Jahedah goodbye. Her nephew Shahzad was in his mother's arms but turned his face away, so Homeira couldn't kiss his cheek.

"Take us, too," the boy pleaded.

Homeira tried to say goodbye to her mother while they were still in the apartment. She worried how any extremists outside their building might react to Ansari's bright floral blouse.

"Don't come downstairs, Mom. If the Taliban sees you, they'll beat you."

"My child," Ansari said, "no one beats a living person over a few dead flowers." She wrapped a scarf over her silver hair and walked regally out the door.

They crowded inside the elevator with Wakil Ahmad, Siawash, Jaber, and Basir. They couldn't wait for Khalid and Qasem to return home, and they didn't have time to stop at the fourth floor to say goodbye to her uncle's family.

Ansari trembled as she leaned against the elevator wall and held Homeira's hands.

"Good thing I didn't go to the shrine," she said. "Now my house is a shrine. I'll miss my daughter."

Homeira fought back tears. She felt a burning pain in her throat that felt as though she'd swallowed hot coals.

Mushtaq had a taxi waiting as they stepped outside the building into the half-light of sunset. He kissed Homeira on both cheeks, then gave the driver the address of the Panjshir Pump: "Brother, get them there as fast as you can."

Jaber slid into the back seat with Siawash, while Basir sat up front with the driver.

Homeira took a last look around. She thought about how precious her neighborhood felt to her. She wanted to run back inside, but she reminded herself that she needed to raise Siawash far from the Taliban, somewhere safe, somewhere his heart wouldn't beat like a hummingbird's every time he left home. Somewhere he couldn't be taken from her again.

She climbed inside the taxi.

Ansari stepped away. Wakil Ahmad reached through the window and squeezed Homeira's hand. He looked ashen, older than Homeira had ever seen him. He took short breaths, his chest rising and falling. In Wakil Ahmad's glistening eyes, Homeira saw her father's joy that she would escape the Taliban's whips, and also his sorrow at her departure.

"No one can take your house away from you," Wakil Ahmad said.

Homeira understood her father meant her family and all of Afghanistan.

Wakil Ahmad turned to Siawash: "Sir, study your lessons well."

He let Homeira's hand slip from his, knowing he might never see her again.

As the taxi pulled away, Homeira heard a mournful cry. She craned her neck to look back, but her parents and oldest brother were gone, swallowed by the darkness.

INSIDE THE JOC, Sam and Mustafa told Ambassador Bass and Jim DeHart they were headed to Glory Gate. They said they hoped to recover a few more people, but offered only cursory details, under the theory that sometimes it's better to ask forgiveness than permission.

Bass and DeHart neither objected nor asked for more information. They were busy with their own work, Sam's day shift was over, and Mustafa's senior status gave him a long leash. DeHart insisted only that Sam and Mustafa get protection from the security team.

The new partners gave a fuller account of their plan to the senior security official on the night watch in the JOC. The security chief understood they wanted to keep the mission low profile, so he assigned only one shooter instead of the usual complement of three. He told Sam and Mustafa that two State Department Regional Security Officers were already near Tajikan Road, awaiting the overdue White Scarves from the Serena Hotel. If needed, they could provide backup.

Sam also spoke with a military intelligence officer who told him about a report of a man in a suicide vest on a bus heading to a gas station near the airport. The report was vague, so it hadn't been shared widely, but Sam interpreted the potential target to be the Panjshir Pump. Sam watched as the intelligence officer repositioned a drone above Glory Gate to provide a live video feed to the JOC. The officer promised to radio them if they needed to evacuate quickly.

As they prepared to leave, Mustafa volunteered to go to the Panjshir Pump to collect their evacuees, just as Asad had done. Sam felt certain the offer was sincere, but Mustafa hadn't been to Glory Gate. He didn't know how unsafe it could be for an unarmed middle-aged diplomat in American body armor. Asad's missions were risky enough in daylight, even with Zero Unit escorts, and those operations happened before a bomb exploded at an airport gate.

Ignoring Mustafa's seniority, Sam told him, "No fucking way."

They walked with their assigned shooter to a silver Land Cruiser. Sam glanced up to see tracer rounds flash across the dark sky. The red streaks seemed to connect the dots of white light from distant stars.

Sam spent the ten-minute ride with his nose buried in his phone, examining photos Marly sent of Homeira and Siawash. He also reviewed copies of their identification documents. One showed Homeira had a temporary work authorization in the United States, which Sam thought might be useful if anyone second-guessed his actions.

The contract shooter drove them through the opening in the wall to the curving service road that led north out of the airport. They parked near the small bridge, more than a hundred meters back from

Tajikan Road. The darkness was complete. A vehicle with U.S. Special Operators and last-minute evacuees drove past in the opposite direction with its headlights off, the driver navigating by night-vision goggles.

Sam climbed out of the Land Cruiser and heard a tinny loudspeaker faintly broadcasting a muezzin's call for the evening *Isha* prayer.

Not far from where they parked, the trio found the white armored Sprinter van with not two but three State Department Regional Security Officers, two men and a woman.

Sam and Mustafa briefed them on the plan, but none seemed interested in helping. One grudgingly agreed to accompany Sam and Mustafa on foot to seek permission from Glory Gate's keepers. Sam judged him to be either useless or burned out for not carrying his rifle or wearing his helmet as they lumbered toward Tajikan Road behind the beam of a flashlight.

INSIDE THE TAXI, Jaber turned to Homeira: "I wish they would send one of us away, too. We'll be here with no future."

Homeira knew Basir felt the same but didn't want to upset her.

Homeira silently deliberated. Sam had been adamant: "Only two people." She was willing to beg for both Jaber and Basir, and for that matter Zahra, Khalid, Qasem, Mushtaq, and the rest of her family. But she feared the more she asked, the more likely Sam would say no.

Homeira made an excruciating choice, based on her belief that Jaber's work for President Ashraf Ghani placed his life in the greatest imminent danger.

She called Sam's burner phone. He picked up on her second try.

"Can I bring my brother? He has documents."

Sam thought, "For fuck's sake." This felt like Ebad's brother all over again. Or worse.

"Does your brother have any other relatives?" he asked.

"He's on his own. He's not married."

That didn't help. At this point in the evacuation, an unmarried Afghan man in his twenties, with no U.S. passport, Green Card, visa, U.S. embassy employment, or other clear qualification was only slightly more eligible than a member of the Taliban.

"I told you no," Sam said.

He felt remorse but saw no other option.

"Only you and your son."

SAM, MUSTAFA, AND the security officer approached Tajikan Road.

The road had no streetlights near them, and the lights from the Panjshir Pump didn't reach the Hesco barriers near the entrance to the service road. Sam had a small flashlight, but he kept it off to avoid unwanted attention. The crowd along the street was thinner than during the day, but still more than 150 people milled about. Sam got the impression some were hostile.

Near the blast walls close to the gate's entrance, Sam recognized the gatekeeper: Omar, the covert U.S. operative who a day earlier gave Sam access to Glory Gate.

"How're you doing?" Sam said.

"You again," Omar replied.

"Yes, it's our last night. This is the last operation we'll be doing. You'll never have to see me again."

"Good."

Omar warned them that the American gatekeepers and their Afghan Zero Unit guards were on high alert for another suicide bombing. Some reports suggested Glory Gate was the target. He also told them he had bigger priorities than Sam and Mustafa's two families.

"I have seven buses," he said. "I can't even talk to you until these buses get in. Just hold tight. We'll have this conversation in a few minutes."

They backed away.

Mustafa turned anxiously to Sam: "Well, that's not good."

"No, no, no," Sam said. "That's just him. That actually is good."

"Really?"

"The fact that he said we could have a conversation in a few minutes means he'll say yes," Sam said.

Mustafa remained skeptical. Maybe he could pull rank. Mustafa had served as chief of staff to William Burns, a high-ranking former State Department official who'd recently been named director of the CIA, which made him Omar's ultimate boss.

"I can give Bill a call," Mustafa offered.

Sam thought it must be nice to have the CIA director's private cellphone number.

"Let's hold tight," Sam said. "Give him thirty minutes. Let's not throw the nuclear card just yet."

TO APPROACH THE Panjshir Pump, the taxi driver took the long way around to the north side of the airport. The closer they came, the heavier the traffic.

"Mom, we're going to be late," Siawash moaned. "Sam won't wait for us!"

Homeira's heart secretly hoped that was true and they'd return home, but she listened to her head. She called Sam again.

"It's jammed," she said. "We might not get there."

"Just get here," he said. "Let's see what we can do."

She took a chance and again pleaded Jaber's case.

"Sam, I am begging you. One of my brothers used to work in the presidential palace in Kabul. He's with us now. He's been supporting me all this time."

"No, ma'am."

Homeira's conflicted feelings about leaving without her entire family, about leaving at all, reared up with full force. She'd spent her life advocating for herself and others. She'd rescued herself and Siawash. Now, she decided that she could accept Sam's help only if she could help someone else she loved, too.

Raising her voice, Homeira persisted.

"Please let him leave with me!"

Jaber whispered: "Don't worry about me. Don't complain."

Sam heard her anguish. He felt it, too. He wanted to help as many deserving evacuees as possible, and he knew his every refusal might trigger consequences far more terrible than a threat to his career. He collected himself and handed the phone to Mustafa.

"This American tells me I can't take my brother with me," Homeira said, not knowing that Mustafa was also American despite his Afghan roots. "It'll be difficult in the U.S. for me alone."

Sam and Mustafa conferred. Mustafa said he believed Homeira was sincere. Sam softened. He reasoned that Homeira, an accomplished woman with so many supporters, wouldn't advocate for a brother who posed a threat to the United States. Sam nodded his approval.

Gently, in Farsi, Mustafa told her: "Get him here."

Sam reclaimed the phone. With Jaber, the target group had swelled to ten. Sam believed that each added person multiplied the risk of a fatal mistake.

"If you show up with a fourth person," Sam told Homeira, "I'm sending all of you back out."

SAM, MUSTAFA, AND the State Department security officer walked south, back down the service road away from Tajikan Road.

The security officer climbed inside the Sprinter van, while Sam and Mustafa continued on to the Land Cruiser. They waited there with their assigned contractor, a well-built man in his early forties with a short Afro and a scruffy beard, wearing khaki tactical pants and a dark, long-sleeve T-shirt under his armored vest.

All three agreed that the three Regional Security Officers weren't motivated to help them. Sam asked the contractor to return to the JOC to recruit another contract shooter he trusted. The contractor had worked at the U.S. embassy in Kabul since before the evacuation, and his patience with State Department security officers had worn thin. He was happy to oblige.

When Sam spoke to Omar at Tajikan Road, he noticed how the paramilitary operatives used night-vision goggles to move comfortably in the pitch dark. Before the contractor drove off, Sam asked him to look around for an extra set.

HOMEIRA CALLED HER father and asked him to have someone race to the Panjshir Pump with Jaber's passport. Mushtaq found it in Jaber's apartment and bolted outside, where he borrowed a motorcycle from a neighbor and sped toward the airport.

Homeira leaned over the front seat and clasped Basir's hand. She held it tightly, feeling guilty about the choice she made. Basir forced a smile.

"You two should go," her cousin said. "We'll survive. We'll leave at some point."

Homeira felt better until a text arrived from Khalid. Crushed that she was leaving, bereft at being left behind, her journalist-poet brother wrote: "You've just left us here and gone."

She felt a wave of nausea.

The taxi pulled up to the Panjshir Pump and all four got out. Basir intended to help them or, if opportunity arose, sneak in with them. Bursts of gunfire and men walking through the crowd with whips greeted their arrival. Siawash clung to Homeira, who had a flashback to the chaos outside Abbey Gate. They huddled together on the ground outside the Panjshir Pump mini-mart, waiting for Mushtaq.

A text came from Sam: "Are you here yet?"

Jaber urged Homeira not to reply immediately: "We have to wait for my passport."

Homeira fibbed, to buy time.

"We'll be there in ten minutes," she texted.

Meanwhile, Mushtaq texted Jaber that he was diverted by Taliban checkpoints. He told Jaber to walk north, away from the airport. "Make your way towards me. I'll get closer so we can meet up."

As Jaber rose, a teenage Talib with a whip appeared from nowhere. "Why are you waiting here?" he demanded. "Who are you?"

Before Jaber could answer, the man whipped his legs. Siawash began to cry.

"Why were you sitting next to that woman?" the Talib asked.

"She's my sister. Look at our IDs!" Jaber yelled. "We're leaving here. We've got an American contact who is coming to get us."

"If an American is waiting for you, why are you sitting here?"

He lashed Jaber again.

Homeira stood.

"Enough!" she shouted. "You ought to be ashamed of yourself for hitting someone older than you!"

Jaber pulled her away, afraid the Talib would whip her, too. The Talib moved on without looking at her.

Homeira told Jaber to forget about finding Mushtaq. She worried they'd be separated when Sam contacted her next. They called Mushtaq, who answered while arguing with a Talib at an outer checkpoint.

"I'm not going!" they heard him say. "I only want to give my brother his passport. Don't hit me!"

They heard a slap of leather. Mushtaq shouted: "Stop hitting me!" The call cut off.

Mushtaq called back a few minutes later. He'd somehow reached a wall near the rear of the Panjshir Pump parking lot. He told Jaber, "There's no one here, so we can meet up."

Basir volunteered to go, so Jaber could stay with Homeira and Siawash. When he stood, he immediately faced a swarm of men with whips. Homeira flinched at every blow. Siawash cried harder. Frustrated and overwhelmed, Homeira grabbed her son by the shoulders.

"You were the one who kept telling me to go! You told me, 'You are a bad mother for not taking me out of the country.' You see one whipping and you start crying. Be quiet so we can see what we're doing!"

SAM CALLED HOMEIRA again. This time, she told the truth: she, Siawash, and Jaber had navigated their way through traffic, crowds, and Taliban checkpoints to reach the Panjshir Pump.

Relieved, Sam said: "We're waiting to get the approval and we'll be back in touch. We're across the street, but there's no way to move yet."

Sam handed the phone to Mustafa, who again spoke with Homeira in Farsi to describe the seven Uzbek family members in his group. He told her to find them and stay together at the gas station. Mustafa also told her if anyone asked, she should say Jaber was her husband.

After the call, Homeira told Jaber they couldn't wait any longer.

"We'll get you out even if you don't have your passport," Homeira assured him. "Let's go. God will help us."

AS THEY AWAITED the contractor's return from the JOC, Sam and Mustafa stood in the darkness on the packed dirt, not far from where a day earlier Sam met the embassy staff bus, reluctantly took Ebad's phone, and began his Glory Gate missions. The two diplomats-turned-operators killed time talking about their lives and careers. Sam smoked a Marlboro Red, each drag a fresh razor across his throat.

Sam grew curious about several Toyota Hilux pickup trucks abandoned alongside the service road by Afghan Army troops. He clicked on his pocket flashlight, barely larger than his cigarette, and shined it through a truck's windows. He saw old Soviet-style night-vision goggles that wouldn't mount to his helmet, but they'd be better than nothing. The doors were locked and Sam didn't want to break in, so he kept looking. In the truck bed he saw a tableau of the sorry state of the Afghan Army: scattered ammo but no guns, discarded uniforms, and assorted trash. He grabbed two stun grenades and tucked them into a zippered thigh pocket. He'd last carried one in Niger.

Sam would have liked a gun, but at least now he had his bayonet and two flash-bangs.

Chatter increased on their handheld radios about heightened threats of another suicide attack. Blood still stained the street outside Abbey Gate, barely two miles away.

The reports of more potential attacks, plus the inky darkness, plus knowing he might need to go out into Tajikan Road, triggered Sam's nerves. He anxiously clicked his flashlight on and off, holding it between his thumb and pinkie. The light illuminated the tip of his little finger in flashes like Morse code. Each blink made Sam think of a firefly.

The contractor returned from the JOC in the Land Cruiser with a second shooter and an extra set of night-vision goggles. Sam climbed into the back seat to attach them to his helmet using the dome light. But his hands shook so badly he couldn't latch the goggles onto his helmet mount. Embarrassed, Sam handed them to the contractor, who fastened them without making Sam feel worse.

Beyond his team's safety, Sam worried about a political firestorm if anything went wrong. He and Mustafa weren't ambassadors, but they were U.S. State Department officials endangering themselves in a hostile environment. Particularly after Abbey Gate, another disaster would be magnified. A catastrophe at Glory Gate would spark comparisons to the 2012 Benghazi deaths of Ambassador Chris Stevens, State Department technology expert Sean Smith, and security contractors Glen Doherty and Tyrone Woods. Even the numbers lined up: two members of the American Foreign Service and two contractors hired to protect them.

Before Sam could reconsider, seven buses drove past.

SAM AND MUSTAFA checked in again with the State Department security officers in the Sprinter van. They said the seven buses, now headed toward the passenger terminal, were filled with evacuees whose passage was arranged by clandestine government agencies. The State Department security officers needed to await other buses, filled with the overdue White Scarves evacuees from the Serena Hotel. They'd have to sit tight, which meant that Sam, Mustafa, and the two private security contractors were on their own. Sam felt glad, believing that the State Department security team wouldn't tolerate the risks he planned to take.

Sam, Mustafa, and the two shooters, their rifles low but ready, walked north up the service road toward Tajikan Road. Sam handed a shooter one of his flash-bangs. All but Mustafa had night-vision goggles that cast their dodgy little corner of Kabul in an eerie shade of green.

The foursome met the gate operator Omar in the U-shaped area protected by concrete blast walls, seventy meters south of Tajikan Road.

"Hey," Sam said, "I saw your buses came in."

"Yeah. You guys have some of your own?"

"We have a few more over at the gas station," Sam said.

"Do whatever you want, bro."

Omar paused, then asked, "Remind me, what agency are you with again?"

Sam began to answer "State De—" then realized he'd been played. Omar couldn't resist one last jab at a young diplomat who'd initially mistaken an American operative for an Afghan commander.

SAM CALLED HOMEIRA. He told her to move west along Tajikan Road, toward the crowd that congregated around the market stalls doing steady business in the dark.

"Walk toward the sound of gunfire. It's going to be loud and scary," Sam said. "This is the only way to make this happen."

Homeira said she understood.

He told her that as they moved west, her group would see soldiers and gun trucks on the other side of Tajikan Road, outside the entrance to the service road. He instructed her to stop at a spot where it would be a straight-line sprint through the median, across Tajikan Road.

"Once you get there I'll tell you—'Now!' and I'll need you to run toward the opening in the street."

An idea for a signal popped into Sam's head: a tiny lighthouse that would guide the two families toward him in the dark without drawing too much attention. He told Homeira he'd hold his flashlight against his finger.

"It's going to look orange," he said. "It'll light up just a little bit, so you really have to look for it. Look for that and run. Run toward it, and we'll get you to safety."

In Sam's plan, Homeira heard an echo of her father's command the first time she became a refugee, more than thirty years earlier: "Run, Homeira!"

Homeira told Sam she was afraid.

"Don't worry," he said. "We have soldiers here."

Sam ended the call and put his phone in his pocket, to keep his hands free.

Mustafa made a similar call to the Uzbek family, telling them to stay with Homeira's family. The pregnant woman who had difficulty walking since childhood polio, said she felt certain she'd be killed. "This is the only way," Mustafa told her.

He also spoke in Dari to several nearby members of the Zero Unit guards, explaining what he and Sam had planned and showing them photos of the Uzbek family on his phone.

HOMEIRA, SIAWASH, JABER, and the seven Uzbeks walked west from the Panjshir Pump toward the sounds of gunfire outside the entrance to the Glory Gate service road. In the darkness, Homeira could see only red flashes from tracer bullets flying above her head.

Spent rounds littered the ground.

As they neared the crossing point of Tajikan Road, Homeira's long black dress snagged on a coil of concertina wire. A Zero Unit soldier approached them, his face twisted, yelling in Pashto, which she didn't understand.

"We've got someone waiting for us," Homeira said in Farsi. "Sam is our contact."

He continued yelling. All around them, gunfire sounded and people screamed as they were beaten away from the entrance path to Glory Gate.

Jaber tried to calm the Afghan soldier: "Yes, brother. We'll go. Just hold on."

Jaber's fears rose that he'd be turned away for his lack of documents. He feverishly texted Basir, who'd somehow survived the Talib gauntlet and found Mushtaq.

Homeira realized they needed a delay. With her dress still snarled in the razor wire, she pretended to have twisted her ankle.

She screamed, "Ouch!"

The Zero Unit soldier stopped yelling. He lowered his gun and patiently untangled her. He kindly asked if her foot was injured.

By the time Homeira was free, Basir had sprinted to them and handed Jaber his passport. The cousins hugged goodbye, and Basir vanished into the crowd, back toward the Panjshir Pump.

WITH HIS NIGHT-VISION goggles, Sam spotted ten people—five women, three men, and two children—on the far side of Tajikan Road. He couldn't make out faces, but he felt certain they were Homeira's group and the Uzbek family.

His heart racing, Sam flashed his penlight through his finger as the two families approached the crossing point. More than thirty meters separated them, and it wasn't clear if anyone saw his firefly signal.

With no cars passing, the ten people stepped into Tajikan Road, headed toward the opening in the center median and beyond that to Sam and Mustafa.

At the same moment, a scrum of more than a dozen young Afghan men stormed into Tajikan Road, shouting as they barreled toward the service road entrance. Sam spotted them and realized they were trying to exploit a small gap in the concertina wire the Zero Unit guards had created for the incoming evacuees.

The outnumbered Afghan paramilitary guards didn't know if the onrushing men were gatecrashers, suicide bombers, or both. The Zero Unit guards ran toward the interlopers, yelling in Dari and firing their weapons just over the men's heads. The muzzles of their AK-47s flashed orange in the darkness.

In the chaos, two Afghan guards mistook one of the Uzbek men for a gatecrasher. They pushed him back and stood ready to beat him with their rifle butts.

Homeira stopped. She felt paralyzed by a need to witness people so desperate to escape the Taliban they were willing to trample one another and ignore a hail of bullets.

Frantic, Sam and Mustafa ran into Tajikan Road.

Sam yelled at the guards in English, "They're good! They're with us! Let them go!"

Mustafa yelled in Dari: "Those are ours! Let them in! Let them in!"

Sam and Mustafa were fully exposed, outside the wire at night, two U.S. diplomats sprinting into a dark Kabul street amid gunfire and gatecrashers, a day after a suicide bombing at a nearby gate. Sam's bayonet bounced against his body armor. His flash-bang rattled in his thigh pocket. He pulled neither. Somewhere in his mind he knew the Zero Unit guards were supposed to be on their side. He also knew a knife and a flash-bang wouldn't stop assault rifles.

The two security contractors followed Sam and Mustafa into the road.

Sam kept shouting, but the Zero Unit guards couldn't hear him over the heavy gunfire. He and Mustafa rushed to the terrified Uzbek man near the median in the center of Tajikan Road.

One of the Zero Unit guards, who'd spoken earlier with Mustafa, finally understood. He lowered his weapon and his partner followed suit. They released the Uzbek man to Sam and Mustafa's custody, then left to help their fellow guards.

Through continued volleys of gunfire, Homeira, Siawash, Jaber, and the Uzbek family dashed toward the service road entrance. The disabled pregnant woman's husband carried her in his arms. Siawash's glasses fell to the ground, cracking the right lens. Homeira bent to find them and shouted to Siawash to keep running with Jaber. He hesitated then did as he was told. Homeira ran her hand over hot bullet casings until she felt the glasses. She rose with them and kept running.

Homeira was the last of the ten to reach the far side of Tajikan Road. She glanced back, hoping to see Mushtaq and Basir, but saw only throngs of people still trying to break through.

AMPED AND SWEATING, Sam lifted the night-vision goggles and stood sideways in the meter-wide gap in the concertina wire.

"You're safe now," Sam called. "You're safe. Follow me."

As each evacuee passed him, Sam counted aloud—"One, two, three . . ."—to be sure no would-be intruders snuck in. When Homeira entered, he loudly asked for her name, as a safety precaution. Taken aback by Sam's tone, she formally introduced herself, Jaber, and Siawash. He ushered them forward then took inventory of the Uzbek family.

They walked several meters from the road to the door-sized opening into the square of Hesco bastions. As they entered, Homeira tapped Jaber on the shoulder. Nodding toward Sam, she joked that he looked like a movie star. A hint of a smile curled on Siawash's lips.

Inside the square, Sam was struck by Homeira's composure. She carried herself like a professor entering a classroom, not a mother who'd just led her young son and brother through gunfire to escape the Taliban. Even more surprising to Sam was her shoulder bag.

"What the fuck is this?" Sam yelled.

He jerked the pink bag off her shoulder, pulling Homeira off balance. Jaber grabbed her arm, to steady her. Homeira saw a flash of anger on Jaber's face.

Inside the bag, Sam saw what looked like a computer in a padded case. He knew terrorists turned laptops into suicide bombs that detonated when powered on. In 2016, a laptop bomb blew a hole in a Somali airliner, killing one man and forcing an emergency landing.

He yelled louder, "I said no bags!"

"No!" Homeira shouted. "You said no suitcases! This is my purse."

"You weren't supposed to bring anything!"

"It's just my laptop!" she yelled, grasping for the bag. "Give it to me. I am a writer. I haven't just brought myself. I've brought my stories. I need my stories."

Jaber echoed her: "Please, she needs the laptop. Her book is on there, all of her documents are on there."

Sam couldn't believe it. He wanted all of them to be far from the darkness and dangers of Tajikan Road, safely buckled into the Sprinter van and the Land Cruiser, headed to the passenger terminal. He silently questioned his decision to help them.

"No," he insisted. "You cannot bring any large electronics!"

Homeira appealed to Mustafa, but on matters of security he deferred to Sam.

"We'll save you, Ms. Qaderi," he said, "so you'll write a thousand stories."

Homeira refused to relent.

"I'll go back if you take away my laptop," she threatened.

Sam ignored her. He handed the bag to the second contractor: "Deal with this."

Homeira watched in horror as the contractor exited the Hesco barriers and tossed her bag with the laptop to the edge of Tajikan Road.

She trembled with anger and humiliation.

"I'm still in Kabul," she thought, "and look what an American is doing to me."

Homeira felt an overwhelming urge to make good on her threat. She wanted to retrieve her MacBook, call Basir and Mushtaq, and tell them to take her home. But Siawash and Jaber depended on her.

"Mom, let's go," Siawash pleaded. "It's all good."

"It's not all good," she hissed.

Realizing his emotions were running hot, Sam tried to explain more calmly: "You literally can't bring a bag—I can't get you on a plane with a bag—and this could be a bomb."

Even as he said it, Sam doubted Homeira carried a bomb along with her son and brother. But after Abbey Gate, he needed to be extra careful. Also, he genuinely worried the bag alone might disqualify Homeira from a seat aboard a military C-17.

Homeira wouldn't surrender. "I need that. Please, can I have someone pick it up for us?"

As Homeira argued with Sam, Jaber called Basir, who remained nearby: "Come back to the place where you gave me the passport and take a laptop from the soldiers!"

Sam took a beat. Maybe he could let someone retrieve her laptop. If it was a bomb, at least it wouldn't pose an immediate threat to the American operatives and their Afghan allies.

Sam asked how long it would take for someone to get it. Five minutes, Jaber said. Sam agreed.

When Jaber called Basir again, gunfire and yelling crackled in the background.

Basir shouted: "They're shooting, Jaber! I can't get there!"

"Come get the laptop!" Jaber insisted. "Homeira's whole life is in there!"

Homeira quivered uncontrollably. She feared Basir would be shot.

With minutes passing and no sign of Basir, Sam announced they needed to get farther away from the road. Sam used the night-vision goggles to guide the ten evacuees single file away from the Hesco bastions, south toward Glory Gate's blast walls. Mustafa walked in back and the contractors flanked each side. Sam shined his flashlight behind him, to light a path.

When they reached the concrete walls, Sam asked one contract shooter to stay with Mustafa to search the evacuees. Sam and the other contractor turned to go back to Tajikan Road to recover Homeira's bag and wait for Basir.

THE GUNFIRE WAS heavier when Sam reached the road. Agitated Zero Unit guards roughly pushed potential intruders and curious pedestrians away from the concertina wire.

Homeira's pink shoulder bag lay untouched where the contractor tossed it. Four years had passed since the Niger prison incident when Sam drew his gun on the al-Qaeda bombmaker with wires protruding from his waistband. The episode was never far from his mind.

Sam saw no sign of anyone looking for the bag. His anxiety rose as several minutes passed. Sam thought about Homeira and everyone else who'd come through Glory Gate and the other airport entrances. All left behind their lives, their loved ones, and their homeland. If Sam could give Homeira her laptop, he could restore a small but priceless piece of her world.

With gunfire intensifying and Basir nowhere in sight, Sam turned to the contractor.

"What if we take the laptop?"

"Dude, it could still be a bomb," the contractor said.

"What if we check to make sure it's not?"

"I'm not going to stop you, but I'm not going to do that."

Sam picked up the bag and opened it wide. He peered inside for wires or residue that might indicate explosives. Seeing none, he gingerly pulled out the black foam sleeve. He tossed the pink bag back into the road, unaware it held Homeira's favorite earrings.

Sam slid out the silver laptop and dropped the sleeve in the dirt.

Carrying the laptop, Sam and the contractor returned to the blast walls but found no one there. Mustafa and the other contractor had already searched the evacuees and led them farther south down the service road to the vehicles.

Sam placed Homeira's MacBook on a waist-high wall. He knew he had to be certain it wasn't a bomb before bringing it to the Sprinter van.

"Man, I don't know," the contractor said. He walked several meters away and ducked low behind a concrete barrier.

Sam steeled himself and decided to repay Homeira's trust.

"It looks fine," he said aloud to reassure himself. "Let me just make sure."

Sam slowly lifted open the clamshell.

He pressed the power button. The laptop stirred to life with a familiar chime. A white Apple logo appeared on the black screen. The only explosives in Homeira's laptop were her stories about the subjugation of Afghan women.

Sam exhaled. He sat on the concrete ledge, basking in the familiar glow of a computer screen.

As he relaxed, Sam noticed two black bags in the dirt. Small backpacks or purses, they'd been carried by two of the women from the Uzbek family. Sam realized that the women had been forced to abandon their bags while being searched, just as he'd taken Homeira's bag.

Sam reached for one of the bags. He told himself he should check to be sure they didn't contain explosives that would endanger Omar and other Glory Gate operators.

"You're nuts," the contractor said.

The bag was almost empty so he set it aside. The second one was smaller, nylon, no bigger than a toaster. Sam looked inside and saw a woman's makeup products. He picked them out jar by jar, tube by tube. He dropped them one by one on the ground at his feet.

Soon the bag was empty. Sam struggled to compose himself.

"These women have nothing left," he thought. "She just wanted to look as nice as she could. And I'm taking it away. This is the last bit of dignity, and I'm taking it away."

Sam dropped the bag.

Too much time had passed. He and the contractor ran to the Sprinter van, where every seat was already filled. Sam jumped inside and knelt awkwardly in the aisle.

"Here you go," Sam said as he handed Homeira her laptop.

The mood in the van brightened

"Oh!" Homeira exclaimed. Jaber smiled. Siawash and the Uzbeks, who'd seen Sam yelling at Homeira minutes earlier about the laptop, looked shocked.

Homeira thanked Sam as she cried and hugged the MacBook to her chest.

OUTSIDE THE PASSENGER terminal, Sam let the adrenaline drain from his system. He unwound with a cigarette as he stood beside Mustafa while Marines searched Homeira's group and the Uzbeks, who were among the final evacuees who would leave Kabul as part of the American withdrawal.

Sam and Mustafa led the two groups inside the terminal to be certain no one questioned their qualifications, seized their remaining belongings, or declared them "Red." Sam especially wanted to be sure that no one took Homeira's laptop.

Mustafa told his bosses in Washington about the mission. As he guided the Uzbeks into the terminal, he told a consular officer he had approval from the "Seventh Floor," a powerful code in State Department lingo that referenced the location of the secretary of state's office.

Sam had no such authority. At the first checkpoint, he mumbled that Homeira, Siawash, and Jaber were "special interest cases." Then he upped the ante, to be certain no one tried to stop him or seize Homeira's laptop.

"White House priority," Sam said, lying without regret.

After a week of teeming crowds, the passenger terminal was empty of evacuees. Marines packed up computers and belongings. The last of hundreds of civilian evacuation flights would soon board.

After the two families received plastic ID bracelets, Sam and Mustafa escorted them down a back staircase to a dirty patch of tarmac called Ramp Eight, where perhaps two hundred other Afghans awaited a C-17. Homeira noticed families waiting to leave had made improvised tents by tying together women's headscarves.

Jaber went in search of scraps of cardboard they could sit on. Siawash sank into a funk. Exhaustion set in. He pined for the rest of his family, his friends, his home, his school, and Sangi.

Homeira and Sam set aside the hard feelings and harsh words they exchanged at Tajikan Road. Homeira thanked Sam for bringing them into the airport and retrieving her laptop. Sam apologized for cursing and for snatching away her bag. She forgave him.

Homeira had one last request: could Sam help her youngest brother, Khalid.

He winced.

"I'm afraid I can't," Sam said. "You're the last people getting out of here."

Sam promised to make sure they reached Doha safely. Before they said goodbye, Sam asked a consular officer to take a few photos on his phone, so he could send one to Marly and always remember the last family he brought through Glory Gate. Homeira, Siawash, and Sam clustered together amid the trash outside the old airport terminal.

In each image, Siawash's red T-shirt peeks out from under his blazer. Through his broken glasses, he stares toward the camera and an uncertain future. The blank expression on his round face makes him look serene or shell-shocked. Maybe both.

Sam stands at attention over Siawash's left shoulder, unshaven, wearing body armor, night-vision goggles, and a dirty checkered REI shirt. Black Sharpie marks snake up his forearm. He's fifteen pounds lighter than when he arrived in Kabul seven days earlier. He looks older and wiser, too.

Homeira stands at Sam's right, close behind the son she fought so hard to save. A fringe of brown hair peeks from under her patterned scarf. She clutches her MacBook and her iPhone. In the first several photos, she looks tired and sad, with a faraway gaze.

But in the last frame, Homeira tilts her head toward Sam and breaks into a smile.

EPILOGUE

AFTER GLORY

A FTER SEEING OFF Homeira, Siawash, Jaber, and the Uzbek family, Sam and Mustafa returned to the second floor of the JOC coated in a sheen of dust, sweat, and satisfaction. Sam plopped his helmet with the contractor's night-vision goggles onto the table amid the laptops.

"We got her," he announced.

John Bass and Jim DeHart looked up, confused.

"You what?" DeHart asked. "What did you do?"

Sam caught his breath and explained the mission. He began to describe the scene on Tajikan Road: "You wouldn't believe it. We were out on the street in pitch-black with gunfire—" when Bass gently cut him off.

Sam realized the ambassador wasn't uninterested or unkind. He wanted to protect Sam from disclosing details of an operation far outside the proper boundaries of diplomacy.

Bass and DeHart gave Sam and Mustafa a round of applause, then returned to work.

THERE WAS NO shortage of mistakes, waste, and dysfunction during the United States' twenty years of war in Afghanistan, with the losses measured in lives and trillions of dollars spent. Republican and Democratic administrations were both to blame. The failure to anticipate and adequately plan for the rapid Taliban takeover was the final tragic misjudgment.

Yet from a logistical standpoint, the August 2021 airlift largely defied critics' predictions of disaster. In a matter of days, the United States and its allies evacuated more than 123,000 people from Kabul, including about 6,000 American citizens. Nevertheless, the deaths and injuries of Afghans and Americans from the Abbey Gate bombing left a deep scar, and thousands of at-risk Afghans with ties to the United States were left behind.

The reactions of Bass and DeHart to the last mission at Glory Gate reminded Sam of the adage that success has many fathers, while failure is an orphan. His unauthorized actions helped vulnerable people without triggering a catastrophe, so Sam was hailed for his initiative rather than punished for his defiance. DeHart formalized that conclusion in a commendation letter that described Sam as a hero amid the "apocalyptic" scene in Kabul.

"Sam Aronson displayed exceptional teamwork, courage, and creativity in rescuing and evacuating American citizens and our Afghan allies," DeHart wrote. "In dangerous and stressful conditions, he remained determined, positive, and mission-focused. He weighed the risks, acted decisively, and improvised proactively to solve problems as they arose."

The commendation added: "Risking his own safety, Sam saved lives."

A separate letter from Secretary of State Tony Blinken praised Sam for his "commitment, bravery, and humanity." It concluded: "I am honored to be part of your team."

Sam left Kabul on the night of Saturday, August 28, less than twenty-four hours after helping Homeira, Siawash, and Jaber. After a stop in Doha, Sam returned to Washington on a charter flight with other American diplomats. A rousing ovation from State Department officials greeted their arrival at Dulles Airport. As soon as he arrived home, Sam recorded his memories of Kabul in what became a 14,000-word journal.

Still in Mali, Liana hid her distress about the risks Sam took, focusing instead on her admiration for what he accomplished. She forgave his broken promises. Sam's parents did the same for keeping them in the dark.

FOR SEVERAL MONTHS after his return, Sam suffered nightmares that jolted him awake screaming. He limped from infected blisters on his feet and his nose bled for weeks. He drank bourbon or wine to fight insomnia. A woman in a headscarf with two young children begging for money outside a Target in Washington, D.C., sparked harrowing flashbacks. He felt the dry air, heard the gunshots, and began to tremble. He broke out in tears on the ride home.

Moments like that triggered the guilt Sam carried for having denied entry to families and individuals who posed no threat but didn't meet that day's shifting priorities for evacuation.

"I followed those orders," he said. "If I could do it all over again, I'd say screw the rules and let them in."

Sam also was haunted by some of the people he helped at Glory Gate. He couldn't shake the desperation on the face of Asad's sister, or how Homeira shielded Siawash from gunfire, or their arguments about who she could bring and whether she could keep her laptop.

Some State Department colleagues expressed support, but others voiced jealousy, wrongly imagining, as Sam once had, that the evacuation was only a career-enhancing adventure, with little or no danger. Sam's supervisor denied his request for a couple of days off to recover. Despite a pledge from Blinken that no one returning from Kabul would be penalized for seeking therapy, Sam's supervisor told him to inform the medical office that he'd seen a State Department psychologist, which could have triggered a career-threatening mental health review. Sam got the order overturned.

Not long after he returned, Sam realized he couldn't envision doing consular work in Iraq, where he'd be deciding who to approve or reject from travel to the United States. After complicated negotiations, Sam convinced the assignments division to select him for a job newly close to his heart: a position at State Department headquarters in Washington focused on diplomatic issues involving Afghanistan. Ultimately, though, Sam decided he needed a larger change altogether. He resigned from the State Department and took a job in private industry, on the strategic response policy team of a major tech company. "Just like my time in government," Sam said, "I hope to contribute to a safer world every day."

Shortly before he left government service, Sam and other members of the evacuation team received the State Department Award for Heroism, which came with a silver medal with a blue-and-gray ribbon, a $2,000 bonus, and a citation that described their valor "in the face of gunfire, rioting, injury and death."

Sam remained in regular contact with Asad, who lived in Michigan near his family as he tried to establish a new life. Sam sent warm clothes that Liana picked out for Asad's niece and nephew. When Asad visited Washington, Sam took him to an Afghan restaurant to catch up. As Asad awaited U.S. citizenship, he explored joining the National Guard. Sam promised to help however he could.

Sam also stayed in touch with Homeira. When she landed in Doha, he asked an aide to Zalmay Khalilzad to keep tabs on her, Siawash, and Jaber. In the months that followed, he relished their text exchanges and looked forward to the photo updates she sent of her new life with Siawash.

Months after his return, Sam understood how deeply he'd been changed by his time in Kabul.

"I'd never seen anything like it," he said. "Seeing the fear and the courage from people like Homeira, from Asad's sister—it just made me realize that I took for granted the things in my life. I know I can't just move on from this."

ON THEIR EVACUATION flight from Kabul, Homeira and Jaber sat back-to-back, with Siawash nestled against her chest. On the twelve-hour flight, the military transport plane stopped in Doha, Qatar, flew to Germany but wasn't allowed to land, then returned to Doha.

During the next few days, they were herded from one refugee camp to another, collecting a half dozen colored identification wristbands along the way. They slept on cots surrounded by dozens of people, some of whom recognized Homeira and were surprised to see her there. They bathed in their clothes, which somehow made them smell worse, and stood in long lines for food.

"It's chicken and rice," Homeira said one day, offering Siawash a bowl.

"My hands are dirty. Bring me a spoon."

"There are no spoons, jan."

By the time they left Doha, the pain of leaving her home had set-tled into Homeira's bones. Some days she struggled to rise from her cot, forcing herself to her feet only so she could care for Siawash.

After a brief stop in Philadelphia, they flew to Fort Bliss, outside El Paso, Texas, one of eight U.S. military sites chosen to house Afghan refugees. Homeira, Siawash, and Jaber were among nearly ten thou-sand Afghan "guests" at the fort's "Doña Ana Village" awaiting reset-tlement.

They lived in white tent dormitories that housed up to a hundred people each. They sloshed through muddy alleys between tents when

it rained. They used brooms to sweep away thick carpets of dung bee-
tles. Women cried themselves to sleep under their blankets. One
woman who lost her husband in the Abbey Gate attack suffered volatile bouts of rage. Siawash feared falling asleep because he often woke
to grasshoppers crawling on his face. For weeks on end, Homeira wore
the same ripped dress she'd worn to pass through Glory Gate.

After nearly two months there, life vastly improved when Homeira,
Siawash, and Jaber left Fort Bliss for Massachusetts. Homeira began a
fellowship at Harvard arranged by the University of Iowa's Christopher Merrill and the author Jane Unrue, director of Harvard's Schol-
ars at Risk Program. Siawash returned to school, where he applied the
English he'd learned at his international school. Jaber found work as
an immigration coordinator and translator for fellow refugees.

AFTER HOMEIRA, SIAWASH, and Jaber left Kabul, their family
members packed up the two apartments, locked the doors, and returned home to Herat.

Homeira's cousin Qasem, who feared that his work as a prosecutor
made him a certain Taliban target, crossed the border illegally into
Iran. He spent a night in custody, paid a fine, then flew to France with
help from Gaël Perdriau, the mayor who'd promised to continue
working on the family's behalf. Homeira remained hopeful the rest of
her family would eventually be able to join Qasem in Saint-Étienne.
However, that prospect grew increasingly uncertain as Perdriau found
himself under investigation in late 2022 for allegedly blackmailing his
former deputy. He denied the charge.

Separately, in late 2022, Homeira's brother Mushtaq, his wife Jahedah, their son Shahzad, and Jahedah's younger brother obtained refugee status in France. "They left all they had. They will have bad days,"
Homeira said, "but they will be safe."

Homeira worried most about her brother Khalid, the radio journalist and poet who was abducted in March 2022 by Taliban intelli-

gence agents. For weeks, Homeira's father and other relatives tried without success to learn his condition and get him freed. Homeira posted about him repeatedly on social media and enlisted human rights groups on his behalf. Amnesty International demanded an end to his "arbitrary detention [for] exercising his freedom of expression."

Homeira feared that Khalid was being tortured, and she wondered if he was being punished partly for her high-profile activism. In April 2022, Homeira learned that a military court had sentenced Khalid to a year in prison, without a chance to appeal, for speaking against the Taliban. "I feel anger and sadness in my every cell," Homeira said.

Amid their heartbreak and worries for Khalid, family members who remained in Afghanistan suffered along with the rest of the country from a brutal drought and a ruined economy that left as much as 95 percent of the population at risk of starvation. United Nations Secretary-General António Guterres said some Afghans resorted to "selling their children and their body parts" to buy food. Homeira's family hadn't reached that point, but they had no money for electricity and little to eat.

"My country is sliding back into the dark age," she said.

THE TRAUMA OF leaving her home and much of her family caused Homeira complicated feelings about her passage through Glory Gate. On one hand, she felt deeply grateful for the risks Sam took and the rules he bent.

"Sam is our friend," she often said. "He is a hero in our life because of his heart."

Yet Homeira fumed about the politics and the forces that led to her departure. Among her most prized possessions was her apartment key. She fantasized often about using it again, regardless of how the Taliban might treat her.

In the meantime, she worked to build a new life. As a fellow in fiction and poetry at Harvard's Radcliffe Institute for Advanced Study,

Homeira worked on a novel called *Tell Me Everything*, about a girl kidnapped during the Soviet-Afghan War and taken to St. Petersburg. The girl returns home under Taliban rule and eventually immigrates to the United States.

In spring 2022, Homeira stood before a rapt audience in a small auditorium on the Harvard campus to discuss her novel in progress and the lives of Afghan women. She'd let her hair grow back, and it again flowed down her back.

"Every woman in Afghanistan is a soldier who has to fight for her rights," she told the crowd. Despite the repression they faced, "Our destiny is not always clad in black."

Yet sometimes it seemed that way. The day after Homeira's talk, the Taliban banned girls from returning to school after the sixth grade. Weeks later, Afghanistan's supreme leader and Taliban chief decreed that women should cover themselves head to toe whenever they appeared in public. The Ministry of Women's Affairs was abolished. Its building became home to the reestablished Ministry of Vice and Virtue.

Even seven thousand miles away, Homeira continued her advocacy. She created an updated version of the Golden Needle Sewing Class where she'd learned storytelling techniques as a girl. With help from a former student, Homeira taught a writing class for several hundred girls and boys in Afghanistan that assembled weekly online via Google Meet. Class members shared their writing and studied great works of fiction and nonfiction.

A class favorite was *The Diary of a Young Girl* by Anne Frank. Despite the tragic end of Anne's story, despite their religious, historical, and cultural differences, Homeira's students were stirred by Anne's bravery, her vibrant writing, and her unbridled emotions.

"They identify with her," Homeira said. "Women and girls in Afghanistan are trying to learn to express themselves freely. Anne Frank expressed herself openly."

One passage from the diary that had special resonance reads: "Let me be myself and then I am satisfied. I know that I'm a woman, a woman with inward strength and plenty of courage."

For Homeira, the diary was a reminder that her own story remains unfinished.

"It shows that we can be creative even when we're in a bad situation. We can always have hope."

ACKNOWLEDGMENTS

I'm grateful beyond words to Homeira. Despite her anguish over being separated from her family and her homeland, she was unfailingly generous and patient as she shared her story.

Working with Sam was a privilege and a delight. His eagerness to spread credit and deflect praise are even more proof that he's a man of rare character.

I consider Homeira and Sam to be kindred spirits, heroes who put the safety and interests of others above their own. My admiration for them is boundless.

Thanks also to Siawash, who sharpened Homeira's memories and endured the many hours she spent recounting these events. He's a smart, brave boy with a bright future.

Fifteen years ago, the extraordinary editor Claire Wachtel changed my life by believing in an idea I had for a book. I'm again in her debt for connecting me to Marly Rusoff, a wonderful person who's the fairy godmother of this story.

Richard Abate is a world champion literary agent. His friendship is an even greater gift.

Special thanks to J. P. Feldmayer, who played an essential role in the evacuation and whose careful reading of the manuscript saved me from unforced errors. Thanks also to Mustafa Popal, Asadullah "Asad" Durrani, Jim DeHart, Jacob Aronson, David Roth-Ey, Deborah Rodriguez, and Jessica Donati, who wrote the first news story about the secret gate in The Wall Street Journal. Extra thanks to Liana Aronson, who shared her insights and surrendered Sam for a weekend of interviews shortly after they reunited following months apart.

I'm thankful to the entire Random House team, starting with my editor, Ben Greenberg, an ace co-pilot who saw what I missed and steered me straight. Publicity boss London King demonstrated again why she's the best in the business. Thanks also to Kaeli Subberwal, Benjamin Dreyer, Dennis Ambrose, Sheryl Rapée-Adams, (MORE TK).

My students and colleagues at Boston University inspire me. Grad research assistant Emma Glassman-Hughes unearthed a mountain of material that enabled me to write with confidence. I'm forever grateful to my friend and fellow professor Dick Lehr, a best-in-class author and peerless sounding board. Thanks to Dean Mariette DiChristina and journalism faculty stars David Abel, Jerry Berger, Chris Daly, Anne Donohue, Shannon Dooling, Noelle Graves, Michael Holley, Meghan Irons, Sarah Kess, Greg Marinovich, Tina McDuffie, Bill McKeen, Maggie Mulvihill, Caryl Rivers, Peter Smith, Susan Walker, and Brooke Williams.

My life is enriched by my long friendship with Brian McGrory, whose jump from editor of The Boston Globe to chairman of the BU Journalism Department (and, apparently, now my boss) is a windfall in every way. I'm thankful for the friends who've nurtured me and my work, among them Naftali Bendavid, Chris Callahan, Dan Field, Colleen Granahan, the Hajer family, John King, Joann Muller, and the late Wilbur Doctor. My pal Caper keeps me relatively sane.

The extended Kreiter and Zuckoff families rock. The Pierceys, too. My brother, Allan, lights the path. Our retired history teacher father, Sid, is a mensch and an expert line editor. No one delivers criticism more gently in the margins: "Could you do better here?" My late mother, Gerry, gave enough love for two lifetimes. I cherish her memory.

Eve Zuckoff is a precious gift and an exceptional storyteller in her own right. Isabel Zuckoff makes the world and my life better every day. Suzanne Kreiter, to whom this book is dedicated, is a brilliant journalist and an even better person. Thanks for my life.

NOTES ON SOURCES
AND METHODS

Although written as a narrative, this is a work of nonfiction. No facts, scenes, or chronologies were created or altered for dramatic or other purposes. No dialogue or characters were invented. No names were changed.

Thoughts and emotions reported on these pages came directly from individuals to whom they are attributed. Descriptions of people, places, and events came from witnesses and other primary sources, as well as from verified accounts, photos and videos, military and government records, responsible media organizations, and other sources, cited in the endnotes where relevant. No government or military entity reviewed or approved the manuscript prior to publication.

By far the most important sources were Homeira Qaderi and Sam Aronson. Each participated in more than two dozen hours of recorded interviews. Each also answered hundreds of phone, email, and text inquiries to correct or verify information and to elaborate on details. They provided emails, texts, photos, videos, social media posts, and other materials, cited in the endnotes where relevant. Marly Rusoff supplied an invaluable cache of emails, notes, and texts, as did other sources cited in the endnotes. Any errors are the sole responsibility of the author.

The sources of this book neither sought nor received editorial control over content, structure, or presentation. Because Homeira arrived in the United States with little more than her laptop, a portion of the proceeds are being shared with her. Another portion is being devoted, under Marly's direction, to Afghan refugee relief.

NOTES

I: HOMEIRA

ooo *Homeira Qaderi:* The account and descriptions of Homeira's life, and primarily her experiences in Kabul during August 2021, are based on more than twenty-five hours of recorded interviews, translated from Farsi, in response to questions and prompts in English. Although Homeira speaks fluent English, answering questions in her first language enabled her to express herself more comfortably and completely. Additional sources include scores of telephone calls, email exchanges, texts, documents, photographs, maps, and social media postings, attributed or cited where appropriate.

ooo *Farsi:* The Afghan dialect of Persian is typically Dari, but having grown up in Herat, near the Iran border, Homeira's first language is Farsi. Numerous conversations recounted here among Homeira, Siawash, and other family members took place in Farsi but are rendered in English. Homeira confirmed the accuracy of the translations.

ooo *"the use of Afghan soil":* Joint Declaration between the Islamic Republic of Afghanistan and the United States of America for Bringing Peace to Afghanistan, https://www.state.gov/wp-content/uploads/2020/02/02.29.20-US-Afghanistan-Joint-Declaration.pdf.

ooo *suicide by self-immolation:* Numerous academic studies and media accounts have documented the continuing tragedy of women setting themselves on fire amid domestic despair even years after the Taliban's defeat. See, for instance, two news stories from Herat: Muhammad Lila and Aleem Agha, "Desperate Afghan Women Setting Themselves on Fire: Self-immolation of desperate young women on the rise," ABC News, December 11, 2012, https://abcnews.go.com/International/desperate-afghan-women-setting-fire/story?id=17935217. See also Alissa J. Rubin, "For Afghan Wives, a Desperate, Fiery Way Out," *The New York Times,* November 7, 2010, https://www.nytimes.com/2010/11/08/world/asia/08burn.html.

ooo *targeted . . . assassination:* Saphora Smith and Ahmed Mengli, "Wave of killings targets Afghan female judges, journalists, intellectuals," NBC News, January 24, 2021, https://www.nbcnews.com/news/world/wave-killings-targets-afghan-female-judges-journalists-intellectuals-n1255302.

ooo *live on Facebook:* https://www.facebook.com/100002303605636/videos/143607917908362/.

ooo *Taliban reasserted itself:* Human Rights Watch 2016 World Report, https://www.hrw.org/world-report/2016/country-chapters/afghanistan#.

ooo *largest and deadliest attack:* Christina Goldbaum, "Taliban Claim Responsibility for Major Attack in Afghan Capital," *The New York Times,* August 4, 2021, https://www.nytimes.com/2021/08/04/world/asia/afghanistan-kabul-taliban-attack.html. See also Mujahid's Tweet: https://twitter.com/Zabehulah_M33/status/1422760620215132167.

ooo *2019 presidential election:* Pamela Constable, "Afghanistan's Ghani wins slim majority in presidential vote, preliminary results show," *The Washington Post,* December 22, 2019, https://www.washingtonpost.com/world/afghanistans-ghani-wins-slim-majority-in-presidential-vote/2019/12/22/73355178-244f-11ea-b034-de7dc2b5199b_story.html. See also website of Dr. Faramarz Tamanna, http://www.faramarztamanna.af/.

ooo EN TK?

ooo *one-eighth of her husband's estate:* Gayle Tzemach Lemmon et al, "Reforming Women's Property Rights in Afghanistan," Council on Foreign Relations, September 5, 2017, https://www.cfr.org/blog/reforming-womens-property-rights-afghanistan.

2: SAM

ooo *Sam Aronson:* Throughout this book, the account of Sam's background and his experiences in Afghanistan is based on more than 350 pages of transcripts from recorded interviews, plus numerous corroborating documents and photographs, as well as several hundred emails, texts, and phone calls with Sam. It also relies on memories, documents, and text, email, and voicemail messages supplied by others, cited where appropriate. Sam also wrote a detailed journal more than 14,000 words long about his time in Kabul that he shared with the author.

ooo *"such wonderful news":* Email from Samantha Power to Sam Aronson dated April 5, 2019.

ooo *"the obedient child":* Interview with Jacob Aronson, December 28, 2021.

ooo *attack in Benghazi, Libya:* Mitchell Zuckoff with the Annex Security Team, *13 Hours: The Inside Account of What Really Happened in Benghazi,* New York: Twelve, Hachette Book Group, 2014.

ooo *biometrically scan:* As a member of the Niger Biometrics Enrollment Team, Sam shared a National Intelligence Meritorious Unit Citation for the work, signed by the Director of National Intelligence and dated April 25, 2018.

ooo *sense of adventure:* Interview with Liana Cramer, January 14, 2022.

ooo *"risked his life":* Remarks of Secretary Colin L. Powell at the at the American Foreign Service Association awards ceremony, June 27, 2002, https://2001-2009.state.gov/secretary/former/powell/remarks/2002/11507.htm. See also https://www.smithsonianmag.com/history/saving-the-jews-of-nazi-france-52554953/ *and*

https://exhibitions.ushmm.org/americans-and-the-holocaust/personal-story/
hiram-bingham-jr, retrieved December 26, 2021.

000 *Holocaust heroes:* Yad Vashem: The World Holocaust Remembrance Center, The
Righteous Among the Nations Database, https://righteous.yadvashem.org/?searc
h=Schindler&searchType=righteous_only&language=en&itemId=4017377&
ind=2.

000 *a sunset proposal:* Sam and Liana's wedding was featured in *The New York Times*
in November 2020, https://www.nytimes.com/2020/11/06/style/how-to-grow-an-
international-relationship-while-preserving-international-relations.html.

3: KABUL

000 *At the news conference:* See live news conference August 10, 2021, https://www.
facebook.com/AISSAfghanistan.

000 *"fight for themselves":* Remarks by President Biden on August 10, 2021, https://
www.whitehouse.gov/briefing-room/speeches-remarks/2021/08/10/remarks-by-
president-biden-on-the-senate-passage-of-the-bipartisan-infrastructure-
investment-and-jobs-act/.

000 *Mohammad Ismail Khan:* Sharif Hasan, "An Afghan warlord who steadfastly resisted the Taliban surrendered; Others may follow his lead," *The New York Times*,
August 13, 2021, https://www.nytimes.com/2021/08/13/world/asia/afghanistan-
mohammad-ismail-khan.html.

000 *an interview:* IWP Periscope: Homeira Qaderi, https://iwp.uiowa.edu/page/
periscope-on-homeira-qaderi.

000 *an attack:* Hamid Shalizi, "Death toll from Kabul University attack rises to at
least 35 as anger grows," Reuters, November 3, 2020, https://www.reuters.com/ar-
ticle/afghanistan-attack-university-int/death-toll-from-kabul-university-attack-
rises-to-at-least-35-as-anger-grows-idUSKBN27J17T. See also Thomas
Gibbons-Neff and Fatima Faizi, "Gunmen Storm Kabul University, Killing at
Least 19," *The New York Times*, November 21, 2020,https://www.nytimes.
com/2020/11/02/world/asia/kabul-university-attack.html.

000 *"preventing further instability":* Adam Nossiter, "Under pressure to quit, Afghanistan's president pledges only to end 'instability,'" *The New York Times*, August 13,
2021, https://www.nytimes.com/2021/08/13/world/asia/afghanistan-ghani-
president-isolated.html.

000 *U.S. troops:* Statement by President Biden, August 14, 2021, https://www.white-
house.gov/briefing-room/statements-releases/2021/08/14/statement-by-president-
joe-biden-on-afghanistan/.

4: VOLUNTEER

ooo *American flags:* Susannah George, Missy Ryan, Tyler Pager, Pamela Constable, John Hudson and Griff Witte, "Surprise, panic and fateful choices: The day America lost its longest war," *The Washington Post,* August 28, 2021, https://www. washingtonpost.com/world/2021/08/28/taliban-takeover-kabul/.

ooo *Jonathan Karl objected:* Transcript of *This Week with George Stephanopoulos* on ABC News, Sunday, August 15, 2021, https://abcnews.go.com/Politics/week-transcript-15-21-sec-antony-blinken-rep/story?id=79458722.

ooo *"Did you know anyone":* Text exchange between Mark and Sam Aronson, starting at 10:09 P.M., Sunday, August 15, 2021.

ooo *"I'm left again to ask":* President Biden's televised address, August 16, 2021. Transcript found at https://www.whitehouse.gov/briefing-room/speeches-remarks/2021/08/16/remarks-by-president-biden-on-afghanistan/.

ooo *"Whoa, super cool":* Sam preserved thousands of texts from multiple people during this period and shared them with the author.

ooo *plunged to their deaths:* Videos of the incident were shared widely and aired on multiple U.S. broadcast outlets. See https://www.cnn.com/videos/world/2021/08/16/kabul-clinging-to-airplane-taking-off-tarmac-afghanistan-ward-vpx.cnn. See also Helene Cooper and Eric Schmitt, "Body Parts Found in Landing Gear of Flight from Kabul, Officials Say," *The New York Times,* August 17, 2021, https://www.nytimes.com/2021/08/17/us/politics/afghans-deaths-us-plane.html?smid=tw-nytimes&smtyp=cur.

ooo *world's deadliest mission:* Susanna D. Wing, "Another Coup in Mali? Here's What You Need to Know," *The Washington Post,* May 28, 2021, https://www.washingtonpost.com/politics/2021/05/28/another-coup-mali-heres-what-you-need-know/.

ooo *crushed to death:* Dan Lamothe and Alex Horton, "Documents reveal U.S. military's frustration with White House, diplomats over Afghanistan evacuation," *The Washington Post,* February 8, 2022, https://www.washingtonpost.com/national-security/2022/02/08/afghanistan-evacuation-investigation/.

ooo *Taliban fighters with Kalashnikov rifles:* These scenes were witnessed by numerous journalists and others. See Shashank Bengali, Lara Jakes, Annie Karni and Kenneth P. Vogel, "Amid Desperation at Kabul Airport, Evacuation Picks Up Pace," *The New York Times,* August 20, 2021, https://www.nytimes.com/live/2021/08/20/world/biden-afghanistan-taliban.

ooo *several thousand more Americans:* The number of Americans and others awaiting rescue was difficult to pin down during the chaotic last weeks of August. Several times, Biden administration officials said they did not have a precise figure. See, for instance, Lara Jakes, "How Many People in Afghanistan Need to Be Rescued? The Number Remains Elusive," *The New York Times,* August 24, 2021, https://www.nytimes.com/2021/08/25/world/how-many-people-in-afghanistan-are-seeking-to-be-evacuated-the-number-remains-elusive.html.

ooo *hungry in a good way:* Interview with James DeHart, January 20, 2022.

ooo *threw or passed young children:* The incident Sam described reportedly happened at East Gate. Media reports about multiple similar events spread widely in the days that followed. See Katie Rogers, "A Baby Passed Over a Wall in Kabul is Reunited With His Family, the Military Says," *The New York Times*, August 20, 2021, https://www.nytimes.com/2021/08/20/world/asia/afghanistan-kabul-baby. html#. See also https://www.nbcnews.com/news/world/videos-show-american-soldiers-help-woman-child-over-wall-kabul-n1277142.

ooo *"safe passage to the airport":* U.S. embassy in Kabul security alert issued August 19, 2021, https://af.usembassy.gov/u-s-embassy-kabul-august-19-2021/.

5: TALIBAN

ooo *withdrawal agreement:* "Agreement for Bringing Peace to Afghanistan between the Islamic Emirate of Afghanistan which is not recognized by the United States as a state and is known as the Taliban and the United States of America, February 29, 2020, which corresponds to Rajab 5, 1441, on the Hijri Lunar calendar and Hoot 10, 1398 on the Hijri Solar calendar," https://www.state.gov/wp-content/ uploads/2020/02/Agreement-For-Bringing-Peace-to-Afghanistan-02.29.20.pdf.

ooo *adherence to the agreement:* Lead Inspector General for Operation Freedom's Sentinel | Quarterly Report to the United States Congress | April 1, 2020–June 30, 2020, Publicly Released: August 18, 2020, https://www.dodig.mil/reports. html/Article/2316028/lead-inspector-general-for-operation-freedoms-sentinel-i-quarterly-report-to-th/.

ooo *an Islamic emirate:* Lynne O'Donnell, "Taliban Map Out Future Vision for Afghanistan," *Foreign Policy,* June 8, 2021, https://foreignpolicy.com/2021/06/08/ taliban-future-afghanistan-war-zabiullah-mujahid-interview/.

ooo *a powerful message:* Video posted on Homeira's public Facebook page, subsequently deleted and replaced with a still image from the appearance, https:// www.facebook.com/photo/?fbid=4259902274096517&set=a.856621631091282.

ooo *crushed to death:* Numerous media reports described the deaths of children outside the airport. See, for instance, Ahmad Seir, Tameem Akhgar, and Jon Gambrell, "Crush at Kabul airport kills 7 as Afghans try to flee," The Associated Press, August 22, 2021, https://apnews.com/article/afghanistan-kabul-airport-deaths-8254e2e79a1a88dd1bd8802b6b9dedac.

6: ASAD

ooo *abandoned American Humvees:* Brad Lendon, Jessie Yeung, Kara Fox, Aditi Sangal, Meg Wagner, Melissa Macaya, and Melissa Mahtani, "The Latest on Afghanistan as the Taliban Take Charge," CNN airdate Friday, August 20, 2021, last updated online 8:27 P.M. With the 8.5-hour time difference between New York and Kabul, these were the among the news stories being aired when Sam woke early Saturday, Kabul time, https://www.cnn.com/world/live-news/afghanistan-taliban-us-news-08-20-21/h_3a1c4e5d11e9502da4e8900c728252b7.

ooo *stun grenades:* CNN Report, "Watch Chaos Unfold At Kabul Airport's North Gate," https://www.cnn.com/videos/world/2021/08/20/kabul-airport-chaos-afghanistan-taliban-npw-dlt-intl-vpx.cnn.

ooo *U.S. military veterans mobilized:* Media reports covered numerous accounts of these efforts. See, for instance, Ben Kesling, "U.S. Military Veterans Rush to Help Afghan Interpreters Escape," *The Wall Street Journal,* August 17, 2021, https://www.wsj.com/articles/u-s-military-veterans-rush-to-help-afghan-interpreters-escape-11629232144.

ooo *Pineapple Express:* James Gordon Meek, "US Special Operations Vets Carry Out Daring Mission to Save Afghan Allies," ABC News, August 27, 2021, https://abcnews.go.com/Politics/us-special-operations-vets-carry-daring-mission-save/story?id=79670236.

ooo *"safest boarding":* Hotel Baron website, accessed January 5, 2022, at https://kabul.thebaronhotels.com/.

ooo *169 American citizens:* President Biden first mentioned the Baron Hotel rescue on Friday, August 20, 2021. See Dan Lamothe, "Americans Rescued by Army Helicopter From Hotel Near Kabul Airport," *The Washington Post,* August 20, 2021, https://www.washingtonpost.com/world/2021/08/20/afghanistan-kabul-taliban-live-updates/.

ooo *28,000 people:* "Remarks by President Biden on Tropical Storm Henri and the Evacuation Operation in Afghanistan," August 22, 2021, https://www.whitehouse.gov/briefing-room/speeches-remarks/2021/08/22/remarks-by-president-biden-on-tropical-storm-henri-and-the-evacuation-operation-in-afghanistan/.

ooo *a panicked crush:* Unbylined story, "Crush At Kabul Airport Kills 7 As Afghans Try To Flee," The Associated Press, August 22, 2021. Published widely, seen at https://www.npr.org/2021/08/22/1030167259/crush-at-kabul-airport-kills-7-as-afghans-try-to-flee.

ooo *A text exchange:* Sam was not one of the two State Department officials involved in this exchange, which occurred between 6 A.M. and 6:10 A.M. Kabul time on the morning of August 22, 2021.

ooo *Asad's full name:* Interview with Asad Durrani, January 9, 2022.

ooo *email from Secretary of State Tony Blinken:* Blinken email to all hands in Kabul, dated August 23, 2021, 2:50 P.M. EST.

ooo *more than 82,000:* Remarks to the Press, Antony J. Blinken, Secretary of State, August 25, 2021, https://www.state.gov/secretary-antony-j-blinken-on-afghanistan/.

ooo *"Every day we're on the ground":* Remarks by President Biden on the Ongoing Evacuation Efforts in Afghanistan and the House Vote on the Build Back Better Agenda, August 24, 2021, https://www.whitehouse.gov/briefing-room/speeches-remarks/2021/08/24/remarks-by-president-biden-on-the-ongoing-evacuation-efforts-in-afghanistan-and-the-house-vote-on-the-build-back-better-agenda/.

000 *press briefing a day earlier:* State Department press briefing, 3:38 P.M. EDT, August 23, 2021, https://www.state.gov/briefings/department-press-briefing-august-23-2021/.

7: WHITE SCARVES

000 *White Scarves:* Interview on March 11, 2022, with a spokeswoman for the White Scarves Coalition who asked not to be identified by name. She acknowledged the failure of initial efforts to bring Homeira and other high-priority women on the list through the airport gates. "It was more chaotic than anybody anticipated," she said. Eventually, the White Scarves Coalition helped to evacuate more than 1,100 Afghan women and their family members, with flights that extended through late October 2021, she said.

8: GLORY GATE

000 *The son (Feldmayer):* Interview with J.P. Feldmayer, February 10, 2022.

000 *Glory Gate:* The gate's existence and the CIA connection were first reported by *The Wall Street Journal* nearly two months after the withdrawal. See Jessica Donati, "A Secret CIA Gate at Kabul Airport Became an Escape Path for Afghans," *The Wall Street Journal,* October 14, 2021, https://www.wsj.com/articles/a-secret-cia-gate-at-kabul-airport-became-an-escape-path-for-afghans-11633545417.

000 *flown by helicopter:* Later reporting by *The New York Times* and other news organizations found that a secret CIA compound called Eagle Base, three miles from Kabul International, was being used during the withdrawal as an evacuation hub for American citizens, Afghan commandos, at-risk Afghans, and their families. See Christiaan Triebert and Haley Willis, "Covert Evacuations and Planned Demolitions: How the C.I.A. Left Its Last Base in Afghanistan," *The New York Times,* September 1, 2021, https://www.nytimes.com/2021/09/01/world/asia/cia-afghanistan-evacuations-demolitions.html. See also https://www.politico.com/news/2021/09/01/afghanistan-commandos-evacuated-secret-cia-base-508646.

000 *"Because of security threats":* Security Alert—Embassy Kabul, Afghanistan, August 25, 2021, https://af.usembassy.gov/security-alert-embassy-kabul-afghanistan-august-25-2021/.

000 *a "specific" threat:* Eric Schmitt and Traci Carl, "U.S., Others Warn of Threat at Airport in Kabul and Tell Citizens to Leave Immediately," *The New York Times,* August 25, 2021, https://www.nytimes.com/2021/08/25/world/asia/us-kabul-airport-threat.html.

000 *Glory Gate:* The gate's existence and the CIA, Delta, and Zero Unit connections

were first reported by *The Wall Street Journal* nearly two months after the with-drawal. See Jessica Donati, "A Secret CIA Gate at Kabul Airport Became an Es-cape Path for Afghans," *The Wall Street Journal*, October 14, 2021, https://www.wsj.com/

articles/a-secret-cia-gate-at-kabul-airport-became-an-escape-path-for-afghans-11633545417.

ooo *sniper at North Gate:* This incident was widely reported. See Nick Paton Walsh, Sam Kiley, and Sheena McKenzie, "Afghan Visa Applicants Told to Stay Away From Kabul Airport as US Races to Meet Exit Deadline," CNN, August 23, 2021, https://www.cnn.com/2021/08/23/asia/kabul-airport-afghanistan-intl-hnk/index.html. See also Jane Ferguson and Steve Inskeep, "An Afghan Soldier Is Killed Amid Gunfire at Kabul Airport's Northern Gate," NPR Morning Edition, August 23, 2021, https://www.npr.org/2021/08/23/1030223373/an-afghan-solider-is-killed-amid-gunfire-at-kabul-airports-northern-gate.

9: WOLVES

ooo *claimed responsibility:* Reuters Staff, "Islamic State claims responsibility for deadly mosque attack in Afghan capital," Reuters, October 12, 2016, https://www.reuters.com/article/us-afghanistan-ashura-idUSKCN12C17E.

ooo *suicide bomber:* Craig Nelson, "Suicide Bomber, in Crowd of New Year Pilgrims, Kills Dozens in Kabul," *The Wall Street Journal*, March 21, 2018, https://www.wsj.com/articles/suicide-bomber-in-crowd-of-new-year-pilgrims-kills-dozens-1521630534.

ooo *16,000 people:* "WATCH: Pentagon's John Kirby and Gen. Hank Taylor hold briefing as Afghanistan exit continues," August 23, 2021, https://www.pbs.org/newshour/nation/watch-live-pentagons-john-kirby-and-gen-hank-taylor-hold-briefing-as-afghanistan-exit-continues.

ooo *exceed 21,000:* Pentagon Press Secretary John F. Kirby and Major General Hank Taylor, Deputy Director of the Joint Staff For Regional Operations Press Brief-ing, August 24, 2021, https://www.defense.gov/News/Transcripts/Transcript/Arti-cle/2744360/

pentagon-press-secretary-john-f-kirby-and-major-general-hank-taylor-deputy-dire/.

ooo *Gaël Perdriau:* Both Homeira and Perdriau shared copies of their text and Twit-ter message exchanges. Perdriau also explained his efforts during email exchanges with the author in March 2022.

ooo *publicly invited:* Unbylined article, "Gaël Perdriau ready to welcome Afghan ref-ugees in Saint-Étienne," *Le Progrès*, August 19, 2021, https://www.leprogres.fr/politique/2021/08/19/gael-perdriau-pret-a-accueillir-des-refugies-afghans-a-saint-etienne.

ooo *Zarifa Ghafari:* Joshua Nevett, "Young Afghan mayor who fled Taliban hidden in car," BBC News, August 26, 2021, https://www.bbc.com/news/world-asia-58343250.

10: ABBEY GATE

ooo *email an embassy staffer sent that day:* Email from U.S. embassy Kabul leadership sent Thursday, August 26, 2021, 11:41 A.M. Kabul time.

ooo *Abdul Rahman Al-Logari:* The Islamic State took responsibility for the bombing almost immediately and identified Al-Logari as the bomber. Thomas Joscelyn, "Islamic State claims responsibility for suicide bombing in Kabul," *FDD's Long War Journal*, August 20, 2021, https://www.longwarjournal.org/archives/2021/08/islamic-state-claims-credit-for-suicide-bombing-in-kabul.php.

ooo *plotting a suicide bombing:* Oren Lieberman and Natasha Bertrand, "ISIS-K suicide bomber who carried out deadly Kabul airport attack had been released from prison days earlier," CNN, October 6, 2021, https://www.cnn.com/2021/10/06/politics/kabul-airport-attacker-prison/index.html. See also Praveen Swami, "Kabul Airport suicide attacker was freed b Taliban after four years in CIA custody for New Delhi terror plot," *Firstpost*, September 19. 2021, https://www.firstpost.com/india/kabul-airport-suicide-attacker-was-freed-by-taliban-after-four-years-in-cia-custody-for-new-delhi-terror-plot-9976961.html. See also Eric Schmitt, "U.S. Military Focusing on ISIS Cell Behind Attack at Kabul Airport," *The New York Times*, January 1, 2022, https://www.nytimes.com/2022/01/01/us/politics/afghan-war-isis-attack.html. Logari's release also was reported by U.S. Rep. Ken Calvert of California, https://calvert.house.gov/media/press-releases/national-security-officials-confirm-rep-calvert-kabul-bomber-was-previously. Note: Media outlets spelled Logari's name several different ways, including Abdul Rehman Al-Loghri.

ooo *Ball bearings:* Defense Department press brief, "Attack on U.S. Forces at Hamid Karzai International Airport," released February 4, 2022, https://www.defense.gov/News/Transcripts/Transcript/Article/2924617/general-kenneth-f-mckenzie-jr-commander-us-central-command-holds-a-press-briefi/.

ooo *climb the airport walls:* Descriptions of the scene come from multiple sources. See, for instance, Susannah George, Ezzatullah Mehrdad, and Sudarsan Raghavan, " 'Dead People Were Everywhere': Carnage and Chaos at Kabul Airport," *The Washington Post*, August 27, 2021, https://www.washingtonpost.com/world/asia_pacific/kabul-airport-afghanistan-isisk/2021/08/26/69466456-0674-11ec-b3c4-c462b1edcfc8_story.html.

ooo *Marines returned fire:* Brian J. Conley and Mohammad J. Alizada, of Alive in Afghanistan, and Joshua Kaplan and Joaquin Sapien, of *ProPublica*, "Report: U.S. Marines Returned Fire After Suicide Bombing, but No Enemies Were Shooting at Them," *ProPublica*, January 21, 2022, https://www.propublica.org/article/report-u-s-Marines-returned-fire-after-suicide-bombing-but-no-enemies-were-shooting-at-them.

000 *cradling an Afghan baby:* The Marine was Sgt. Nicole Gee, https://www.insta-gram.com/nicole_gee__/?hl=en. The ten other Marines killed were Staff Sgt. Darin T. Hoover, Sgt. Johanny Rosario Pichardo, Cpl. Hunter Lopez, Cpl. Daegan W. Page, Cpl. Humberto A. Sanchez, Lance Cpl. David L. Espinoza, Lance Cpl. Jared M. Schmitz, Lance Cpl. Rylee J. McCollum, Lance Cpl. Dylan R. Merola, and Lance Cpl. Kareem M. Nikoui. Also, Navy Hospitalman Maxton W. Soviak, and Army Staff Sgt. Ryan C. Knauss, https://www.defense.gov/News/Releases/Release/Article/2756011/dod-identifies-Marine-corps-navy-and-army-casualties/.

000 *"continue these attacks":* Pentagon Press Briefing, August 26, 2021, https://www.centcom.mil/MEDIA/Transcripts/Article/2789438/pentagon-press-secretary-john-f-kirby-holds-a-press-briefing-aug-26-2021/.

12: FINAL SPRINT

000 *Mustafa Popal:* Interview with Mustafa Popal, January 19, 2022.

000 *updated security alert:* Security Alert: U.S. embassy Kabul, August 27, 2021, https://af.usembassy.gov/security-alert-u-s-embassy-kabul-august-27-2021/.

000 *"Children, women, and men":* Email from Secretary of State Antony Blinken, titled "A Message for Team Kabul," sent at 6:32 A.M. Kabul time, Friday, August 27, 2021.

000 *a retaliatory drone airstrike:* This strike took place early Saturday, August 28, 2021, Kabul time, and was declared a success by U.S. officials. It is distinct from a separate drone strike on August 29, 2021, that was later described by the Secretary of Defense Lloyd Austin as a "horrible mistake" that killed ten civilians. For details of the strike briefed by Vasely at the JOC, see U.S. Central Command statement on counterterrorism strike on ISIS-K planner, August 27, 2021, https://www.centcom.mil/MEDIA/STATEMENTS/Statements-View/Article/2755890/us-central-command-statement-on-counterterrorism-strike-on-isis-k-planner/. See also Adam Nossiter and Eric Schmitt, "U.S. Launches Strike on ISIS-K as Bombing's Death Toll Soars," *The New York Times*, August 27, 2021, https://www.nytimes.com/2021/08/27/world/asia/kabul-afghanistan-airport-bombing.html. See also Sune Engel Rasmussen, Ehsanullah Amiri, Gordon Lubold, and Nancy A. Youssef, "U.S. Targets Islamic State Planner in Afghanistan Airstrike," *The Wall Street Journal*, August 27, 2021, https://www.wsj.com/articles/afghan-crowds-return-to-kabul-airport-after-deadly-explosions-11630065498. For more on the mistaken drone strike, see Statement by Secretary of Defense Lloyd J. Austin III on the Results of Central Command Investigation Into the 29 August Airstrike, September 17, 2021, https://www.defense.gov/News/Releases/Release/Article/2780404/statement-by-secretary-of-defense-lloyd-j-austin-iii-on-the-results-of-central/. See also Alex Horton, Joyce Sohyun Lee, Elyse Samuels, and

Karoun Demirjian, "U.S. military admits 'horrible mistake' in Kabul drone strike that killed 10 Afghans," *The Washington Post*, September 17, 2021, https://www.washingtonpost.com/national-security/2021/09/17/drone-strike-kabul-afghanistan/.

13: "RUN, HOMEIRA!"

ooo *"Are you Homeira?":* This account of their phone calls and in-person interactions is based on multiple interviews with both Homeira and Sam. Initial separate interviews with each revealed broad agreement on the conversations and events described here. During follow-up interviews, details and dialogue from each refreshed the memory of the other and refined the account presented here. When their memories diverged, every attempt was made to reconcile their accounts, including interviews with other witnesses, such as Mustafa Popal, to be certain the version presented here is as accurate as possible.

ooo *laptop bomb:* "Somali officials: Suicide bomber may have blown hole in jet," CBS News, February 6, 2016, https://www.cbsnews.com/news/somali-officials-suicide-bomber-may-have-blown-hole-in-jet/.

EPILOGUE: AFTER GLORY

ooo *123,000 people:* State Department Press Briefing by Spokesperson Ned Price, August 31, 2021, https://www.state.gov/briefings/department-press-briefing-august-31-2021-2/. See also remarks by President Biden, August 31, 2021, https://www.whitehouse.gov/briefing-room/speeches-remarks/2021/08/31/remarks-by-president-biden-on-the-end-of-the-war-in-afghanistan/.

ooo *described their valor:* U.S. Department of State, Award for Heroism Nomination, approved April 20, 2022.

ooo *Amnesty International:* Quote from Amnesty International tweet on March 30, 2022, https://twitter.com/amnestysasia/status/1509054241020649474.

ooo *"selling their children":* Jamie Keaten and Kathy Gannon, "UN seeks record $4.4B for Afghans struggling under Taliban," the Associated Press, March 31, 2022, https://apnews.com/article/russia-ukraine-afghanistan-business-taliban-united-nations-620d87cc04b692b5cd132bc254509128.

ooo *cover themselves head to toe:* "Afghan Supreme Leader Orders Women to Wear All-Covering Burqa," Agence France-Presse, [https://www.afp.com/en/ -ce] May 7, 2022.

INDEX

Leave 15 pages for Index

ABOUT THE AUTHOR

MITCHELL ZUCKOFF is the Sumner M. Redstone Professor in Narrative Studies at Boston University. He is the author of eight previous nonfiction books, including four *New York Times* best-sellers. As a member of *The Boston Globe* Spotlight Team, Zuckoff was a finalist for the Pulitzer Prize in investigative reporting and the winner of numerous national journalism awards. He lives with his family outside Boston.

ABOUT THE TYPE

This book was set in Garamond, a typeface originally designed by the Parisian type cutter Claude Garamond (c. 1500–61). This version of Garamond was modeled on a 1592 specimen sheet from the Egenolff-Berner foundry, which was produced from types assumed to have been brought to Frankfurt by the punch cutter Jacques Sabon (c. 1520–80).

Claude Garamond's distinguished romans and italics first appeared in *Opera Ciceronis* in 1543–44. The Garamond types are clear, open, and elegant.